Crafting Wonders

Unleashing Your Cricut Creativity for Timeless Masterpieces

Mark Ready

TABLE OF CONTENTS

15

BOOK ONE: INTRODUCTION TO CRICUT MACHINE

INTRODUCTION
What is Cricut?

The Cricut Machine is one of the most advanced machines available for use in arts and crafts. It enables you to create a wide range of works by combining specially created software and transforming it into a tangible form of art.

The Cricut Machine is essentially a cutting machine. It can cut a variety of materials based on programmed patterns created in specifically specialized software. You may take a material and have the Cricut Machine cut out the designs you desire in these masterpieces.

So, if you need to make a lot of cuts, the Cricut Machine is what you require.

This is essential for creating crafts with complicated patterns. Assume you have lofty goals for the designs you want to create. In such situation, the Cricut Machine can supply you with the technological means to create detailed designs that come in a variety of sizes.

Here is a some crafts you can make using the Cricut Machine:

- Cards
- Clothing
- Bags
- Leather
- Cardboard cutouts
- Stamps
- Embossing
- Stencils
- Molds
- Patterns

It should be noted that this instrument is solely intended to cut. It does not print anything. That is a crucial consideration to bear in mind. For example, using a piece of leather, you may carve out a complex design and then color it to your preference. If you're designing a birthday card, you may cut out the design you want and then color it with the method of your choosing (pastels, crayons, paints, watercolors, and so on).

The Cricut Machine is ideal for cutting. Even if you don't cut out too much, it's still useful to have on hand in case you need it. You may not, however, get as much out of it. That is why it is ideal for individuals who chop away a lot of form.

Having saying that, the Cricut Machine is a fantastic tool for any project.

The Benefits of the Cricut Machine

Anyone can benefit from the Cricut Machine. All sorts of folks can use this device to make any type of design they wish. It's perfect for home projects, students, art majors, and businesses. In particular, businesses can make the Cricut Machine roar into action. As you will see, projects can be quite elaborate, depending on the type of materials and designs you use.

Furthermore, you don't need any type of technical expertise or specific experience with electronics or design. If you are brand new to this type of device, you might need to take some time to figure out the Cricut Machine's ins and outs. Beyond that, all you need is the imagination to make it work.

It is better for children to use this machine without adult supervision. It's just a safety thing. But kids can put it to work in their school projects. It is intuitive when it comes to making your projects come to life.

On the whole, there is no limit to what anyone can do with the Cricut Machine. So, it's worth taking a closer look at the various features that this device offers. That way, you can make up your mind on how you would like to use your very own Cricut Machine.

Common Considerations

Depending on where you purchase your Cricut Machine, it can get to be pretty pricey. But that shouldn't be a drawback, especially if you are ambitious about the projects you wish to pursue. Consider that it can pay for itself if you plan to use it as part of a business.

It's important to consider that the Cricut Machine is ideal for those who carry out projects regularly. As such, if you are not a regular hobbyist or crafter, you might think twice about getting one of these machines. But if you are a serious hobbyist, then the Cricut Machine is an excellent way to bring your ideas to life.

The device itself is certainly worth it, especially when you can see everything it can do. You can produce original creations in such a manner that no one else will be able to produce. That alone makes the machine worth its cost.

On the flip side, if you want one of these devices but are unsure about investing in them, you might want to consider picking up a used one. Depending on the price, it could be a good option for you. Don't overpay it as there is no guarantee regarding the device's condition. Nevertheless, these are pretty reliable and robust machines. As such, you are picking up a used one that might not be the craziest idea.

Conclusion

The Cricut Machine is ideal for serious hobbyists and crafters. Also, it's great if you are planning on using it for business purposes. It's the type of machine that can take a heavy workload. It will also make a good investment, especially when considering how much it would cost you to get these types of creations made elsewhere. It can also provide a great means for family fun and entertainment.

On the whole, the Cricut Machine is the type of device that is reliable. While it might get a bit pricey, this machine's cost-benefit relationship makes spending the cash worthwhile. The only consideration in this regard would be to avoid spending too much money on it, especially if you are only a casual crafter or don't plan to use it very often. Otherwise, you can bet that this device will provide you with the type of versatility you need to make the most of your imagination. In the end, you will have the opportunity to set your imagination free truly. If you are on the ropes, you go for it! The worst thing that can happen is that you fall in love with the creations that you produce.

WHAT IS A CRICUT MACHINE

Have another Cricut and don't perceive where to begin? Get creating with this posting of more than one hundred innovative and astounding simple DIY activities with a Cricut that is best for fledglings! Are you considering using Cricut to reduce the allocation of tasks that can be done by the machine? Or then again thinking what particular substances a Cricut can cut? With a Cricut, the potential outcomes are tremendous! To help energize you and supply you thinking about the numerous great Cricut ventures you can make, I've assembled a rundown of some beautiful undertakings underneath.

The Cricut machine is a fantastic creation. This poor boy can help you cut paper, cloth, and vinyl sheets to whatever pattern you would like. These actual production designs may be achieved via software tools like the Cricut layout studio or via capsules using pre-engineered structures assembled into them. Therefore, if you're an enthusiastic scrapbooker, this system is essential-have.

Different Uses

There are vast amounts of one-of-a-kind issues you can utilize a Cricut. While you know what type of task you want to perform, and at the same time considering what kind of decoration and supplies you need to use the machine, please take a look at the rest of the other projects and parts that Cricut has just started. Demand (and what are basically "decent possessions" that you can spend when you need them) Scrapbooking and Card Making

There are loads of scrapbooking thoughts and scrapbook designs you can discover for your Cricut!

Or once you don't want the opportunity to make cards yourself, here are some pointers and special effects for making cards quickly.

Weddings and Gatherings

Cricut machines are great for making custom stylistic themes for weddings and gatherings!

Occasions

Utilize your Cricut to make occasion stylistic layout for any event!

Home Stylistic theme. You can make loads of various undertakings to improve your home!

Everything from cushions and divider craftsmanship to big business thoughts!

Clothing and Extras

One of my preferred things to make with my Cricut is shirts, onesies, and tote sacks. You can put warmness switch vinyl on exceptionally much any material surface. However, you can likewise utilize a Cricut to make adornments, headbands, and then some!

Vinyl Decals and Stickers

Our assortment one intrigue is lessening vinyl decals and stickers, and you can do this with the Cricut Maker.

It can cut through any vinyl in no time easily — you should simply make your format in Cricut Design Space, teach the PC to begin cutting, at that point, weed and change the arrangement to your picked surface.

Texture Cuts

One of the essential selling elements of the Maker is the truth that it comes outfitted with the produce-new Turn Cutting edge.

On account of uncommon coasting and moving movement — by and large with the gigantic 4kg of power at the back of the Cricut Maker — this ability that the work area can lessen unmistakably any texture.

The truth is out. Denim? Check. Overwhelming canvas? Check. Silk? Check. Chiffon? Check. We've continually constrained using a particular texture shaper sooner than as the registering gadget lessening machines essentially weren't compelling to deal with more massive textures. We cherish the truth that the Maker is an across the board machine. It comes furnished with a texture-cutting mat so that you can lessen bunches of textures aside from the utilization of any support. Astonishing! Sewing Examples

Another key prepared of the Maker is the gigantic sewing test library that you'll get passage to when you've purchased the machine.

It comprises of earnestly many examples — comprehensive of some from Effortlessness and Riley Blake Designs — and capacity you can genuinely pick the model you like, and the Maker will remove it for you. No additional removing designs physically yourself (and not any more human blunder ruins)!

Additionally, secured is a launder-able texture pen that will call attention to the spot the example parts intend to stable together.

Balsa Wood Cuts

On account of the incredible 4kg of weight and the Blade Sharp edge (sold independently), the Cricut Maker can slice using substances up to 2.4 mm thick. That limit thick texture that had before been beyond reach with the Cricut and Outline machines are currently open to us. We can hardly wait to start cutting wooden with it!

Thick Cowhide Cuts

In a similar vein as factor #4, thick cowhide can cut with the Maker!

Natively constructed Cards

Paper crafters aren't forgotten about with the Maker either.

Paper and card cuts will be less complicated and snappier than at any other time because of the machine's vitality and exactness.

Your Scratchpad playing cards just went up a level.

Jigsaw Riddles

We comprehend that the Cricut Maker can cut through significantly thicker substances with the Blade Edge than any time in recent memory.

The central perspective we give it a shot? Making our special jigsaw confound. We'll save you, refreshed!

Christmas tree Adornments

The Revolving Cutting edge that vows to lessen through any texture is the ideal gadget for designing occasion improvements. Scour the sewing design library for Christmassy designs (we've purchased our eye on the gingerbread man adornment!), lessen out the example utilizing felt or whatever texture you want, and after that, sew it all in all independently.

Blankets

Cricut has collaborated with Riley Blake Designs to give various sewing designs in the sewing design library.

This capacity that you can utilize the Maker to remove your sewing correctly divides before sewing them aggregately independently.

Felt Dolls and Delicate Toys

One of the Effortlessness designs we have our eye on in the sewing design library is the 'felt doll and garments' example. We understand a couple of little women and young men who'd love a natively constructed dish to add to their accumulation. Just pick the bar, cut, and sew. Simple peasy!

Shirt Moves

You need to arrange the switch in Design Space, load the glow switch vinyl to the manufacturer (or flash it drastically on the HTV if you may feel timid); it recommends that the PC start cutting and ironing your switch the shirt.

Texture Appliques

Additionally, available to get individually is the fortified texture sharp edge in lodging, which will allow you to lessen additional unpredictable material designs, similar to applique.

In contrast to the sharp rotating edge, the fortified texture edge requires reinforced sponsorship on the material to diminish adequately.

Calligraphy Signs

The Cricut Maker's significant selling element is its Versatile Apparatus Framework. It is the element that will verify that you keep up your Maker until the end of time. In reality, it's a gadget machine that never again exclusively suits every one of the instruments and sharp edges of the Explore family. However, it will fit as a fiddle with every future device and cutting edges made using Cricut.

The vitality of the Cricut Maker limit that you can cut thicker substances than sooner than that is appropriately perfect for intricate gems designs.

And keeping in mind that you aren't in any way, shape, or form to cut gold, silver, or jewel on there at whatever point soon, an excellent pair of cowhide rings are just inside reach.

Wedding Solicitations and Spare the Dates

As a whole, we know about how 'little' costs like welcomes and sexually transmitted diseases can add to the super price of a wedding.

As makers, we also know how to counterbalance a portion of those costs using making matters like ourselves.

The Cricut Maker is perfect for making staggering welcomes — presently, not exclusively, would you remove confusing paper designs, anyway that calligraphy pen will come in reachable once more.

Wedding Menus, Spot Cards, and Support Labels

You're nearly no longer compelled to creates before the wedding function — you can likewise utilize your Maker to adorn for the gigantic day itself. The sky is just the confinement directly here; however, in all actuality, make menus, region playing a card game, and lean toward labels. Attempt and ensure you utilize a practically identical arrangement for all your stationery to protect the subject upfront.

Shading Book

Do you know these 'careful shading' books that are extremely popular at present? And after that, the Maker's total direction is to make your own unique, unquestionably extraordinary, shading book utilizing the Fine-Point Pen device.

Liners

Another part we can hardly wait to make with our new Maker is liners.

The world you claim as far as substances go — whatever from cowhide to sew, to steel sheets and everything in the middle.

There are likewise some fabulous liner designs in the sewing library to investigate as well.

Texture Keyrings

Something different that got our attention in the sewing test library was, at one time, a couple of simple designs for fabric key-rings.

Once more, the Maker makes it advantageous — totally decrease out the example, and after that, sew it together.

Headbands and Hair Adornments

Presently, Cricut has propelled a registering gadget that is lessening through thick calfskin; we are fearless thought for mind-boggling, steampunk-motivated hair designs and even headbands.

Who realized the Maker ought to be so convenient for significant pattern articulations?

Cut-Out Christmas Tree

We know we know every individual needs a real Christmas tree eventually of the get-away season. As the Cricut Maker successfully decreases thick substances like wood, we guess an interlocking wood tree is an incredible task to check with this year. No laser is required when the Maker is available to you, no matter what!

Models

Cricut Explore One

Explore One is ideal for beginners and inexperienced users who want to get into die-cutting, craft cutting, and plotting. The machine is not advance like the other Explore models, and it is also the cheapest Cricut machine you can get.

Capability:

The machine is also highly capable, even if it's an old model. The system can also handle scoring and writing smoothly.

Materials:

Regardless of the simplicity and the inexpensive nature of the machine, it is still highly capable.

Cricut Explore Air

While this is quite similar to the Explore One model, it also comes with some additional features. The main difference between them is the presence of the inbuilt Bluetooth adapter. If you don't enjoy seeing cables and wires all around your workplace, especially with the danger of tripping over them, then this model solves that problem.

Capability

The Explore Air is also different from Explore One because it features a double carriage. It means that you can draw, write, or score while you cut because it has two clamps to hold both tools. It saves you money because you don't have to purchase a tool adapter.

Cutting Force

The system is more powerful than the older model when it comes to the cutting force. It features a Cut Smart technology made by Cricut, which enhances the blade control of the system and gives your creations a more professional look. It can cut anything that is as wide as 23.5 inches accurately and precisely.

It also has the Smart Set dial, which increases the control you have over your project's cutting.

The features of the Cricut Design Space are very similar. But, when using Explore Air, you get more freedom, and you are allowed to use .svg, .gif, and .dxf files in addition to the standard files allowed with the Explore One.

Sadly, Explore Air does not have either a knife or a rotary blade. Because of these two types of blades, the Explore Air recommends for more light crafts and scrapbooking. It does have an inbuilt cutter, though.

A brand new Explore Airbox comes with these tools:

A 25.4 x 10 x 9.2 inches Cricut Explore Sir machine with inbuilt Bluetooth technology

It has an inbuilt accessory adapter.

Inbuilt blade.

USB and power cord.

Metallic silver marker.

Iron-on sample.

Cardstock sample.

Over 100 images,

Over 50 ready-to-cut projects.

12" x 12" Standard Grip cutting mat.

Welcome guide.

<u>Cricut Explore Air 2</u>
It is the youngest sibling of the Cricut Explore line. It is the best of the machines in this line.

Explore Air 2 as efficiently as the other ones, but it does its work even better. It even has a better design, and it comes in different colors.

Cricut Maker

The newest Cricut die-cutting machine is the Cricut Maker. If you thought that the Explore Air 2 was a great model, then you should get ready to be blown away.

The Cricut Maker is a rare unit amongst other die-cutting machines. The rotary blade is already enough to attract experienced users.

For beginners, it provides an avenue for improvement and unlimited creativity.

The Cricut Maker, as an updated version of others, is mighty and flexible. It comes with a toolkit that includes a rotary blade, knife blade, deep cut blade, and fine point blade.

It also comes with a single and a double scoring wheel and a collection of pens. The pens include a fine point pen, a washable fabric pen, a calligraphy pen, and a scoring stylus.

The machine also improves its efficiency by adding some unique features. We have the adaptive tool system, which means that the device can automatically adjust the blade's angle and the edge's pressure depending on the material. It doesn't need the Smart dial feature because the Cricut Maker determines your cutting force for you, and its decisions are usually accurate. It has two clamps, one for the pen or scoring tool and the other for the cutting blade. This system works for any paper, cardstock, and vinyl.

Materials

As expected, the Cricut Maker will handle more and thicker materials than the Cricut Explore series machines. From light materials to basswood and leather, this machine will exceed your expectations.

Cricut Design Space also provides a lot of benefits for Cricut Maker users/. It allows .jpg, .gif, .png, .svg, .bmp and .dxf files.

The system also supports a wireless Bluetooth adapter. You can also enjoy the Sewing Pattern Library if you own a Cricut Maker. The library contains 50 ready-to-cut projects, and it is a result of a partnership between Cricut and Riley Blake Designs.

Another great benefit you get when using Cricut Maker with Design Space is to get Cricut Access free membership for a trial period.

How to Choose Your Cricut Machine

Assuming that all Cricut machine templates are great, the ones recommended for beginners and professionals are the Cricut Maker or Explore Air templates. These two models are the first choice for most people, regardless of their experience level.

The Cricut maker is the right choice for the brave people who want to work with Cricut, such as woodworking seriously, sewing and quilting. It's a professional machine, and it works for any experience level. His system has many advantages, many of these over design space.

If instead you are a beginner and want to get your feet wet in the fantastic Cricut world, you could still opt for the Cricut Maker. It makes no sense to gain experience with a basic model and then buy a better version.

In the future, you may opt to use the Cricut machine to create designs for sale, which means that you will use it more often.

To do this you can use Cricut explore air 2 because it is much faster and has a lot of other advantages.

In summary, beginners, enthusiasts, and people with a little budget will be better off with the Cricut explore one and explore air.

BOOK TWO: HOW TO USE A CRICUT MACHINE

TOOLS AND ACCESSORIES

Tools for Cutting

We will start with the tools that you can mount on your Cricut devices to achieve the perfect cut, scoring, and writing for a variety of your projects.

Deep-Point Blade

The Cricut deep-point blade facilitates the effortless cutting of a wider range of products. You can use chipboard to build customized wall calendars, cut personalized stamps using rubber sheets, and even create unique magnets. With this blade, any 1.5 mm. thick material can be easily cut, such as poster boards, heavy cardstock, and much more. This blade can be used with the Cricut Maker and the Cricut Explore line (including the Explore, Explore One, Explore Air, and Explore Air 2). It is recommended to be used for these materials: Magnet, chipboard, stamp material, thick cardstock, stiffened felt, foam sheets, cardboard. You can buy the deep-point blade with the housing for $34.99.

Premium Fine-Point Blade

The premium fine-point blade can deliver highly durable precision cutting to ensure your DIY projects are a total win. This high-strength blade has been built with German carbide steel with a special design to allow cutting of even the most intricately designed graphics with the Cricut machine. It is resistant to regular wear and tear and is capable of cutting through the lightest and medium-weight materials such as iron-on, vinyl, and cardstocks. This blade can also be used with the Cricut Maker and the Cricut Explore line (including the Explore, Explore One, Explore Air, and Explore Air 2). It is recommended to be used for these materials: faux leather, iron-on, vinyl, cardstock, poster board. It is also available for purchase with the housing for $34.99.

Bonded-Fabric Blade

The bonded-fabric blade as the name suggests it is specifically designed to cut through bonded fabric and fabrics with iron-on by ensuring that the blade is capable of precisely cutting and will stay sharp for a long time. It is constructed with premium carbide steel from Germany and is developed to bring your intricately designed graphics to life with the Cricut Maker. It allows the creation of fantastic DIY projects such as personalized applique and sewing projects that will take your fabric crafting skills to the next level. Although, this blade can be used with the entire Cricut Explore line (including the Explore, Explore One, Explore Air, and Explore Air 2) and not just the Cricut Maker. It is also available for purchase with the housing for $34.99.

Rotary Blade

The rotary blade is a uniquely designed sharp blade that can cut exquisite designs from soft textiles for your dream sewing projects much faster and easier than ever before. You will be able to effortlessly cut silk, cotton, denim, canvas, and even burlap. With this blade, you will also be able to cut through delicate materials such as crepe paper and create parts to make stunning quilts, plush toys, bags, accessories, decorations, among others. It is recommended that when you start noticing uncut threads or if the material configurations on Design Space are not as precise, you should replace your rotary blade to keep getting high-quality results. This blade can only be used with the Cricut Maker and doesn't support the Cricut Explore line or any older models. The rotary blade replacement kit is available for purchase at $16.99.

Knife Blade

The knife blade is designed with extra depth to easily and safely cut through thick and dense materials up to 2.4 mm. (3/32). It is good to use if you are interested in adding dimensions to your project. It can be used for a broad spectrum of practical and artisan materials such as chipboard, balsa wood, basswood, mat board, craft foam, garment leather, and tooled leather. You can easily create puzzles, models, dinosaur skeletons, dioramas, wood decor, leather goods, toys, and much more. It is better to avoid cutting designs smaller than 0.75 inches. This blade can only be used with the Cricut Maker and doesn't support the Cricut Explore line or any older models. The knife blade with drive housing is available for purchase at $45.99.

Scoring Wheel Tip

The scoring wheel tip can be used to transcend creative barriers and create in-depth scoring lines. This helps you create professional-looking and high finish tags, cards, and gift boxes to marvelous wearable art, 3D home décor, and structures by generating professional-level precision on every crease-and-fold project that comes to your mind. You can create crisp creases and perfect folds without struggle; all marked with a flawless finish. The patented design of the wheel can effectively work on basic materials while generating 10 times more pressure than the scoring stylus. This blade can only be used with the Cricut Maker and doesn't support the Cricut Explore line or any older models. It is available for purchase at $29.99 and the scoring wheel tip with drive housing for $49.99.

Maker Tools

Every craftsman has a distinctive approach to bringing their ideas to life, and you may want to supplement your artistic tools by employing one or more of the tools listed below to create stunning projects.

Engraving Tip

The Cricut engraving tip will help you generate customized texts and monograms. You can design ornamental embellishments and flourishes as well as inscribe any famous quote of your choice on a keepsake. This tip is made with high-quality carbide steel that will allow engraving on Cricut aluminum sheets and anodized aluminum, so you can highlight the silver underneath for a professional-looking effect. This tip can be used only with the Cricut Maker machine. The Cricut engraving tip will help you create intricate dog tags with personalized engraving, customized nameplates, engraved art and decoration, jewelry, monograms, wood sculptures, and mementos. It is recommended to be used with aluminum flat, soft metals, leather, acrylic, plastic, among others. You can buy the Cricut engraving tip for $24.99.

Fine Debossing Tip

The fine debossing tip (2.0 mm.) is the ultimate tool to create elegant papercrafts by incorporating professional finish and elevation to the base material. It will help you achieve crisp debossed designs with fine details. This tip is uniquely designed with a rolling debossing ball, that will provide you the freedom to create customized and personalized designs with exceptional intricacy, unlike standard embossing folders available in the market that limit you to a predefined layout.

You can easily create dimensional wedding cards, monogrammed "thank you" notes, or attached flourish to the gift boxes and gift tags, and much more. You can also create an amazing effect on coated paper, shimmer and glitter paper, and foil cardstock. This tip can be used only with the Cricut Maker machine. It is recommended to be used with cardstock, foil poster board, foil cardstock, foil kraft board, poster board, and kraft board. You can buy the fine debossing tip for $24.99.

Basic Perforation Blade

The basic perforation blade is uniquely designed with 2.5 mm. teeth and 0.5 mm. gaps to quickly generate smooth tears with accurate and consistent perforation cuts for all your craft projects. For all your perforated design needs, this blade will allow you to create models with finely perforated and uniform lines that would eliminate the need for folding the paper prior to tearing it up and is very handy particularly for shapes with curves. You can effortlessly create tear-out booklet pages, raffle tickets, homemade journals, or any project requiring a tidy tear, such as Christmas decorations, paper dolls, tear-away cards or gift coupons, advent calendars, and much more. It is recommended to be used with fabrics like paper, cardstock, foam, acetate, and foil. This blade can be used only with the Cricut Maker machine. You can buy the basic perforation blade for $29.99, exclusively through HSN.

Wavy Blade
The wavy blade will help you create decorative edges much faster than a drag blade for a broad range of projects with smoothly molded cuts. This uniquely designed blade made from stainless steel is perfect to create original vinyl decals, iron-on designs, envelopes, cards, gift tags, and collage projects, or when you are looking to add stylish accents with a whimsical wavy edge to your craft. It is recommended to be used with iron-on, vinyl, paper, cardstock, and fabric. This blade can be used only with the Cricut Maker machine. You can buy the wavy blade for $29.99, exclusively through HSN.

Craft Tools
Cricut also offers a variety of crafting tools such as rulers, fabric shears, seam rippers, thread snips, knives, trimmers, rotary cutters, measuring tape, and much more. All the tools are carefully designed to help you take your crafting skills to the next level resulting in professional-looking crafts with a premium finish. For instance, the True Control Knife Kit contains 5 replacement blades along with a storage cartridge to help you monitor and discard the used blades. This knife is designed with a razor-sharp edge, piercing tip, and superior blade lock system to provide you better control and stunning finishes every time. It can be used to create precision cuts on paper, cardstock, thin plastics, canvas, and various other material. Their patented hands-free blade changing system means you can safely change your blades without needing to touch them and accidentally hurting yourself. It also boasts an anti-roll design to ensure that the knife will stay in place when not being used along with a padded grip for a comfortable handling experience.

Weeder Tool
So, the following tools are from the Cricut company, and one of the things that you might want to get for yourself is a weeder tool. A weeder tool is one of the most essential tools that you can have because while the spatula and the tweezers that come with the machine are beneficial, the weeding tool is necessary if you're trying to lift vinyl off of your mat.

There are a lot of different tools that people can use for weeding, and they all work to raise the vinyl from the backing sheet in a safe way so that the project doesn't get ruined and your mat doesn't get ruined.

However, if you want a tool that's direct from the company itself, you can use the weeder tool, or you can buy the weeder toolset because it has finer points, and it might be able to do more for you.

Some of the other popular tools that people use for weeding are dental picks, but the handles may be uncomfortable; however, you can also use an Exacto knife, but you'll have to be very careful not to damage the project or cut yourself open. They also use an old gift card or a credit card, but you should be aware that this might scratch the project, so you'll have to be very careful with this as well.

Spatula Tool

The next tool we're going to talk about is the spatula. The spatula is for lifting material from the cutting mat when you don't want to worry about tearing the fabric. It will take care of this by lifting the material from the mat as easily as possible, and it can also be used with a scraper tool to keep the mat clean and debris-free. Cricut sells the scraper and spatula together for a very reasonable price as well.

Scraper Tool

Now that we talked about the spatula let's talk about the scraper tool. A clean mat is essential for getting a good project done and making sure that your material isn't moving around during the cutting. The last thing you need when you are spending a lot of money on the material is to have it move halfway during the project, and then you have to start completely from the beginning, and you wasted all that money as well. Other tools remove that issue, but the scraper tool is much faster, and it ensures that you have a nice clean mat. There are different sizes, but most people prefer the extra-large as it's easier to hold, and it's faster than the smaller one, which means that it can also help get the bubbles out of your vinyl.

Extra mats are always something that is recommended because there's nothing more irritating when you're working on a project than realizing that your mats are no longer sticky. There are definite ways to re-stick your mat, and they can save you money, but just in case, it is still always a good idea to have a couple of extra mats on hand just in case you need them. The mats do different things for different projects, such as the following.

- The pink that's for fabric is, of course, only for fabric.

- A strong grip, which is purple, would be better for thicker projects like leather, poster board, or thicker card stock.

- A standard green would be for iron-on and vinyl.

- The light blue would be for paper and card stock projects.

Toolset

They also offer an essential toolset that has almost every item that we're talking about it. The toolset includes the following items.

- Tweezers.

- Weeder.

- Spatula.

- Scraper.

- Scissors.

- Scoring stylus.

By buying this, you can cut down on a lot of money instead of buying the items individually if you just buy the set instead.

<u>Bright Pad</u>

A Bright Pad is great for many different reasons because it makes weeding so much easier. After all, it makes the cut lines much more visible, but if you have anything more than a simple cut, this is really going to help you out because you'll be able to see exactly where the lines are, and you could even use it for adapting patterns and tracing.

<u>EasyPress</u>

An EasyPress is great as well. If you're still using the iron for heat transfer vinyl, the EasyPress makes things so much easier than iron because there's no peeling after 1–2 wares, and it takes out all the guesswork of the right time and temperature as well. If you have space, you can get a real heat press for just a little bit more if you can afford it, but we would recommend considering a beginner heat press first, especially if you're doing anything in a large quantity or for commercial purposes.

Brayer Tool

A brayer tool is good for larger vinyl projects or working with fabric; then you should use a brayer. This fixes the problem of not fully stabilizing your material before cutting. A brayer makes the material stick to the mat but without damaging it.

Trimmer

A paper trimmer is super handy if you want to get a straight cut. You do not have to use scissors, and you don't have to use a ruler. As such, it makes cutting a lot easier on you, especially if you're working with vinyl.

The company also sells their trimmer; however, there are other places where you can get a trimmer as well. If you go with a shortcut paper trimmer, it has the option for scoring to get a perfect fold, so that may be something that you would want to look into.

Scissors

Scissors make a world of differences well. The company scissors are made with stainless steel, which creates an even cut while remaining durable, as stainless steel is one of the most durable materials that we have. The scissors are quite sharp, and they come with a micro-tip blade, which means that working on the fine details in a smaller area is easier and clean right down to the point. It also has an interchangeable colored cap, which is protective as well; therefore, your scissors can be stored safely.

Tweezers

The tweezers are super helpful, and many people have more than one type. They usually have one for small items and one for vinyl. This tool is in the Cricut toolset, but if you want to go for something else, there are Pazzlee needle point tweezers, and they have a very sharp point, which makes them excellent for vinyl. The points are also sharp enough to pick fine pieces from the mat without using the edges or any other little trick, and they can also pick up the tiniest small scraps. If you don't want to get the company's tweezers, you can go with this other company instead.

Pens

Pens are a big part of the Cricut world as well, and you can purchase these pens in a variety of places. However, you can use other pens that you can find just about anywhere and for really cheap prices.

Other

There're other tools you can get for yourself if you find that you are a busy person and that you go to other people's houses or you go on business trips or things of that nature, such as a tote bag to carry all of your Cricut supplies and machine. The company sells a great tote for a reasonable price, and you would be able to use it for your benefit because you will be able to keep everything organized and neat the way it needs to be. If you don't like their price point, there are actually a lot of other places where you can get a great tote as well.

You can also get rotary blades or a control knife. A control knife is basically like an Exacto knife, so you'll have to be careful with this because even though it adds precision and accuracy to your projects, you could end up cutting yourself pretty badly. You'll have to make sure to be careful.

If you need rulers because you feel like you're not accurate enough, they have these as well, and they have all different types and kits that have all the tools you need so that you don't have to buy everything individually. This is a great thing to look into so that you can see everything that you need. There are many different websites on the Internet where you can find tools for your machine, and each of them claims that their materials are better than the rest.

Cricut offers everything you would need on their site, and they offer very reasonable prices, but you can also do some additional searching if you feel like their stuff isn't what you would want, and you would want something else. As we've already listed examples from other companies, this will help you get an idea of what we're talking about. If you decide to get these additional tools, you'll find that your projects will be able to go a lot easier, and you'll be able to have more precision and more accuracy with them as well. Many people who like the Cricut and their company recommend getting these items just for that purpose.

Mats

There are 3 different categories of mats offered by Cricut which are compatible with different Cricut machines and heat presses, as described below:

Machine Mats

The Standard Grip machine mat is 12 by 12 inches and compatible with all the Cricut machines. These mats are designed to hold the material firmly in place while you cut through it and then easily remove the material when ready. It is recommended to be used with cardstock, patterned paper, embossed cardstock, iron-on, and vinyl.

They also offer the LightGrip machine mat, which is also 12 by 12 inches and specifically designed for the adhesion of lightweight and delicate materials such as standard paper, light cardstock, and vellum.

Self-Healing Mats

Cricut offers a wide variety of self-healing mats and claims them to be twice more self-healing than their competitors. They are designed with larger numbers on a 1-inch-wide border, for easy readability. These mats cannot be used inside the Cricut machines. Some of these offerings include Decorative Self-Healing Mat—Mint, Decorative Self-Healing Mat—Blue, Decorative Self-Healing Mat—Lilac, and more.

EasyPress Mats

The Cricut EasyPress mat is uniquely designed to work with the Cricut EasyPress for impeccable heat transfer projects. The long-lasting cover offers even thermal conduction and uniform distribution of the heat. The interior liner can easily absorb moisture resulting in clean and dry heat. The foil membrane can reflect heat onto the material, preventing the transfer of moisture vapors, while the silicone foam insulates the surface and protects it against heat damage. They come in 3 different sizes, namely, 12 by 12 inches, 20 by 16 inches, and 8 by 10 inches, and special Decorative Polka Dot Mats in blue/mint and rose/lilac in 14 by 14 inches.

Storage

There are 3 different categories of storage bags specifically designed for Cricut machines and tools as described below:

Machine Totes

These premium storage bags are 26 inches long, 9.25 inches wide, and 9.25 inches tall and carefully designed so you can organize and store your Cricut machine at home and easily transport it if needed. The bag has side pockets and compartments to allow storage of craft tools and supplies and comes with a sturdy double-snap handle. These bags have soft padding to provide additional protection and shock absorption. You can buy these bags in different colors (purple, navy, tweed, and raspberry) for $149.99.

Rolling Craft Tote

These bags are equipped with rollers for easy portability and storage at home. They are 26 inches long, 10.25 inches wide, and 14.38 inches tall but remember these bags are designed to store your craft supplies and will not fit any Cricut machines. These bags are also available in different colors (purple, navy, tweed, and raspberry) for $199.99.

EasyPress Tote

These bags are specifically designed for storage of Cricut EasyPress along with its safety base, mat, and other small accessories at home or on the go.

They are made from robust and heat-resistant material to protect your device against bumps and scratches while you work through your heat-transfer projects. A convenient shoulder strap and powerful gripped handle will allow for easy carrying around with the Velcro strap to secure your device for travel. A back pocket and front pocket are added to store the mats and iron-on accessories.

Cricut BrightPad

The Cricut BrightPad is an electronic crafting pad that looks like a tablet. You can use this to light up your paper designs for easier drawing, tracing, weeding, quilting, and lower the strain on your eyes in the process. It is thin, lightweight, and sturdy for comfortable use and portability, with 9 by 11.5 inches of the uniformly LED-lit area and 5 different brightness settings. It is made of a 6H Hardness Surface, which makes it highly resistant to scratches. You can use it to weed vinyl or iron-on designs and paper piecing quilt blocks. Bas well as for models, jewelry, needlepoint. You can buy a Cricut BrightPad in a rose or mint color for $79.99.

Cricut Cuttlebug Machine

The Cricut Cuttlebug is a machine to cut and emboss a range of different materials. With clean and crisp cuts as well as uniform and deep emboss for professional quality results. Cricut also offers an entire line of compatible Cuttlebug embossing folders and cutting dies, while you can still use other folders and dies that are offered by other leading brands. You can use this machine to not only cut and emboss paper but a variety of other materials, including tissue paper, foils, acetate ribbon, and thin leather. You can buy a Cricut Cuttlebug machine in rose or mint color for $89.99. A variety of accessories for this material are also offered, including cutting spacers and embossing folders.

Cricut Accessories

Generally, almost all machines need specific accessories to function properly; the same goes for Cricut machines. There are some accessories you need to possess to use a Cricut machine effectively. Although the accessories you will need will be dependent on the nature of the project you want to work on, and how you want to work on it. Several different accessories work with Cricut machines; however, some are more important than others. Below are accessories you must have when using a Cricut machine, no matter what you are planning to create.

Cricut cutting machines come with quite a few accessories that you can purchase to add to your machine's functionality. There are some accessories that most of the machines can use and others that are designed only for a specific machine.

The newly designed Cricut Explore Air 2 machine comes with all the tools you need to get started for your regular cutting project. Every project will determine what tools you will need, and apart from the Cricut Explore Air 2 and the starter guide.

ACCESS TO A CRICUT MACHINE

Cricut Access is the program that allows you to access pictures, fonts, and other resources. You must acquire this if you intend to use your Cricut machine, and if you do not already have the software, I recommend that you do so.

The monthly plan is ideal for novices, as it includes over 400 distinct typefaces and 90,000 additional pictures. It also includes a 10% discount on any further Cricut purchases, as well as a 10% discount on premium pictures and fonts, such as Disney fonts. In addition, you'll have access to a priority member line. The next membership choice is yearly, which is exactly the same as the basic, and is only $7.99 each month.

If you're serious about getting into Cricut, this is an excellent place to start. Finally, there is the premium option, which is the same price as monthly and provides unlimited access to the same fonts and pictures, discounts on both goods and licenses, and a 50% discount on licensed images and fonts, as well as certain ready-to-make projects. If you buy more than $50 in the Cricut store, you will receive free delivery.

If you intend to spend a lot of money on Cricut things and are in it for the long run, I believe this is the best option. If you're just starting out, the monthly subscription is generally a better option because you may cancel at any moment. Membership entitles you to a small discount on premium ideas and licensed designs - the more you create with your Cricut machine, the more you save, and you'll quickly realize that you might save a lot.

CARTRIDGES

The final item you'll need is, of course, Cricut cartridges. These are little cartridges that you put into the machines that are loaded with different fonts, images, and graphics. You can buy themed cartridges, too, with the idea to create the design that the Cricut machine will make for you.

There are many different ways to use just one cartridge, even though the designs are limited.

Now, if you are getting the Cricut access package, this might not be worth it. This could be a good option to try out.

You can also import images, of course, with the Cricut design space on the most current machines, and these machines also work with Cricut cartridges. For crafters who don't want to design their cuts, this is ideal. You can also use both together, and there are benefits to this, too.

To use the cartridge, you just put it into the machine, go to Design Space, and then follow the steps. Once they're linked up, you can essentially choose the cartridge you want to work on, and you're ready to go.

For newbies, these especially great as you learn how to get better at designing. They are a bit bare-bones, but they're worth it.

The cartridges are a little more expensive than the Design Space and Cricut access alternatives. They're about $20 each unless you're lucky enough to find them on clearance, but here's the thing – you could get hundreds of designs out of that small investment, and if you're not yet sure how to use your Cricut machine, these are great for you to work with.

These aren't used as much these days when compared to the Cricut Access option. However, you'll soon realize that the ability to do different designs is limited on a Cricut machine with just cartridges, and in truth can be almost a bit boring, so you may want to consider an alternative.

With Cricut, there are many materials you can use. While it might seem like a lot, getting them early on or buying even just the basic toolset is a great option.

MATERIALS FOR A CRICUT MACHINE

Certain materials can cut on various Cricut machines, but it does vary from device to machine. The newer engines have more functionality with more materials.

No matter the machine, though, there are some materials you may have thought of, like those listed on the Cricut's website, while there are others you may not have considered. Just like you may not have thought of some out-of-the-box ideas for projects to do!

Main Materials

Cricut.com is a treasure-trove of information for both the new and experienced Cricut users.

One helpful feature is the list and store for materials:

• Cling for windows

• Washi sheets

• Vinyl

• Vellum

• Posterboard

• Iron-on materials

• Foils

• Leather-like materials

• Craft foam

• Papers, including cardstock

Within these categories, multiple items list. For example, under vinyl, items are included like basic vinyl, transfer vinyl, and adhesive vinyl. Ultimately, the Cricut website lists over 100 different materials that the machines can cut, many of which they sell on the site.

Other people prefer to try more out-of-the-box materials and projects to test their creative powers and those of their machines.

Alternative Materials

While vinyl and paper are the most popular materials to cut with your Cricut, they are only the "tip of the iceberg." There are several different materials that crafters have successfully employed with their Cricut machines. Here is a list of some of the things to think about:

Balsa Wood

Balsa is a quick-growing, American tree. The thin wood it produces uses in model making or rafts. It is because it is very lightweight and slightly pliable.

Craft projects from balsa wood include favor tags for wedding or parties, rustic-looking placeholders for the table, or a natural-themed sign for a door or wall.

Duct Tape

The popularity of duct tape as a fashion or crafting item has blossomed over the past few decades, producing projects from wallets to prom dresses.

It is still a material that some Cricut DIY-ers underestimate. This material can be durable and fashionable. Projects made using Duct Tape include Bold and textured gift tags for packages or an art portfolio that showcases the artist's vibrancy and precision with the added touch of this material.

Fabric

Fabric is not an unusual material for some Cricut users. Still, because the variety of fabric available to choose from is complete, it needs to be mentioned again because some techniques and materials are a little more unusual. For example, cutting a lace-like pattern into fabrics can immediately add a color-palette of fancy lace to any project.

Faux Leather and Leather

Cricut.com does not sell real leather. They offer a variety of different leather-like or "faux" leathers. "Faux" means "fake."

Depending on your preference, you can use either material. Despite what you choose, both are suitable materials to cut with the Cricut. Custom jewelry, like necklace pendants or earrings, are simple and stunning projects. These make beautiful and personal gifts or add the right touch to a particular outfit. Leather can also use for making fashionable bracelets or cuffs.

The bracelet is finely cut in cute leather or artificial leather and attached to an adjustable strap. You can also add a hair bow or bow to your clothes or handbag. For a hair bow, hot glue a hair clip to the back when the bow finish. Use hot glue or other adhesives to fix the bow to your clothes or wallet. You can make other hair accessories, such as flowers and different shapes. These can be attached to hair clips, like the bows, or linked to hard or stretchy headbands. Leather can also be used as an embellishment to pillows or other fabrics, like chair backs, or made into manly coasters.

Felt

Felt is another multi-functional material that You can use for a host of projects. Because this item is reasonably sturdy but has good flexibility, it is perfect for just about anything. Also, it comes in all different colors and is relatively inexpensive. Some unique projects that can make from felt including garlands of multi-layered flowers to hang over a window curtain or above a bed, a textured phrase attached to a pillow, an interactive tree-shaped advent calendar, banners, ornaments, and a cupcake or cake toppers.

Magnets

Magnets can use refrigerators, but Cricut can also help create novel and exciting ways to make magnets for all these different purposes. Be selective about the type of interest you choose to cut. Thick and solid magnets do not work well for these projects, but magnets' thinner sheets are suitable for fun crafts.

Some ideas that are outside the fridge-box include:

- Magnet to be attached to the dishwasher that indicates if the machine load with dirty or clean dishes

-Magnetic busy boards such as a mermaid scene with underwater characters or a race track with cars and spectators (do not forget a trophy for the first across the finish line!). Magnetic words to spell out messages on the side of the car or, yes, on the fridge, or school pride or mascots to attach to the vehicle.

Crafting Blanks

The objects you decorate using your Cricut can refer to as blanks. It can be absolutely any object, and it can be something you stick vinyl to, etch, paint, draw on, write on, or anything else you think. They called blanks because they provide a mostly blank surface to decorate, though they can also have colors or designs.

Some popular blanks are cups, mugs, wine or champagne glasses, travel mugs, tumblers, and other such drinking vessels. Craft stores will usually sell these, but you can find them at almost any store. They don't need to be considered a "craft" supply for you to use. Most stores have a selection of plain cups and mugs or travel mugs and tumblers with no designs. As long as you can imagine a Cricut project with it, it's fair game.

Drink wares aren't the only kitchen or dining-related blanks.

Get creative with plates, bowls, and serving utensils. Find blank placemats or coasters at most stores.

Decorate mason or other types of jars. Dry goods containers, measuring cups, food storage containers, pitchers, and jugs—anything you can put in your kitchen can serve as an excellent blank for your projects.

Clothing

Clothing is another popular choice for Cricut projects. T-shirts are easy to make with iron-on vinyl, and you can find cheap blanks at any store or a more extensive selection at craft stores. Craft stores will typically have a large selection of clothing blanks, such as T-shirts, long sleeve shirts, ball caps, plain white shoes, plain bags, and so on.

Thrift stores or consignment shops can be an unusual option as well. You could find a shirt with an interesting pattern that you'd like to add an iron-on to something similar.

Glass

Glass is fun to work with and has many project options with your Cricut machine. Glass blocks can found at craft or hardware stores. Many stores that carry kitchenware will have bare glass cutting boards, or you can find them online. Craft stores and home goods stores could sell glass trinkets or décor that you can decorate. You can even buy full panes of glass at your local hardware store and have them cut it to your desired size.

There are plenty of blanks related to electronics, as well. Electronics stores, online stores, and some craft stores offer phone and tablet case blanks. They might be clear, white or black, or colored. Portable battery packs are another option as well. These blanks are often significantly cheaper than already decorated ones, or you can buy them in bulk for a lower price. Get your phone case for a lower price and customize it how you like.

Book covers

Book covers make great blanks, as well. Customize the outside of your sketchbook, notebook, or diary.

Fix the cover of an old book. Or, create a new book cover for the regular.

If you have old books that you aren't going to read, create a new fake cover for them and use them as décor.

COMPLEX OPERATIONS

Cricut machines are pretty straightforward with what you need to do in order to make simple designs, but you might wonder about some of the more complex operations. Here, we'll tell you how to accomplish these with just a few simple button presses.

Blade Navigation and Calibration

The blades that come with a Cricut machine are important to understand, and you will need to calibrate your blades every single time you use your machine.

Each blade needs this because it will help you figure out which level of depth and pressure your cut needs to be. Typically, each blade needs to be calibrated only once. Once you've done it once, it will stay calibrated, but if you decide to change the housings of the blades or if you use them in another machine, you'll need to calibrate it again.

So, if you plan on using a knife blade and then a rotary blade, you'll want to make sure that you do recalibrate – and make sure you do this before you start with your project.

To calibrate a blade, you just launch the Design Space, and from there, you open the menu and choose calibration. Then, choose the blade that you're going to put in. Assume you're using a knife blade for the purposes of this discussion.

Place the blade in the clamp B region and make a test cut through the mat, such as using copy paper, before loading it into the machine.

Continue by pressing the "continue" button, then the "go" button on the machine. It will then complete all of the necessary tasks for the object and begin to cut.

You may then select the calibration that is ideal for your blade, although typically the initial one is sufficient.

You may do this with every blade you use, and I strongly recommend you do it every time you use a fresh blade on your machine - for optimal results, of course.

Set Paper Size

Setting paper size in a Cricut machine is actually pretty simple. You will want to use this with either cartridge or with Design Space for what you'd like to make. This also comes with a cutting mat, and you'll want to load this up with paper so that you can use it.

To accomplish this, first ensure that it is plugged in, then navigate to the project preview panel. If you pick a material that is larger than the mat size, it will be altered automatically and modified as needed based on the size of the material that you chose.

You may select the color, size of the material, and whether or not it will mirror – and you can also skip the mat entirely if you don't want that picture printed just yet.

Load Last

It is really straightforward to load that paper and image last. Remember the preview we spoke about in the last section? Do you recall the "skip this mat" step? Simply press that and then leave. You'll be able to quickly avoid this. It's one of those activities that's clearly different from what you're used to, but if you want to avoid design and don't want to work with it right now, this is probably the greatest alternative for you to employ. If you're concerned about forgetting, don't be; Cricut will remind you.

Paper Saver

Saving paper is something you should think about doing if you have a Cricut machine since it eats up the paper before you ever start embellishing. If you conserve paper, the Explore Air 2 will undoubtedly appreciate it, and there are a few methods to do it.

The first is, of course, to cut your mats in half. But you don't have to stop there.

You may also use the machine's material saver feature, which will automatically modify and align your paper to the best of its ability. Unfortunately, it is not explicitly mentioned on newer computers, however there is a technique to conserve paper on them.You'll want to create tabbed dividers to organize your projects and save them directly there.

First you need to create a shape. Make sure that the paper looks like a background. Go to shapes, and then select the square to make the square shape.

Next, once you've created squares to represent the paper, arrange this to move to the back so that the shapes are organized to save the most space on each mat.

Rotating is your best friend – you can use this feature whenever you choose objects, so I do suggest getting familiarized with it.

Next, you hide the background at this point, and you do this by choosing the square, and in Design Space, literally hiding this on the right side. Look at the eyeball on the screen, and you'll see a line through the eyeball. That means it's hidden.

Check over everything and fine-tune it at this point. Make sure they're grouped around one object, and make sure everything has measurements. Move these around if they're outside of the measurements required.

Once they're confirmed, you then attach these together on the right-hand side of Design Space, which keeps everything neatly together – they're all cut from the same sheet.

From here, repeat this until everything is neatly attached. It will save your paper, but will it save you time? That's debatable, of course.

Speed Dial

So, the speed dial typically comes into play when you're setting the pressure and speed. Fast mode is one of the options available on the Explore Air 2 and the Maker machines, which make the machine run considerably faster than other models. You can use this with vinyl, cardstock, and iron-on materials. To set this, go to the cut screen. You'll have a lot of speed dials here, and various different settings. If you have the right material in place when choosing it, you'll be given the option to do it quickly with fast mode. From there, you simply tap or click on that switch in order to toggle this to the position for on. That will activate fast mode for that item.

It will make everything about two times faster, which means that if you're making complex swirl designs, it will take 30 seconds instead of the 73-second average it usually takes.

However, one downside to this is that because it's so fast, it will sometimes make the cuts less precise – you'll want to move back to the regular mode for finer work.

This is all usually set with the smart-set dial, which will offer the right settings for you to get the best cuts that you can on any material you're using. Essentially, this dial eliminates you having to manually check the pressure on this.

To change the speed and pressure for a particular material that isn't already determined with the preset settings, you will need to select custom mode and choose what you want to create. Of course, the smart-set dial is better for the Cricut products and mats. If you notice that the blade is cutting too deep or not deep enough, there is a half-settings option on each material that you can adjust to achieve the ideal cut.

Usually, the way you do this with the pre-set settings is to upload and create a project, press go, and load the mat, then move the smart-set dial on the machine itself to any setting. Let's select custom and choose the speed for this one.

In Design Space, you then choose the material, add the custom speed, and you can adjust these settings. You can even adjust the number of times you want the cut to be changed with the smart-set dial, too. Speed is something you can adjust to suit the material, which can be helpful if you're struggling with putting together some good settings for your items.

Pressure Dial

Now, let's talk about pressure. Each piece of material will require different pressure settings. If you're not using enough pressure, the blade won't cut into the material, and if you use too much pressure, you'll end up cutting the mat, which isn't what you want to do.

The smart-set dial kind of takes the guesswork out of it. You simply choose the setting that best fits your material, and from there, you let it cut. If you notice you're not getting a deep enough cut, then you'll want to adjust it about half a setting to get a better result. From there, adjust as needed.

But did you know that you can change the pressure on the smart-set dial for custom materials? Let's say you're cutting something that's very different, such as foil, and you want to set the pressure to be incredibly light so that the foil doesn't get shredded. What you do is you load the material in, and you choose the custom setting. You can then choose the material you plan to cut, such as foil – and if it's not on the list, you can add it.

From here, you're given pressure options. Often, people will go too heavy with their custom settings, so I do suggest that you go lighter for the first time and change it as needed. There is a number of draggers that goes from low to high. If you need lots of pressure, obviously let it go higher. If you don't need much pressure, make sure it's left lower. You will also want to adjust the number of times the cut is done on a multi-cut feature item.

This is a way for you to achieve multiple cuts for the item, which can be incredibly helpful for those who are trying to get the right cut, or if the material is incredibly hard to cut. I don't suggest using this for very flimsy and thin material, because it'll just waste your blade and the mat itself.

That's all there is to it! This is a great way to improve on your Cricut designs. Personally, I love to work with custom cuts, and you can always delete these if you feel like they don't work. You just press the change settings button to adjust your pressure, speed, or how many cuts you want, and then choose to save when you're done.

What if you don't like a setting, period? You can delete it, of course!

To delete, go to materials settings, and you'll see a little trash can next to it. Press the trash can, and the setting will be removed.

Adjusting the pressure and cuts is part of why people love using Design Space, and it's a great feature to try.

Cricut Design Space

Design Space lets you do many things with your Cricut machine. Here are a few things you can do with this convenient app:

- Aligning various items right next to one another.

- Attaching items to hold images in place, and lets you use score lines.

- Arranging these to make them sit on the canvas in different layers.

- Canvas, a tool that lets you arrange prints and vectors so you can use the various tools with them.

- Contouring, which is a tool that lets you hide image layers quickly, so they're not cut out.

- Color sync, which lets you use multiple colors in one project to reduce the material differences.

- Cut buttons, which will start cuts.

- Make it button: this is the screen that lets you see the designs being cut.

- Draw lines: lets you draw with the pen to write images and such.

- Fill: lets you fill in a pattern or color on an item.

- Flipping items flip it horizontally or vertically by 180 degrees.

- Group: puts different text and images on a singular layer, and everything is moved at once so that it doesn't affect the layout.

- Linetype: an option that you can do with your piece, whether you want to cut a line, draw a line, or score a line.

- Mirrored image: reverses it, which is very important with transfer vinyl, so everything reads correctly.

- Print then Cut: it's an option that lets you print the design, and from there, the machine cuts it.

- Redo: does an action again and reverses it.

- Reverse Weeding: removes the vinyl that's left behind, and it's used mostly for stencil vinyl

- Score lines: helps you make creases in the papers so you can fold it.

- SVG: this is a scalable vector graphic that lets you cut a file that's scaled to be larger or smaller so that the resolution is kept, and made up of lines that consist of infinite white dots.

- Texts and fonts: let you use put specialized fonts and words within Design Space.

- Weeding: lets you remove the excess vinyl from designs. Press this when you're cutting vinyl.

- Welding: a tool you use when you want to combine two line shapes into one shape, and it's used to make seamless cursive words.

These are most of the functions you can do in Design Space. To use these, simply choose an image or font that you want to use and put it in Design Space. From there, you can do literally whatever you need to do with it – within reason, of course – and then put the image onto the material that you're using. For the purposes of learning, I suggest not getting in too deep with vinyl just yet, and get used to using these tools. You also have pens, which can be implemented to help you write images with a tool that looks sharp and crisp. We'll go over the purpose of pens and what you can do with them in the next section.

Cricut Pens

Pens for your Cricut machine are essentially another way to get creative with your projects. I love to use them for cards, handmade tags for gifts, or even fancy invites and labels.

Now, each pen offers a little different finish and point size. They aren't toxic, and they are permanent once they're dried. You've got the extra-fine points for small lettering, up to a medium tip for making thicker lines. There are also glitter and metallic pens, so you have a lot of options to choose from!

But do you have to use them? Well, the answer is no. You can use different pens, but test them on paper first and get adapters to use with them. Cricut pens are your best option.

To use these, choose the wording or design, or whatever you want to do. You want to go to the layers panel that's on the right-hand side, and choose the scissors icon – change that to the write icon. From there, you'll want to choose the pen color that you would like to use.

You can then have the design printed out on the material you're using.

Some people like to use different fonts, whether it be system fonts or Cricut fonts, or the Cricut Access fonts. However, the one thing with Design Space is that it will write what will normally be cut, so you'll get an outline of that font rather than just a solid stroke of writing.

This can add to the design, however – you essentially change the machine from cut to write, and there you go.

You can also use the Cricut writing fonts, which you can choose by going to a blank canvas, and then choosing the text tool on the left-hand side, along with the wording you'd like for this to have.

Once you're in the font edit toolbar, you are given a font selection. You choose the writing font filter, so you have fonts that you can write with. From there, choose the font, and then switch from the scissors to the pen icon, and then select the pen color. That's all there is to it!

You can also use this with Cricut Access – if you're planning on using this a lot, it might be worth it.

To insert the pens into the Cricut machine, you want to choose to make it, and from there, you'll then go to the prepare mat screen. It will say draw instead of writing in the thumbnail this time around, so you press continue in the bottom right-hand corner, then put the pen into clamp A – you just unlock it and then put it in. Wait until it clicks, and that's it!

Cricut pens are super easy, and it's a great idea to consider trying these out.

Easy Cricut Pen
<u>Fruity Tray</u>
Materials:

An octagonal tray, crealia coral, light yellow, white, and leaf green decorative paints

One or two flat brushes

A pencil

A 10cm paper disc and brown

Black and glitter green poscas

Polish glue to varnish spray and masking tape.

Steps:

Draw disks on your board and paint them green (mix leaf green with light yellow). It will be necessary to make two layers. After drying, make yellow ovals in the center (light yellow and white) and paint in two coats. All this can be done using the Cricut template

Trace the outlines of the discs in brown. Draw the green lines (see photo) in the green area and then the pips. Apply a spray varnish to prevent the posca from drooling in the glue varnish in the next step.

Stick the stickers with the varnish glue at the bottom of the tray. After drying, apply a little varnish in spray to prevent the ink of the stickers from dissolving in contact with the resin.

Attach the little wooden fruit ornaments using a glue gun.

Here are some indications for a successful resin.

- First of all, the bottom of the tray must be varnished to prevent inks/colors/paints from bleeding into the paint. It is not systematic, but it could happen, so you better take the lead.

- Then, respect the dosages of the packaging and check that you pour the hardener first. - Mix for a long time—10 minutes minimum per cup. Here there are two cups. I have mixed over 20 minutes. Don't hesitate to transfer your mixture to a new cup and mix it again. - pour the resin in the center of the tray and distribute the whole by tilting it.

- Let dry two days, even if the packaging says 24h.

Craft Paper Pencil Holder
The necessary equipment:

Imitation leather kraft paper braiding tape - 9.5 cm

Self-healing cutting mat - 60x45 cm

Transparent ruler for creative hobbies 40 cm

Scissors

Mini high-temperature glue gun

Pencil

Salvaged cardboard, glass, and jar or compass

Discover all steps below:

Beginning by taking a glass and a jar with different diameters. Then you need to trace the outlines of the circles on recycled cardboard. You may also cut it with a cutter. In addition to this, you need to know more about it.

Glue the cardboard discs together with the glue gun. Cut strips of kraft paper braiding 20 cm long. Glue them one by one in radiation. Superimpose them slightly at the base: the bands must be the edge to edge at the circumference of the cardboard disc. In addition to this, you need to know more about it.

Cover the larger cardboard disc in this way. Glue with a glue gun. Fold the braiding strips, measure the cardboard disc's circumference, and cut five braiding strips of this size. In addition to this, you need to know more about it.

Slide a strip of braiding perpendicular under one of those welded to the cardboard base. Stick one end to it, as close as possible to the base. Pass it alternately under one vertical strip and over the next one. Attach a dot of glue to the glue gun under a few vertical strips.

To close, glue the second end of the strip under the first end. In the same way, slip the second strip of braiding, mount a second row, tightening to avoid gaping spaces.

Set up the braiding of the pot with five strips in all. Fold a base strip towards the inside of the pot. Mark the fold in the pot to mark the length. Cut off the excess. In addition to this, you need to know more about it.

Cut a strip of braiding a little larger than the circumference of the pot. Glue to the top edge of the pot with a glue gun. Fold the strips one by one towards the inside of the pot. Glue them with a glue gun. R with a glue gun.9. The pot is ready to accommodate the pencils in your office.

Birth Announcement Card
Make an announcement using different Parisian ties to celebrate the birth of your child.

To make this invitation, you will need:

    i.   An assortment of Parisian ties "newborn girl."

    ii.   An assortment of 80 Parisian ties - Pink

    iii. Alphabet Glitter uppercase - Pink

    iv. 25 Pollen folded cards 135x135 mm - White

v.   Mahé sheet 30.5 x 30.5 cm white

vi.   Mahé sheet 30.5 x 30.5 cm pale pink

vii. Tube of universal gel glue - Cultura - 30 ml

viii.   Precision cutter and three blades

ix.   Self-healing cutting mat - 30x22 cm

x.   An assortment of 3 precision tools

xi.   Transparent ruler for creative hobbies 30 cm

xii. Template to download and print

Discover all the steps below:

STEP 1/8 To start, download, print, and reproduce the heart template. Hollow out the pattern using the cutter to create a stencil.

STEP 2/8 Cut an 11 x 11 cm pink square and a 10.5 x 10.5 cm white square.

STEP 3/8 Center the stencil on the square of white paper and secure it with adhesive paper to prevent it from moving.

STEP 4/8 Place a few Parisian ties to guide you in their positioning inside the cutout heart.

STEP 5/8 Using a precision cutter or paper punch, pierce your card and insert the Parisian clips.

STEP 6/8 Once the heart is filled, glue the white part on the rose.

STEP 7/8 Finish by pasting the desired text (first name.) to finalize the card.

STEP 8/8 The invitation is ready.

Cloud Shelf

Decorate this shelf cloud beautiful papers to Koala's reasons for decorating children's room very softly.

To make this cloud shelf, you will need:

Créalia "Clouds" wooden shelf

Acrylic tube 120 matt white

Flat synthetic brush n ° 18

Straight scissors - 17 cm

Transparent ruler for creative hobbies 30 cm

Precision cutter and three blades

Self-healing cutting mat - 45x35 cm

Cardboard stickers - Little baby

Extra strong double-sided adhesive tape - 6mm x 10m

Discover all the steps below:

STEP 1/6 Paint the cloud shelf white. Let dry.

STEP 2/6 Download and transfer the templates to different papers from the collection and compose the decoration.

STEP 3/6 Glue the cut papers on the cloud shelf using the extra-strong double-sided tape.

STEP 4/6 Personalize the shelf with stickers from the collection.

STEP 5/6 Tip: the 30 x 30 cm block of paper offers visuals to frame to decorate your child's room or make scrapbooking albums.

STEP 6/6 The cloud shelf is ready to decorate your child's room

<u>DIY Bookmark Cat-page</u>
Materials used:

-block of 20 multi-colored cartoline sheets

Glue

Pouch of 24 decorated colored pencils

6 round movable eyes Ø 12mm

PERFO ROUND CLAMP 6MM

5m roll of Glitter masking tape - Green

5m roll of Glitter masking tape - White

Discover all the steps below:

Print the template and choose its paper colors.

Cut out the template along the lines.

Copy the drawing of the body, front legs, and back legs on the brown sheet, do the same in the purple sheet for the belly and cut out.

Glue the elements together with glue.

** To facilitate the gluing, put a little glue in a cardboard plate and use a brush to spread the glue well. Then clean the brush with warm water and soap.

Glue the movable eyes, glue a piece of masking tape to make the collar, cut a piece of pink paper in a triangle for the nose, and draw the mouth, mustaches, and legs with a black pencil.

With the hole punch, make a small circle in the yellow paper and glue it to finalize the cat's collar.

** To get an easy triangle nose, first cut out a square and cut it in half diagonally.

Write your name on the cat's belly with a colored pencil.

And there you have a nice cat-page bookmark for your summer readings. I'm going to reread the adventures of the little wizard, and what will you read?

You can even do it in other colors so that it doesn't get boring!

<u>Table Decoration</u>
Create a fresh and summery decoration for a tropical atmosphere, both on your walls and on your tables! Ideal for your summer evenings to share without moderation!

 To make this tropical decoration, you will need:

Set of 6 Scrapbooking paper sheets - Tropical Paradise

Mahé Leaf - 30.5x30.5cm - petrol blue

Mahé Leaf - 30.5x30.5cm - menthol green

Mahé Leaf - 30.5x30.5cm - lime green

Mahé Leaf - 30.5x30.5cm - spring green

Slate scrapbooking sheet - Mahé - 30x30cm

Sheet of 34 epoxy stickers - Tropical Paradise

Eight card stock polaroid frames - Tropical Paradise

An assortment of 40 die-cuts - Tropical Paradise

100m two-tone spool - Sky blue

16 mini clothespins 35 mm

Vivaldi smooth sheet A4 240g - Canson - white n ° 1

Precision cutter and three blades

Blue cutting mat - 2mm - A3

Black acrylic and aluminum ruler 30cm

Precision scissors 13.5cm blue bi-material rings

3D adhesive squares

Mahé Tools - Easy Mounter - scrapbooking

Pack of 6 HB graphite pencils

Gather the materials.

Using the template and a pencil, reproduce the palm tree on the papers in the collection.

Download and print the template here.

Cut out with a cutter or scissors.

Assemble the trunk of the palm tree. Glue the foliage. Using the template, reproduce the traces of the cocktail support on thin cardboard, following the dimensions indicated. Cover it with the collection paper.

Download and print the template here.

After having cut in the slate sheet: 1 x (8.5 x 8.5 cm), choose a Polaroid. Glue the slate sheet to the back of the Polaroid. Using a chalk pen, write "Cocktail of the day." Decorate with the stickers. Fold the support at the dotted lines.

Using the templates and a pencil, draw the leaves and flowers on the Mahé paper and the collection paper. Draw.

Download and print the leaf and flower template.

Choose photos. Next, cut them to size: 8.5 x 8.5 cm. Stick to the back of the Polaroids.

Glue the leaves and flowers together. Cut the string to the desired dimensions and glue it to the back of the flowers. Glue the birds on the string and hang the photos using mini clips.

And here is a pretty summer and tropical decoration! Beautiful evenings in perspective!

Clothespin Card

The necessary equipment:

Clothespin

Glue

Painting

Color paper or illustrations to download

Decorations: eyes, sequins

The stages of realization:

Start by painting your clothespins.

Cut out the illustrations or your colored paper in a heart shape.

Come and cut your shape in half in the middle.

Apply glue to the ends of your clothespin.

And stick your heart or your butterfly on your clothespin.

We now add glue to the back of your clothespin to be able to place the small text "I love you."

You can also add small decorations to customize your clothespin further. Your laundry card is ready!

HOW TO TAKE CARE OF A CRICUT MACHINE

Every Cricut machine needs to be cleaned and taken care of to keep it working for as long as possible.

Cleaning and Care

Cleaning your machine is very important, and you should do it regularly to keep everything in tip-top shape.

If you don't take care of your machine, that's just money down the drain. But what can you do to care for your machine?

Well, I do suggest that you make sure to run maintenance on it as much as you can and keep it clean.

For beginners, keep liquids and food away from the machine; never drink or eat while you use your Cricut machine.

Set up your machine in a location that's free of dust and try to keep it away from excessive coolness or heat, so don't just throw it in the attic or an exceptionally cold basement.

If you're transporting your machine to use it at a different location, never leave it in the car.

Excessive heat will melt the machine's plastic components, so be careful.

Finally, make sure the machine is stored away from sunlight. Keep it out of places in the home where sunlight hits it directly.

Be gentle with your machine. Remember, it is a machine, so you'll want to make sure that you do take some time and try to keep it beautiful and in order.

Don't be rough with it, and when working with the machine parts, don't be too rough with them, either.

Cleaning the Machine Itself

In general, the exterior is pretty easy to clean; you just need a soft cloth to wipe it off. Keep in mind that those chemical cleaners with benzene, acetone, or carbon tetrachloride should never be used on your Cricut machine.

Any cleaner that is scratchy, as well, should be avoided at all costs. Make sure that you never put any machine components in water.

This should be obvious, but often, people may use a piece of a damp cloth, thinking that it'll be fine when in reality, it isn't.

You should consider getting some non-alcoholic wipes for cleaning your machine.

Always disconnect the power before cleaning, as you would with any machine.

The Cricut machine can then be lightly wiped down. Some people also use a glass cleaner sprayed on a cloth but do be careful to make sure no residue builds up.

If you notice there is some dust there, you can typically get away with a cloth that's soft and clean.

Sometimes, grease can build up—you may notice this on the cartridge bar if you use cartridges a lot.

Use a swab of cotton or a soft cloth to remove it.

Greasing the Machine

If you need to grease your machine, first make sure that it's turned off and the smart carriage is moved to the left.

Use a tissue to wipe this down, and then move it to the right, repeating the process.

From there, move the carriage to the center and open up a lubrication package.

Put a small amount onto a Q-tip.

Apply a thin coating, greasing everything evenly, and also clean any buildup that may have occurred.

There are a few other important parts that you should make sure to clean, besides the outside and the carriage.

Any places where blades should be cleaned, you can just move the housing unit of the blade to clean it.

You should also check the drawing area to make sure there isn't any excessive ink there.

Never use spray cleaner directly on the machine for obvious reasons.

The bar holding the housing shouldn't be wiped down, but if you do notice excessive grease, please take the time to make sure that it's cleaned up.

Remember to never touch the gear chain near the back of this unit, either, and never clean with the machine on for your own safety.

When caring for a Cricut machine, try to do this more frequently if you're using the machine a lot or twice yearly.

Cricut machines are great, but you need to take care of making sure that you keep everything in proper order.

Cutting Blade

Your blades will tend to dull over time, but this is usually a prolonged process.

The best way to prevent it is to have different blades to cut different materials.

Having a different blade for each material is a perfect idea. You can get fine-point ones which are good for smaller items; deep-cut, which is great for leather and other fabrics; bonded fabric, so great for fabric pieces; a rotary blade for those heavy fabrics; and finally, a knife blade, which is good for those really thick items.

In order to maintain your blades, you should clean the housing area for every blade after each use since they get gunky fast.

Squirting compressed air into the area is a beautiful way to get the dust out of there.

As for the blades, remember foil? Use a little bit of that over the edges of the blade to help clean and polish them up.

To polish them, you should put them on the cutting mat and, from there, cut small designs on it. It actually does help with sharpening them, and it doesn't require you to remove them altogether. You can do this with every single blade, too!

To change the blades in their housings, just open the clamps, pull up, and remove the housing within the machine. Put a new blade in, and then close it. That's all it takes.

Storing them is also pretty simple. There is a dropdown doorway in the front area of the machine. It's made for storing the blades within their housings.

Put your loose blades in there first, and then utilize the magnet to keep them in place.

In this way, your blades will always be with the Cricut, even if you take the machine somewhere else.

There is also a blade organizer that you can use, too, made out of chipboard with some holders attached. This is also a wonderful means to store all of your items.

Organizing your Cricut blades is very important, and understanding the best places to keep them is, of course, essential.

Cutting Mat

Your cutting mats need to be cleaned because if you don't clean them frequently, they will attract dirt and lose adhesiveness.

That means you'll have to spend more money on mats, which isn't ideal.

There are different ways to clean them, and we'll go over a few of the different means to clean your mats so you can use them for longer.

Cleaning the Mat Itself

First, if your mat is completely filthy, you need to clean it. Of course, you'll also want to do this for just general maintenance too. Once it's been cleaned, you'll notice it's sticky again.

Typically, washing it down with either a magic eraser or a kitchen scrubber can do it.

Sometimes, if it's really dirty, you might want to get some rubbing alcohol onto a wipe.

But what about the really tough grime? Well, get some Goo Gone cleaner. Put a little bit on the troublesome spots and wipe it around, and then let the goo stick on there.

From there, get an old card or something to get it off, and then wash the mat. Once it's dry, check to see if it's sticky. If it is, then great—you don't need to do anything more.

But what if you notice that it's still not sticky? Well, why not restick the cutting mat itself!

Resticking the Mat

Tape the edges, so you don't get adhesive near the edges and mess with the rollers of the machine. Once that's there, use either spray adhesive or glue stick, and then let it dry.

If you notice that it's still not sticky enough when you're finished applying the first coat, apply a second coat.

There are great adhesives out there, such as simple spray adhesive, easy tack, quilt basting, bonding, and also repositionable e glue.

All of these are fairly effective, and if you notice that the mat is actually sticking pretty well, then you're in luck.

However, always make sure that you let this fully dry.

If you don't let the adhesive dry and you start using the mat again, you will run into the problem of the material being stuck to it.

Once it's dried, try it out with some test material.

If you find it too sticky at this point, put either your hands or a shirt on there to help reduce the tackiness.

Caring for Machines and Mats

Here are a few other tips to use with your cutting mats.

First, use different mats. You may notice that you can get more out of one type of mat than another kind, which is something many people don't realize.

Often, if you notice that you get a lot more out of the firmer grip mats, buy more of those.

Finally, halve your mats.

You can save immensely by making sure that they're cut in half. This does work, and it helps pretty well. You can expect anywhere from about 25 to

40 different cuts before you'll need to replace the mat, but cleaning after about half of that can definitely help with improving the quality of your cuts.

Of course, the life of the mat does vary based on the settings and what materials you cut. When you can't get it to stick, try cleaning and resticking it, but if you notice that it's still not doing the job, you're going to need to get a replacement.

Taking care of your Cricut machine will get you more use out of it, so make sure you perform regular maintenance on all your machine's components so it can be used for years.

CRICUT MACHINE PROJECT IDEAS FOR BEGINNERS

The Glitter and Felt Hair Bow
Supplies:

- Hair bow project file in Cricut

- Design Space Cricut Felt Glitter

- Iron-on Vinyl Hair Clips (large and small)

- Cricut Mat Glue Gun Scissors

- Weeding tools Easy Press

Instructions

To start, in Cricut Design Space, open the design (hair bow); then, click "Make it now." If you would similar to make any modifications to the design, click "Customize."

Insert a regular blade into the Cricut machine. Then place the materials and the appropriate board on the Cricut mat.

Send the document to the Cricut machine and cut it out.

After the Cricut machine has cut out the felt and the iron-on, remove the excess vinyl, then cut around each of the bows using scissors.

Heat your Easy Press. For the settings, check the Easy Press Guide.

Place the vinyl on the cut out felt sticky side down, then heat with the Easy Press for 10 seconds. For larger pieces, do this for each section one at a time, after which you should smooth the Easy Press over the entire design.

Remove the transfer paper and repeat this for all the other bows.

Use the glue to stick one side of the bigger bow piece (the piece without the sharp edges) to the other side. This will form a circle.

Apply glue on the inside and on the middle of that bow piece. After this, fold the piece so that it forms a bow.

Stick the bow to its back piece.

Fold the small bow piece to the middle of the bow. Fold it in the back and glue it as well.

Glue the bow to the bigger or smaller bow clips to have your bow.

Halloween T-shirt
Supplies:

- T-shirt Blanks Glam Halloween

- SVG Files Cardstock Transfer Sheets (Black and Pink)

- Butcher Paper (comes with Infusible Ink rolls)

- Light Grip Mat Easy Press (12" x 10" size recommended)

- Easy Press Mat Flint Roller

Instructions

Import the SVG files into Cricut Design Space and arrange them as you want them on the T-shirt.

Change the designs' sizes to get them to fit on the T-shirt.

Using the slice tool, slice the pink band away from the hat's bowler part (the largest piece). Make a copy of this band and then slice it from the lower part of the hat. With these done, you have three pieces that fit together.

You can change the designs' colours as you would like them. When you are done with the preparation, click "Make It."

Ensure that you invert your image using the "Mirror" toggle. This is even more important if there is text on your design, as infusible ink designs should be done in inverse. This is because the ink part is to go right on the destination material.

Click on "Continue"

For the material; Select Infusible ink. After this, cut the design out using your Cricut Machine.

With the designs cut out, weed the transfer sheet.

Cut around the designs such that the transfer tape does not cover any part of the infusible ink sheet. Ensure that this is done well, as any part of the infusible ink that is not in contact with the fabric will not be transferred.

Preheat your Easy Press to 385 degrees and set your Easy Press mat.

Prepare your T-shirt by placing it on the Easy Press mat, then using a lint roller to remove any lint from the front.

Insert the Cardstock in the t-shirt, between the front and back, where the design will be. This will protect the other side. The T-shirt from having the Infusible Ink on it.

If necessary, use the lint roller on the T-shirt again, after which you should heat your shirt with the Easy Press. Do this at 385 degrees for 15 seconds.

Turn the part where the design faces on the T-shirt. Place the butcher paper on the design, ensuring that the backing does not overlap.

Place the Easy Press over the design and hold it in place for 40 seconds. Do not move the Easy Press around so that your design does not end up looking smudged.

Remove the Easy Press from the shirt and remove the transfer sheet.

To layer colours, ensure that your cutting around the transfer sheet is done as close as possible, then repeat the previous three steps for each colour. This will prevent the transfer sheet from removing part of the colour on the previously transferred design.

Bed and Breakfast guest room wood sign
Supplies:

- Vinyl

- Electronic cutting machine

- Folk-art Color shift Acrylic Paint (Aqua Flash)

- Painted panels

- The paintbrush

Instructions

Vinyl is used as a stencil, and therefore the colour does not matter.

You will weed out the positive space instead of weeding out the negative space.

Paint all the pieces you want.

When finished, rub it on top and remove the vinyl back.

Rub it with the squeegee.

Put the wood mark on it, rub the squeegee gently, and then take out the transfer ribbon.

The paintbrush could get too close to the wood's surface edges.

The Acrylic Paint of Folk-art ® Color Shift is very fun.

Squeeze out some on a palette, or just peel off a little of the vinyl backrest.

Tap onto the paint and dab on a palette of the stencil brush.

You don't want a paintbrush loaded or underneath the vinyl stencil to seep it.

Take the whole positive space up and down.

Folk-art ® Color Shift Acrylic Paint has a certain texture when applied, and a second cover is applied.

Allow the paint to dry then.

This is a questionable point. Some people like to wet paint and stencils, but, honestly, it just requires wet paint to be scrubbed everywhere! Let it dry. Let it dry.

Then, in a corner, peel the vinyl. Peel it back over the top, just as it rolls over it.

Watch on now! Now! It is perfection! B&B — you make both of you!

I'm thrilled... thick paint raises words and pops.

That would make for a hostess a substantial gift too!

Are you not loving it? Have you got the right spot for such a sign?

Get to the lobby and collect one supply!

Valentine's Day Classroom Cards
Supplies:

- Cricut Maker Card Designs (Write Stuff Coloring)

- Cricut Design Space Dual Scoring Wheel Pens

- Cardstock Crayons Shimmer Paper

Instructions

Open the Card Designs (Write Stuff Coloring) on the Design Space, and then click on "Make it" or "Customize" to make edits.

Cricut will request you to select a material when all the changes have been done. Select Cardstock for the Cards and Shimmer Paper for the Envelopes.

Cricut will send you a notification when you need to change the pen colours while creating the Card, and then it will start carving the Card out automatically.

You will be prompted later to change the blade because of the Double Scoring Wheel. It is advisable to use the Double Scoring Wheel with Shimmer Paper; they work best together.

When the scoring has been finished, replace the Scoring Wheel with the previous blade.

After that, fold the flaps at the Score lines in the paper's direction's white side, and then attach the Side Tabs to the Bottom Tab's exterior by gluing them together.

You may now write "From:" and "To:" before placing the Crayons into the Slots.

Place the Cards inside the Envelopes and tag them with a sharp object.

Fancy Ironton Vinyl Tote DIY
Supplies:

- Oversize jumbo 100 per cent Cotton Tote

- Cricut Easy Press

- Cricut Easy Press, Mat

- Cricut Easy Press Space

- Gold Glitter Iron-on Vinyl

- Cricut Explore Air 2

Instructions:

Right-click and save this image. I'm so fancy to make it up.

Download and select Cut into Cricut Design Space. Then image size and reflection on the mat with the plastic coating, place glitter vinyl. Cut it then. Get out of the mate and Easy Press. This leads to a hint that iron is attached to vinyl. Put the 340* Glitter Iron-on Vinyl Easy Press in place for twenty seconds.

Top the Easy Press mat with the tote.

Heat 10 seconds of the canvas tote.

Position the Iron on the plastic vinyl side, while warm, on top of the tote.

On the picture's left-hand side, place the Easy Press for 20 seconds.

Repeat the process for 20 seconds on the right side.

Turn over the bag next and apply Easy Press for 20 seconds on the back.

Turn it over and completely refresh the vinyl.

Peel the plastic off if the vinyl is cool and ready for loading and use!

These super cute hotter gold sandals!

Funny Iron-on Vinyl Shirt
Supplies:

- Cricut Explore Air2 Machines

- Cricut Design Space Directions

- Cricut Easy Press, Mat

- Cricut Nature Walk Basics Patterned Iron-on Sampler

Instructions:

This patterned vinyl is amazing!

Right-click to save the following png. Upload and set for cutting into Cricut Design Space.

Before cutting, ensure that the image is reflected. Then continue clicking.

Put down on the mat the Patterned Iron-on Vinyl face and place the iron on the dial.

Set the shirt on the backside facing Cricut Easy Press Mat.

Heat Easy Press to 340* for 510 seconds and place on the shirt. Then set the Iron Pattern on the warm shirt wherever you like it. The Easy Press is then placed on the plastic and heated for 50 seconds. Repeat the other part of the image process.

Turn off the shirt and heat for 20 seconds on the backside of the shirt. Then cool down the vinyl fully.

Peel off the piece of plastic cover after the vinyl is cool... and you're ready to wear it!

The last day of school is perfect!

Making Monogram Pillows
Supplies:

- Cricut machine

- Iron-on vinyl

- Iron

- Pillow cover

- Muslin cloth

- Transfer tape

- Weeding tool

Instructions

Create the alphabetic design you want to use as your monogram and save it as an image.

Log in to the Cricut Design Space and start a new project.

Tick on the Upload icon and upload the saved image.

Click on the image, drag it to the next page, and select the image type.

Select the parts of the image you do not want as part of the last cut.

Select the image as a cut image; you would get to preview the image as a cut image.

Approve the cut image. You would be redirected to the first upload screen.

Click on your just finishcd cut file, highlight it, and insert the image.

The image is added to your design space for size readjusting. The image is ready to cut.

Highlight the image and use the Flatten button to keep the design together.

Place the shiny side of the iron-on vinyl down on the cutting machine.

Mirror the image before cutting.

Cut the image and remove excessive vinyl after the image is cut with a weeding tool.

Put on a layer of transfer tape to the top of the cut vinyl.

Carefully peel away the paperback of the vinyl.

Preheat the iron and press the pillow cover for a few seconds.

Apply the transfer tape to the pillow cover.

Cover the transfer tale with a muslin piece.

Press the image with medium heat iron for thirty seconds.

Remove the transfer tape from the pillow cover.

Place a muslin cloth piece on the designed part of the pillow cover and press for ten seconds.

Your Cricut monogrammed pillow is ready.

Create Christmas Ornament with Cricut machine
Supplies:

- Cricut machine

- Cricut glitter vinyl

- Transfer tape

- Scraper tool

- Weeding tool

- Ribbon

- Ornaments

Instructions:

Log in to the Cricut Design Space and start a new project.

Click on the Input icon.

Type in your Christmas greetings

Change the text font.

Ungroup and adjust the spacing.

Highlight and "weld" to design the overlapping letters.

Select the parts of the text you do not want as part of the final cut.

Readjust the text size.

Select the file as a cut file. You will get to preview the design as a cut file.

Approve the cut file.

The text is ready to cut.

Abode the vinyl on the cutting mat shiny side down.

Load the mat into the machine.

Custom dial to vinyl

Cut the image.

Practice the weeding tool to remove excess vinyl after the image is cut.

Rub in a layer of transfer tape to the top of the cut vinyl.

Peel back the vinyl paperback.

Apply the vinyl onto the glass ornament.

Go over the applied vinyl with a scraper tool to remove the air bubble underneath the vinyl.

Leisurely peel away the transfer tape from the glass ornament.

How to Decorate a Mug
Supplies:

- Adhesive vinyl

- Cricut machine

- Weeding tool

- Scrapper tool

Instructions

Log in to the Cricut Design Space. Create a new project.

Click on "upload image." Drag the image to the design space.

Highlight the image and "flatten" it. Use the Make It button.

Place vinyl on the cutting mat. Push up against the roller.

Custom dial the machine to vinyl. Load the cutting mat into the machine.

Push the mat up against the rollers. Cut the design out of the vinyl.

Weed out the excess vinyl. Apply a thin layer of transfer tape on the vinyl.

Peel off the backing.

Apply the cut design on the mug.

Smoothen with a scraper tool to let out all air bubbles.

Carefully peel away the transfer tape.

How to Etch Glass at Home
Supplies:

- Cricut machine

- Stencil vinyl

- Rubbing alcohol

- Gloves

- Plastic spoon

- Paper towel

- Etching cream

- Transfer tape

- Scrapper tool

- Weeding tool

Instructions

Log in to the Cricut Design Space.

Create your stencil.

Click on the Text icon and input your text.

Highlight the font and change the font.

Ungroup the text.

Adjust the spacing and let them overlap slightly.

Highlight and group the text.

Adjust the text size to the size of the stencil you want to make.

Highlight the text and "attach" to keep them together.

Click on the Insert Shape icon.

Insert a square shape.

Unlock the shape and make it a rectangle.

Move the new shape over the text.

Right-click on the box and select Move to the Back.

Alteration the colour of the shape to whatever colour you want.

Highlight the entire project and attach it.

After attaching it all, the cutline should be shown.

Press the Make It button on your machine.

Place the stencil vinyl onto the cutting mat.

Load the cutting mat into the machine.

Let the machine cut out the design on the stencil.

Tidy out the excess vinyl with the weeding tool.

Apply a layer of transfer tape on the stencil.

Put on the gloves. Prepare the glass by cleaning it with rubbing alcohol. Apply the transfer tape to the glass.

Brush over with a scraper tool to remove the air bubble.

Use the plastic spoon to apply a thin layer of etching cream to the stencilled glass. Let it dry out for twenty minutes.

Scrap off the etching cream. Remove stencils and wipe the body with rubbing alcohol. Rinse with water. Your etched cup is ready.

Creating Wall Decals
Supplies:

- Adhesive vinyl

- Cricut machine

- Weeding tool

- Scrapper tool

Instructions

Log in to the Cricut Design Space.

Create a new project. Click on Upload Image.

Drag the image to the design space.

Highlight the image and "flatten" it.

Click on the Make It button.

Place vinyl on the cutting mat.

Custom dial the machine to vinyl.

Load the cutting mat into the machine.

Push the mat up against the rollers.

Cut the design out of the vinyl.

Weed out the excess vinyl with a weeding tool.

Apply a thin layer of transfer tape on the vinyl.

Peel off the backing.

Apply the transfer tape on the wall.

Smoothen with a scraper tool to let out the air bubble.

Carefully peel off the transfer tape from the wall.

Treat Boxes
Supplies:

- Cricut machine

- Valentine's Day Treat Box cut document

- Cricut 12" x 12" Light Grasp Tangle

- Cricut Cardstock: White Cricut Scoring Stylus

- Cricut Pens: Dark, Jade, Precious stone Pink

- Double-Sided Tape

Instructions:

After the cut is done, deliberately expel the case format from the tangle. To shield the paper from twisting, turn the tangle, look down, and peel the tangle farther from the paper. The tangle will twist far from the paper (rather than the inverse), keeping your container layout decent and level!

Cut a bit of clear cellophane to cover the heart pattern on the front of the container. The cellophane will enable you to perceive any sweet through the pattern, without your treat dropping out!

Turn the case format over and include several lines of twofold sided tape on the two sides of the heart. Place the bit of cellophane down, finished the heart.

Turn the crate back finished and precisely overlay along most of the score lines. Add some twofold sided tape to the tab on the left half of the case. Unite the two closures and stick the tab under the contrary side.

Fold in the tabs at the base to close the crate. Begin with the biggest "U" formed tab and overlap in the side tabs' finishes. In conclusion, overlay toward the finish of the last tab, and the base of the container will remain shut. The crate is shockingly strong; however, you can include a bit of tape over the creases on the off chance you are stressed over it popping open.

Fill the case with your most loved Valentine's treats. To close the crate, unite the two handles, and pop the tabs through the "keyhole" on the case's sides.

Such a "sweet" present for companions, family, or even an instructor for Valentine's Day! You can compose a brief note or even toss a gift voucher into the crate for a fun shock.

You can give the case somewhat of an alternate look by changing the pen hues.

Bachelorette Party Supplies
Supplies:

- Cricut Creator

- Glitter Cardstock

- Cricut Cardstock

- Standard Grasp Tangle

- Printer - Tattoo Paper

- Adhesive

- Bachelorette Solicitations Document

- Straw and Doughnut Ring Document

- Mini powdered doughnuts

- Straws

Instructions

Anything too thick won't pull through. When you have your record printed, put it on your tangle and load it in the Cricut Creator. It will read the enlistment stamps and start cutting and scoring. Dump your tangle. Load your dark pen into the Cricut Producer (this was incorporated) and your customary cardstock and cut your envelope, little card, and your Lady of the hour Clan image. Add your sparkled cardstock to the tangle and cut the envelope.

At that point, you'll print off your tattoo paper pictures and add that to the tangle. The Cricut Creator sensors are superior to anything the Investigate, so these will cut. Place them into your little embed for the card as an extraordinary shock for your companions. To gather these, include your bigger pink sparkle square within the envelope. Next, overlay in your edges and place a little measure of glue to the sides of the envelope and place the end on the glue. The printed welcome will currently be set on the littler sparkle cardstock with the goal that the shading will crest through the openings your Cricut Producer made. Place some cement on the little squares and follow them together. Place your tattoo embeds behind the square and cling to it to the welcome

For the straw and doughnut toppers, cut your white foundation first, at that point the standard cardstock, and last, the pink sparkle cardstock for the lips. Follow your precious stone tops to the bottoms and place them in your doughnuts. For the lips, there are two openings cut in it, and you string your straw through there.

Tassels
Supplies:

- 12" x 18" fabric rectangles

- Fabric mat

- Glue gun

Instructions:

Uncluttered Cricut Design Space and create a new project.

Select the "Image" button in the lower left-hand corner and search "tassel."

Select the rectangle image with lines on each side and click "Insert."

Place the fabric on the cutting mat.

Send the design to the Cricut.

Remove the fabric from the mat, saving the extra square.

Place the fabric face down and begin rolling tightly, starting on the uncut side. Untangle the fringe as needed.

Use some scrap fabric and a hot glue gun to secure the tassel at the top.

Decorate whatever you want with your new tassels!

Paper Ferens Resin Serving Tray DIY
Supplies:

- Bamboo service tray

- High gloss Envirotex Lite resin

- Green shade paper

- Ultra-seal

- Cricut Explore Air 2 machine

- White paint

- Resin instruction manual handles, cups and sticks

Instructions:

Start with paint inside the tray.

Cut the leafy ferns into 3 colours of green paper during drying on the tray.

Sufficient ferns and fronds should be available to fill the tray.

Then make straight lines on the blades with a straightedge and cutter.

It fit snugly on the tray's edges.

Once cut and fit on the tray, cover with the Ultra Seal the bottom of the tray, then place the leaves above and cover the top with an additional Ultra-Seal. It can slightly bubble up. Don't be panic. Don't panic. Completely let it dry.

Mix the resin to the instructions of the package.

Then pour directly into the middle of the tray.

Tilt the tray slightly to cover the tray's entire base with the resin. Twenty minutes let it sit. Then practice a butane torch or a heat pistol for popping any of the forming bubbles. Then cover with a card piece and let it heal overnight.

It's ready to use when the tray doesn't smell like resin!

Filler with a delicious breakfast or use on the couch as a work surface; There are many ways to experience this fun tropical tray.

Gold Foil Rose Iron on Vinyl on Cricut Straw Bag
Supplies:

- Cricut Easy Press 2

- Cricut Easy Press

- Rose Gold Foil Iron-on Vinyl

- Cricut Maker

- Cricut Easy Press Mat

Instructions:

Set it on the top of the bag with a bright side. Remain firm while it presses inside the bag with towels.

Cover with a cover or Teflon board to prevent the bag's melting.

Set the Easy Press 2 at the correct material temperature. Pull down firmly while heating (Check this chart).

Let the project fully refresh before the carrier plate is removed.

The bag is now ready to be gifted or filled!

Cricut Metallic Foil's Pineapple Polka Dot Shirt

Supplies:

- 27 pineapple

Instructions:

Just add the shape into the software of 27 pineapple tops and 27 pineapple bodies.

The software aligns them automatically to avoid overlapping, and • uses the material to its best use.

Select and create one group of all green tops.

Group all the bases of the pineapple as well.

Then, it will appear on 2 mats when you click to cut.

Load on the mat, the first iron colour.

Metallic gold foil, then.

Line it up and inserted it into Cricut on the mat, colour, and plastic side that touches a mat.

Then, on the dial, choose "iron-on."

And click go!

Click on the image mirror button if the design is not symmetrical. No matter this form.

Your tool kit is needed now.

Use the vinyl excess hook tool.

It's easy to peel off.

The small green tops look fine!

Use the scissors and cut all the scissors apart.

Cut near the tuft base so that it fits closely next to the pineapple gold. Fold repeat.

Cut off the body of the pineapple. Then use the crochet to remove vinyl excess.

And cut off all the bodies of the pineapple. On the ironing board or covered table, set your desired shirt. Then put the shirt in a polka dot pattern on every pineapple.

Place the pineapple bases close to the green tops.

Cover thoroughly with a vinyl-free tea towel.

On each pineapple, press iron for approximately 30 seconds. Completely let it cool.

Then peel the plastic gently and slide it over.

If the vinyl doesn't seem to stay, cover and cool and try again.

An abundant way to add a personalized touch to a present. On a baby slut or tote bag, this would be very nice!

Great way to pick up a shirt out of it! So many options for you to do the work for your trimmer!

How to Create the Stencil for Painting
Supplies:

- Cricut machine

- Stencil vinyl

- Weeding tool

Instructions

Log in to the Cricut Design Space.

Click on the Text icon and input your text.

Highlight the font and change the font.

Ingroup the text.

Adjust the spacing and let them overlap slightly.

Highlight and group the text.

Adjust the text size to the size of the stencil you want to make.

Highlight the text and "attach" to keep them together.

Click on the Insert Shape icon.

Insert a square shape.

Unlock the shape and make it a rectangle.

Move the new shape over the text.

Right-click on the box and select Move to the Back.

Transformation the colour of the shape to whatever colour you want.

Highlight the entire project and "attach."

After attaching it all, the cutline should be shown.

Press the Make It button on your machine.

Place the stencil vinyl onto the cutting mat.

Load the cutting mat into the machine.

Let the machine cut out the design on the stencil.

Tidy out the excess vinyl with the weeding tool.

The stencil is ready.

Wooden Hand Lettered Sign
Supplies:

- Acrylic paint for whatever colours you would like

- Vinyl

- Cricut Explore Air 2

- Walnut hollow basswood planks

- Transfer Tape

- Scraper

- An SVG file or font that you wish to use

- Pencil

- Eraser

Instructions

You will need to start by deciding what you will want to draw onto the wood.

Then, place some lines on the plank to designate the grid's horizontal and vertical axis. Set this aside for later.

Upload the file that you wish to use to the Design Space. Then, cut the file with the proper setting for vinyl.

Weed out the writing or design spaces that are not meant to go on the wood.

Using the transfer tape, apply the tape to the top of the vinyl and smooth it out. Using the scraper and the transfer paper's corner, slowly peel the backing off a bit at a time. Do it carefully.

Remove the vinyl pieces' backing, aligning the lettering or design to be fully centred. Place it carefully on the wooden plank.

Again, use the scraper to smooth out the vinyl on the plank.

Take off the transfer tape by smoothing off the bubbles as you scrape along with the wood sign. Discard the transfer tape at that time.

Continue to use the scraper to make the vinyl smoother. There should be no bumps since this creates bleeding.

Now, paint your wood plank with any colour of your choice. Peel the vinyl letters off.

Napkin Holders
Supplies:

- Colored or glitter cardstock

- Vinyl, if preferred

- Your closure method of choice: glue dots, double stick tape, etc.

Instructions

In Design Space, design the text or names that you want to appear on your napkin wraps. Make sure it is adjusted so that the words will appear appropriately on your wrap width. This is also the time to develop a layer with the flourishing details, like the olive branch and your napkin wrap shape. Think about images and different shapes you could include on your napkin holders.

With your napkin wrap base designed, repeat your patterns and words on the number you need for your place settings. This will tell your Cricut to cut multiple pieces and allow you to customize each one if you desire. If you will be closing the wraps with ribbon and need holes or want to slide the ends together with slits, make sure to add those in now.

Once you have your designs laid out, send the file to cut. Weed out any small items you do not want in your design. Assemble your napkin wrap pieces and wrap your napkins or silverware for your big event! Make sure to attach them securely according to the method you have chosen.

Magnetic Paper Flowers
Supplies:

- Cardstock in a variety of colours or patterns

- Hot glue gun

- Magnets

Instructions:

Open Design Space and develop the shape of your petals. These look good as half circles or oval shapes. You can also create bumped petal shapes by stacking oval over one another. Repeat the petal shapes to make enough flower magnets you want. A large flower typically has about 12 petals, while a medium has about eight. Medium petals are about two inches long, while large petals are usually about three inches. Measure the size of your magnet base and develop a circular flower base. You can add a small, ½ inch long slit at the end of every petal for the easiest construction if you want to.

Once you have your petals designed and duplicated, load the cardstock on your cutting mat and get it ready to cut. Send the file to cut. If you did not add the slit in Design Space, use a crafting knife or an Exacto knife to scratch a slit at the bottom of each petal. Once all the petals have a cut, add a dot of glue and glue one side to the other, making them into the petal shape. Do this to all the petals.

Place your magnets down on the table, gather all the base circles, and glue them to the magnets' tops. Begin gluing the petals to the circle bases, starting on the outside and working your way in. Continue adding petals until it looks full. Large flowers will have about three or more layers, while the medium may only have two. Keep playing with your petals until you have a shape and set up that looks best to you. Consent a small space in the centre of the flower open.

Go back to Design Space and create smaller petals. Make them marginally smaller than the first petals. These add to your flowers' centre, so adjust them according to what you want. If you are uncertain, try a few different shapes to try them out. Add the slits to the petals again, or wait until after they are cut to add the slits with an Exacto knife. When you are ready, send the file to cut. Create the petal shapes with a little glue.

Add glue to the flower design's interior and begin adding the smaller petals to the inside of your flowers. Gently pinch your flowers' edges for a more geometric appearance, or gently curve them inside for something more natural. You can add as many petal layers as you like.

Art Journals
Supplies:

- Glue

- Coloured thread

- Large needle

- Paper piercer or something to poke holes in your paper

- Various cardstock in interesting prints

- Various papers in interesting colours and prints

Instructions

In Design Space, create a square on your canvas. Round the corners. You may want to ungroup the layers and delete the bottom layer. Also, adjust the size of your square to the size of your final notebook. For example, in this example, the notebooks are 5" x 7". This means your square will need to measure 10" x 7". Add your score line to the middle of the square or rectangle shape. You will find this line under "lines." Alter the size to fit your project, and then select "Align" and "Center." This should automatically adjust the line, so it is directly in the middle of your project.

Next, add notches to your center score line to tell you where to pierce your paper. You can place another scoreline at 90 degrees from the centerline and scale it down, so it is small. Alternatively, you can place a tiny circle over the place you want to pierce your paper and have the machine cut the little spot out for you. Measure down about one inch from the top and bottom to place your holes or notches.

If you want to add any custom cut-outs or stickers to the front cover, you can now design those as you desire. Otherwise, you can use the shapes and stickers you already have on hand. You can always create these later than well.

Now you are ready to create the inside pages of your book. You will want to copy and paste the cover rectangle piece and make the pages just slightly smaller than the cover. Consider the size 9.8" x 6.8". This means you will also want to realign your center scoreline. You will also need to alter the size. Do not move your notch or hole marks, though! Keep that one inch from the top and bottom of the cover, not the page!

If you moved the notches or complete marks, you can always group the markings from the cover and copy and paste them for as many pages of the book you are creating. Then move, do not resize these markings, and place them over the centerline of each page.

If you want to add images and cut-outs to the internal pages, you can add those now. Keep in mind that any words you cut out on one side of the page will appear back on the other side! Consider using images and shapes to be safe. You can also create vinyl stickers or drawn images to the pages if you do not want to cut them into paper.

If you choose vinyl words or images, some art mediums may struggle to cover them properly.

When you are done designing your pages, send your file to print. Cut, and score your cover and pages. Tail the reminders to load your paper and tools into your machine.

After your pages and cover are cut, fold on the scoreline, place the pages into the cover and line up the notches or holes. If you are using notches, use your paper punch to poke holes in the cover and paper where the notches are located. Depending on your paper, punch holes one at a time.

Thread your needle with the colored thread. Pass your needle through the holes and tie a slip knot. Tighten your knot as tight as possible, and then tie off with a regular knot. You can tie on the outside of the journal or the inside. Trim the threads as short as you want.

If you are decorating your cover, make sure you add stickers or vinyl to the cover as you prefer. Now you are ready to start journaling away!

Unicorn Wine Glass
Supplies:

- Stemfewer wine glasses

- Outdoor vinyl in the color of your choice

- Vinyl transfer tape

- Cutting mat

- Weeding tool or pick

- Additional fine glitter in the color of your choice

- Mod Podge

Instructions

Uncluttered Cricut Design Space and create a new project.

Select the "Text" button in the Design Panel.

Type "It's not drinking alone if my unicorn is here."

Using the drop-down box, select your favorite font.

Adjust the positioning of the letters, rotating some to give a whimsical look.

Select the "Image" button on the Design Panel and search for "unicorn."

Select your favorite unicorn and click "Insert," then arrange your design on how you want it on the glass.

Place your vinyl on the cutting mat, making sure it is smooth and making full contact.

Send the design to your Cricut.

Use a weeding tool or pick to remove the excess vinyl from the design. Use the Cricut Bright Pad to help if you have one.

Apply transfer tape to the design, pressing firmly and making sure there are no bubbles.

Remove the paper backing and apply the words to the glass where you'd like them. Sabbatical at least a couple of inches at the bottom for the glitter.

Smooth down the design and carefully remove the transfer tape.

Coat the bottom of the glass in Mod Podge wherever you would like glitter to be. Give the area a wavy edge.

Sprinkle glitter over the Mod Podge, working quickly before it dries.

Add another layer of Mod Podge and glitter and set it aside to dry.

Cover the glitter in a thick coat of Mod Podge.

Allow the glass to cure for at least 48 hours.

Enjoy drinking from your unicorn wine glass!

Framed Succulents Made from Paper
Supplies:

- Foam brush

- Standard grip cutting mat

- Deco Art acrylic paint for the frame

- Scissors to curl the succulent petals

- A piece of chipboard, cardstock, or cardboard

- 12x12 cardstock in assorted green colors

- Glue gun

Instructions:

Start with painting the picture frame you wish to use. Unless you wish to leave it as rustic and old as I would.

Place your chipboard or cardboard to the inside of the frame. This is for placing the succulents on. Frame it properly using a glue gun.

Press: Go to cut out the succulents.

As soon as all the pieces have been cut from the paper, you can assemble them to make your succulent.

Once the succulents are created, you can glue them aboard.

Live, Love, Laugh Glass Block
Supplies:

- Glass block

- Frost spray paint

- Clear enamel spray

- Holographic vinyl

- Vinyl transfer tape

- Cutting mat

- Weeding tool or pick

- Fairy lights

Instructions

Spray the entire glass block with frost spray paint, and let it dry.

Spray the glass block with a coat of clear enamel spray and let it dry.

Uncluttered Cricut Design Space and create a new project.

Select the "Text" button in the Design Panel.

Type "Live Love Laugh" in the text box.

Use the dropdown box to select your favorite font.

Arrange the words to sit on top of each other.

Place your vinyl on the cutting mat.

Send the design to your Cricut.

Use a weeding tool or pick to remove the excess vinyl from the design.

Apply transfer tape to the design.

Remove the paper backing and apply the words to the glass block.

Smooth down the design and carefully remove the transfer tape.

Place fairy lights in the opening of the block, leaving the battery pack on the outside.

Enjoy your decorative quote!

Vinyl Car Window Decal Sticker
Supplies:

- Cricut Explore Air (used is a suitable solution if you want to save some money)

- 2 Premium Outdoor Glossy Vinyl

- Transfer Tape

- Scraper Tool

Instructions:

You can use Premium Outdoor Glossy Vinyl to transform any cut picture into a window decal. You can select a photo from Cricut Design Space, but I'll explain how to upload an image and generate your cut file. To find the ideal picture, simply google search. There are loads of images to choose from, but the simpler the model, the faster it transfers to a cut file. Note that most images will have copyright, and you will be in breach if you use them for business (so, if this the case, be sure to purchase the copyright before starting the project).

When you discover your picture, right-click to save it to your laptop. Go to Cricut Design Space, click New Project.

Tick the Upload key at the bottom left.

Click Upload Image to drag or drop the picture to the next page.

Click the Cricut Design Space Upload button to pick your picture type. You can go simple or have fun with the colors; there are many possibilities to choose from.

Click when selecting the picture type in the Cricut design room and choose which picture regions are not part of the last cut.

Select the picture area to cut the Cricut machine to generate the window decal, the select the picture you have chosen.

This also provides you a preview of how the cut picture looks.

There is a back button you can press to adjust to the image before.

After approving, you are taken back to the initial upload screen, but this time you can see your latest cut file among the pictures.

Cut your Cricut Machine Vinyl Decal Click the picture to highlight, then select Insert Image.

To create your vehicle decals, select the picture to put it into the canvas. That brings the picture to your design region, where you can adjust the image's size or direction. Now you're ready to cut.

Resize the picture to the size of your vehicle window (remember to be precise and take measures first), then click on the green button that says "Make It" and follows the prompts to cut the Cricut Premium Glossy Vinyl picture. After cutting, thoroughly weed or remove the surplus vinyl. Apply a transfer tape player to the cut vinyl. The transfer tape will help you position the vinyl with none of the parts stretching or moving out of the location.

Apply carefully vinyl transfer paper decal to the window where you want to put the sticker. Then go over again with rubbing alcohol to remove surplus grease or fingerprint smudges.

Carefully peel back the vinyl's paperback to allow all elements of the picture release from the sheet.

Remove the paper backing from the car window decal to apply the vinyl, begin at one end or corner and roll the plastic down.

This will guarantee even placement.

Go over the scraper tool transfer tape and push any bubbles below the vinyl. Scrape over the vehicle decal when applying the transfer tape to a window.

CRICUT MACHINE PROJECT IDEAS INTERMEDIATE LEVEL

When you begin to venture into the types of projects needing more expertise, you will find that you need to branch out to websites providing their own design and cutting files that you can use to create more and more imaginative stuff.

For this reason, I would suggest searching for various online tools for projects you can do to expand your horizons when it comes to more complex projects!

There's a list of 100 crafts you can do with your Cricut device to make your crafts special to you to give you some ideas to get you started on where to look!

False Cowhide Home Keychain
Tools And Materials:

- Cricut Creator
- Faux Calfskin
- Suede
- White Press on Vinyl
- Leather Paste
- Keychain Ring
- Standard Grip Tangle (green)
- Iron or Simple Press

Steps:

1. You must use the false cowhide for the house, the calfskin for the heart, and the iron-on for "home" Use cowhide paste to join the heart to the fluffy side calfskin house that doesn't show some kindness cut out.

2. Put calfskin stick on the house around the heart and connect the other house, fluffy side down. Let sit for 30 minutes. Preheat the false calfskin for 35 seconds before squeezing the home on with the iron or Simple Press.

3. Put the key chain ring through the entire at the highest point of the house.

4. Also, much the same as that: you have the ideal housewarming present for pretty much anybody!

Poster Paper Cricut
Tools And Materials:

- A text-weight or some card stock papers

- A white; vellum of 11 × 17-inch cream

- A card stock, a cotton twine; two wood trim pieces of about 11 inches

- of length

- A double-sided adhesive roller

- A craft tape

- A low-temp hot glue gun

- An IRON-ON PATCH

- A cutting-machine iron-on vinyl

- A wool-blend felt

- A fusible bonding web

- Scissors

- A weeding tool

- An iron and an ironing surface

- A smooth cotton ironing cloth

Steps:

1. Cut all the pieces from the text-weight or the card stock papers and the bee wings' vellum.

2. Place the tape on the back of the top layers of the bugs and the wing edges.

3. Position; then press the layers into place, repeat the same process with the leaf layers.

4. Print the poster design onto a cream card stock of about 11 × 17-inch cream card stock and adhere

5. Finish the design by adding the leaves, tape the cotton twine to the hang poster.

6. Glue about 11-inch-length wood trim pieces to the back and the front of top of the poster art.

Cricut Tassels
Tools And Materials:

- A Fabric of about in 12″ x 18″ rectangles

- A Cricut Maker with a Rotary Blade

- A 12″ x 24″ Pink Fabric Grip Mat

- A Brayer (optional)

- A Hot Glue

- A Cricut Design Space File

Steps:

1. Start by opening up the file in your Cricut Design Space

2. You'll see that the Cricut Design Space is a rectangle with a bunch of lines in parallel structure into either the sides of it; then Click the Make it into the upper right of the canvas

3. There is no need to make any type of changes at this step; so you should click the button 'Continue'.

4. Select the type of fabric that you are using; if you are using cotton; press the setting cotton

5. The cricut Design Space will be automatically changed to the Rotary Blade.

6. Insert the Rotary Blade into the Cricut's housing.

7. Place the fabric on the Cricut mat; then carefully smooth out the fabric or you can also use a brayer so that you can keep the oils on your fingers as far away from the mat adhesive

8. Insert the mat into your machine; then click the blinking "C" to perform the process of cutting

9. Remove the fabric tassel from the mat; then peel off the mat and keep the scraps

10. Put the fabric with the face down onto a table; then start at one uncut end

11. Roll the fabric; then untangle the fringe as you keep going, layout the tassel with the face down; then start to roll

12. Bend into half so that you can create a loop; to do that; use a piece of scrap fabric from the top; then secure the tassel with a little quantity of hot glue

13. Make sure that you can feed one piece of a ribbon or twine through the loop you have made

Monogrammed Drawstring Bag
Tools And Materials:

- Two matching rectangles of fabric

- Needle and thread

- Ribbon

- Heat transfer vinyl

- Cricut EasyPress or iron

- Cutting mat

- Weeding tool or pick

Steps:

1. Launch Cricut Design Space and start a new project.

2. Click the "Image" button in the lower left-hand corner and search for images. "monogram."

3. Select the monogram of your choice and click "Insert.", place the iron-on material shiny liner side down on the cutting mat, send the design to the Cricut.

4. Use the weeding tool or pick to remove excess material, remove the monogram from the mat.

5. Center the monogram on your fabric, then move it a couple of inches down so that it won't be folded up when the ribbon is drawn, iron the design onto the fabric.

6. Place the two rectangles together, with the outer side of the fabric facing inward.

7. Sew around the edges, leaving a seam allowance. Leave the top open and stop a couple of inches down from the top, fold the bag's top down until you reach your stitches.

8. Sew along the bottom of the folded edge, leaving the sides open, turn the bag right side out.

9. Thread the ribbon through the loop around the top of the bag, use your new drawstring bag to carry what you need!

Watercolor Heart Sign
Supplies Needed

- Watercolor paper

- Watercolor paints and paintbrush

- Glue

- Lightstick cutting mat

- Weeding tool or pick

- Frame

Steps:

1. Paint your watercolor paper in soft gradients. Use a lot of water and gradually blend two or three colors into each other. Set aside to dry, open Cricut Design Space, and create a new project.

2. Click the "Image" button. and search for "heart."

3. Select the heart of your choice and click "Insert.", place your watercolor paper on the cutting mat.

4. Send the design to your Cricut, remove the outer edge of the paper, leaving the heart on the mat.

5. Use your weeding tool or carefully pick to remove the heart from the mat.

6. Glue your heart to the center of a blank piece of paper, cut to fit your frame.

7. Place your sign into your frame, set or hang wherever you need a little color!

Cricut basket
Tools And Materials:

- A Pattern Piece SVG file for the Cricut Design space

- A Cricut Maker Machine

- A 1 Fat Quarter of Fabric or about ½ yard for the Basket Outside

- A 1 Fat Quarter of Fabric about ½ yard for the Basket Lining

- A large piece of Shape Flex Interfacing

- A large piece of Decor Bond Interfacing

- A matching Thread

- A Walking foot for Sewing Machine

- A 12″x 24″ Fabric Mat for the Cricut Make

- A Fabric Marking Pen for the Cricut Maker

For the Labels:

- A Cricut Lite Iron on Vinyl

- A Cricut EasyPress

- A Scrap of Canvas

- A Heat N Bond Lite

- Some Cricut SVG Cut files of Words

Steps:

1. Begin by uploading the sewing pattern piece to the Cricut Design space; it will then upload in at a width of about 16″ wide x 10 ½″ of height which will fit on a large fabric cutting mat

2. You can't make any part of your chosen pattern piece larger than about 11 ½ "of width

3. Size the Pattern Piece; then after sizing it; you just need a few marks to pattern this piece accordingly; this will help you sew the baskets altogether and to do this; all you need to do is to click the shape box that is on the lower left-hand side of your design software; then click on the add and the scoring line

4. Now, it is time to add a Stitching Line for your Fabric Pen and to do that; draw a scoring line along the top of the pattern piece about ½″ down from the top edge of your chosen pattern.

5. After you have already drawn the line, start going over to the line attributes box; then click your circle icon and change the line from scoring to Write line; then select the Fabric Marker from the drop-down list

6. And after that is done, all you need to do is to click on the two pieces; then click the 'attach' over the layers panel and this will make your piece cut; then mark at the same time

7. Click the button "Make it"; then it is the time for cutting; all you need to do is to cut the same piece 4 times; 2 for the lining of your basket and 2 for the front basket; if you have a small piece

that you can make it fit both on about one 12″ x 24″ mat; then you will only need no more than 2 mats.

8. In the dialog box and in the upper left-hand corner, change the number of the copies to 4.

9. Cut out the interfacing in a separate way; then iron the interfacing onto your fabric; then just cut out

10. Cut the basket outside fabric, the lining fabric, and the interfacings to about 12″ wide

11. Iron your Shape Flex interfacing onto the wrong side of the basket outside pieces

12. Iron your Decor Bond interfacing onto the wrong side of the basket lining pieces

Unicorn Wine Glass
Tools And Materials:

- Stemless wine glasses

- Outdoor vinyl

- Vinyl transfer tape

- Cutting mat

- Weeding tool or pick

- Extra fine glitter

- Mod Podge

Steps:

1. Launch Cricut Design Space and start a new project., select the "Text" button in the Design Panel.

2. Type "It's not drinking alone if my unicorn is here.", using the dropdown box, select your favorite font.

3. Adjust the positioning of the letters, rotating some to give a whimsical look.

4. Select the "Image" button on the Design Panel and search for "unicorn."

5. Select your favorite unicorn and click "Insert," then arrange your design how you want it on the glass.

6. Place your vinyl on the cutting mat, making sure it is smooth and making full contact.

7. Send the design to your Cricut.

8. Use a weeding tool or pick to remove the excess vinyl from the design. Use the Cricut BrightPad to help if you have one, apply transfer tape to the design, Firmly pressing and ensuring sure there are no bubbles

9. Remove the paper backing and apply the words to the glass where you'd like them. Leave at least a couple of inches at the bottom for the glitter, smooth the design down, and gently remove the transfer tape. Coat the bottom of the glass in Mod Podge, wherever you would like glitter to be. Give the area a wavy edge.

10. Sprinkle glitter over the Mod Podge, working quickly before it dries, add another layer of Mod Podge and glitter, and set it aside to dry.

11. Cover the glitter in a thick coat of Mod Podge, allow the glass to cure for at least 48 hours.

12. Enjoy drinking from your unicorn wine glass!

A pet container
Tools And Materials:

- A Cricut Joy

- Your Smartphone (with the Cricut app)

- A Cricut Joy Pen

- A Cricut Joy Smart Label.

Steps:

1. The Cricut Joy is easy to turn on and lug in

2. Search for a fun font and a Cricut Access image of a balloon dog into the app

3. Now, you are ready to draw and cut; the app will tell you when to switch from the pen to the cutting blade

4. With the Joy Cricut Joy; you don't need a cutting mat

5. Grab a roll of vinyl, a Cricut Joy pen as well as the Cricut Joy; then label the whole house

6. So in a few minutes, you will have a new label of your jar

Patterned Gift Wrap
Supplies Needed

- White kraft paper

- Cricut Pen Tool in color(s) of your choice

- 12x24 cutting mat

- Weeding tool or pick

Steps:

1. Launch Cricut Design Space and start a new project. Select the "Image" button in the lower left-hand corner and search for doodled images appropriate for the gift you're wrapping, for example, "Christmas doodle" or "birthday doodle."

2. Select the images you like and click "Insert."

3. Copy, resize, and rotate the images to create a pattern you like for your wrapping paper's size.

4. Change the doodles' colors if desired—leaving them black creates a coloring-book feel, or you can make them in different colors, place your paper on the cutting mat.

5. Send the design to your Cricut, remove your wrapping paper from the mat.

6. Wrap your gift in your customized wrapping paper!

Flower Coloring
Tools And Materials:

- A Cricut Machine and Cricut Design Space

- A Flower cutouts and heart accessories

- A 12″ x 12″ StandardGrip Cricut® mat

- A Cardstock and paperwhite

- A Black Cricut pen

- Some Colored pencils and markers – optional

Steps:

1. Follow the instructions to draw; then cut the flower coloring card design into the Cricut Design Space.

2. Fold the card along score line; then cover the way you like

3. Fold the score lines; then glue the side flaps inside the back of the envelope, add the confetti inside the envelope and seal; then send.

4. Use the colored pencils and the Tombow markers to color the coloring page, colour with the colored pencils

Rose Gold Leather Earrings
Tools And Materials:

- Cricut Maker

- Cricut Strong Grip Mat

- Clear Contact Paper

- Cricut Metalic Rose Gold Vinyl

- Cricuts tools

- Hook and jump rings

- Criticut Metal leather Gold Cricut

Steps:

1. Start by stitching a clear contact paper to the back side of the leather. This keeps everything from the matt surface and keeps the mat more useful.

2. To design a rope shape with a tiny hole cut at the top, use Cricut Design Space. Cut it off, then. I shouted I was using the blade for the knife, but I was too tired to switch to it.

3. And the leather wasn't really cut all around its rear edge, so there's a bit of fluff. I cut it off with the scissors of Cricut, then use some pins to attach a hook on the leather earring.

4. Cut some sweet shapes out of metallic rose vinyl gold. These are the forms in the Cricut Access file I found on a CDS.

5. Then peel the leather and stick it to the back. The rose-gold and rose-gold vinyl go hand in hand.

6. Under the layers of leather, I like the hit metallic, such a simple DIY for a good declaration pair of earrings.

Cricut Tote Bag
Tools And Materials:

- A Cricut machine and Cricut Design Space

- A Tote bag project canvas

- A few Cricut Infusible ink pens

- A Cricut Easy Press and a mat

- A White paper

- A Parchment paper

Steps:

1. Start by going to the pre-set Cricut project canvas for this personalized tote bag.

2. Now, edit the design you want to use your monogram letter for and the favorite ink colors

3. Follow on the screen instructions to create your monogram design on the white paper and don't forget to mirror the image before creating it, pre-heat the Easy Press to about 400 degrees (As per Infusible ink user instructions), put the EasyPress mat into the tote bag; then iron out any wrinkles on the tote bag

4. With the use of a lint brush, clean off your tote bag

5. Now; put the design with the face down onto your tote bag; then tape into place with heat-safe tape and cover with parchment paper, heat set your infusible ink design onto the tote bag

Baby Burp Cloth
Tools And Materials:

- A Burp Cloth SVG Pattern

- 2 Gutermann Thread

- A Fabric grip mat of about 12 x 24"

- A Cricut Maker

- A Rotary Blade

- A Cricut Rotary Cutter

Steps:

1. Start by uploading the burp cloth svg to the Cricut Design Space, you should first edit the file so that it is about 10" of width and about 20" of length, you can also adjust it to be bigger or smaller to your liking

2. Place the fabric onto the Cricut 12 x 24 Fabric Grip Mat

3. Make sure to change the blade to the rotary cutter; then load the mat into your machine and cut out your own pattern, unload your favorite cutting mat; then peel away any excess of fabric

4. Remove the burp cloth pattern; then place 2 burp cloth pieces with the right sides all together

5. Stitch the 2 pieces altogether, but make sure to leave about 2 to 3" of the opening so that you can turn it side out, use the scissors so that you can clip around the burp cloth; then press

and turn the burp cloth right side out through the opening of about 2 to 3" of opening and Press.

6. Topstitch around the obtained entire burp cloth at 1/8"; then press.

Multi-Day Tee And Koozie
Tools And Materials:

- Cricut

- Cricut Press On Vinyl

- Cricut Toolbox

- Cricut EasyPress

- Cricut BrightPad (discretionary, however super accommodating)

- Blank shirts and can koozies

- Cricut cut record and Bonjour Textual style for this shirt.

Steps:

1. Open the slice documents and change by fit your shirts. Send to the Cricut to cut; make sure to reflect cut iron-on glossy vinyl side down.

2. Weed the vinyl. The BightPad is super useful.

3. Apply the vinyl on the shirts and koozies with the EasyPress. We utilized the Cricut press on the defensive sheet for the koozies and squeezed them at 360* for 30 seconds. We did likewise for the shirts, however, we rehashed the procedure within the shirts as well.

That is it! You have cute amusement day wear for any diversion you are going to!

Pet Bandana
Tools And Materials:

- A Cricut Joy

- A Cricut Easy Press 2 9" x 9" or Cricut EasyPress 2 6" x 7"

- A Cricut Easy Press Mat or fluffy beach towel

- A Smart Iron-On Glitter (I'm using Fluorescent Pink)

- A Weeder tool

- A 100% cotton pet bandana

- A 100% cotton hair tie

Steps:

1. Open the Lucky Pet Bandana and the Matching Hair; then tie the project into the Design Space; you need a Cricut Access

2. First, measure the bandana of your pet; then adjust the size of your bandana pet on the canvas with the help of the arrow; now to customize the name of the pet; click first on the "Lucky Penny" Layer

3. Click on the Detach so that you can separate the three layers; then double click on the "Penny" and change the name of the pet

4. Adjust your design so that it can fit the template of the bandana by typing into a new size with the use of the arrow to decrease or increase the size

5. To customize the pet name, click on the "Lucky Penny" layer; then click on the setting "Detach" to help you separate all the three layers

6. Double click on the button "Penny"; then change the name to the pet name

7. Adjust the design to fit the bandana template by typing into a new font size or just by using the arrow to increase or decrease the size.

8. Hold down the key "shift"; then select all the three layers and click on the button "Attach"

9. Repeat the same steps for the layers of the hair tie; hide the template of the bandana; then click the Make It button and change the type to 'Without Mat'

10. Turn on the feature Mirror; then hit the button continue and let the Cricut Joy to connect via the Bluetooth

11. Set the material to Smart Iron-On Glitter or just click to Browse All the Materials and select another Smart Iron-On material.

12. Now; make sure that the Cricut Joy Blade is very well inserted; then load the Smart Iron-On Glitter with the shiny side down; the machine will automatically be pulled into the material; then measure it to make sure that you have enough to complete the project.

13. Click the button 'Go' and the machine will start cutting and once the cutting process is complete, click the Unload to release the material.

14. Cut the iron-on into the needed pieces for each of the projects and weed out the smaller inner pieces with the help of the Weeder Tool

15. Carefully peel back the rest of the iron-on to reveal the chosen design

16. Now, refer to the Heat Guide so that you can determine the settings for your Easy Press

17. Select the heat-transfer material, the base material and the iron onto the surface (towel); then click the button Apply

18. Turn on your EasyPress 2; then preheat to a temperature of about 3400F. Apply the heat to the bandana for about 5 seconds; then position the iron-on onto the bandana with the face down with the liner side up.

19. Press for about 30 seconds; then flip the bandana over and press for about 15 seconds; finally, let it cool before removing your liner

20. Repeat the same process with the hair tie

Art Journals
Tools And Materials:

- Glue

- Colored thread

- Large needle

- Paper piercer or something to poke holes in your paper

- Various cardstock in interesting prints

- Various paper in interesting colors and prints

Steps:

1. In Design Space, create a square on your canvas. Round the corners. You may want to ungroup the layers and delete the bottom layer. Also, adjust the size of your square to the size of your final notebook. For example, in this example, the notebooks are 5" x 7". This means your square will need to measure 10" x 7".

2. Add your scoreline to the middle of the square or rectangle shape. You will find this line under "lines." Select "Align" and "Center." This should automatically adjust the line so it is directly in the middle of your project.

3. Next, add notches to your center score line to tell you where to pierce your paper. You can place another scoreline at 90 degrees from the centerline and scale it down so it is small. Alternatively, you can place a very small circle over the place you want to pierce your paper and have the machine cut the little spot out for you. Measure down about one inch from the top and bottom to place your holes or notches.

4. If you want to add any custom cut-outs or stickers to the front cover, you can now design those as you desire. Otherwise, you can use the shapes and stickers you already have on hand. You can always create these later as well.

5. Now you are ready to create the inside pages of your book. You will want to copy and paste the cover rectangle piece and make the pages just slightly smaller than the cover. Consider the size of 9.8" x 6.8". This means you will also want to re-align your center scoreline. You will also need to adjust the size. Do not

move your notch or hole marks, though! Keep that one inch from the top and bottom of the cover, not the page!

6. If you moved the notches or hole marks, you can always group the markings from the cover and copy and paste them for as many pages of the book you are creating. Then move, do not resize these markings, and place them over each page's centerline.

7. If you want to add images and cut-outs to the internal pages, you can add those now. Keep in mind that any words you cut out on one side of the page will appear back on the other side! Consider using images and shapes to be safe. You can also create vinyl stickers or drawn images to the pages if you do not want to cut them into the paper. If you choose vinyl words or images, some art mediums may struggle to cover them properly.

8. When you are done designing your pages, send your file to print, cut, and score your cover and pages. Load your paper and tools into your machine.

9. After your pages and cover are cut, fold on the scoreline, place the pages into the cover and line up the notches or holes. If you are using notches, use your paper punch to poke holes in the cover and paper where the notches are located. Depending on your paper, you may want to punch holes one at a time.

10. Thread your needle with the colored thread. Pass your needle through the holes, and tie a slip knot. Tighten your knot as tight as possible and then tie off with a regular knot. You can tie on the outside of the journal or the inside.

11. Trim the threads as short as you want. If you are decorating your cover, make sure you add stickers or vinyl to the cover as you prefer. Now you are ready to start journaling away!

Cricut Notepad
Tools And Materials:

- A Cricut Maker (or Explore)

- A Fine Point Blade

- A Light Grip Mat

- An every day Iron-On in the color of your choice

- An EasyPress 2 (I used the 6″ by 7″ size)

- An EasyPress Mat 8″ 10″

- A Blank Canvas Notebooks (like these)

- Some Watercolors

- Some Watercolor brushes

- A BrightPad

- Some weeding Tools

- A Matte Mod Podge (optional)

- Access to Cricut Design Space

Steps:

1. With the help of a fine point blade; cut out the vinyl, wed the vinyl with BrightPad weeding tools.

2. Now, heat up the EasyPress 2 and just set it to the setting canvas.

3. Heat up your notebook a little bit; then place your design right on top

4. Use the EasyPress 2 onto your book's cover; then open the book and heat your design from the other side.

5. Let the design cool; then remove the film, once the Vinyl has perfectly cooled, use the watercolors to your liking

6. You can also paint the cover with the plain water, coat the cover into a thin layer of Mod Podge so that you can seal it

Holiday Gift Card Holders
Supplies Needed

- Holiday-themed scrapbook paper

- Cricut Scoring Stylus

- Light grip cutting mat

- Weeding tool or pick

- Glue stick

- Ribbon, twine, or string to match your paper

Steps:

1. Create a new project on Cricut Design Space.

2. Select the "Image" button in the lower left-hand corner and search for "gift card."

3. Select the gift cardholder template and click "Insert.", insert the scoring stylus into the Cricut, making sure it is secure and place your paper on the cutting mat.

4. Send the design to your Cricut, use the weeding tool or carefully pick to remove the template from the mat.

5. Bend the large outer piece and the inner cardholder where they have been scored.

6. Bend the three tabs on the inner cardholder inward and the one tab on the other side outward.

7. Apply glue to the three tabs and attach, glue the inner cardholder to the large outer piece with the outward-facing tab and glue two decorative pieces to the inside and two to the outside.

8. Place the gift card in the holder and tie it closed with ribbon, twine, or string, present your gift card to the recipient!

Cricut soap Dispenser
Tools And Materials:

- A Cricut Explore Air 2 or a Cricut Maker

- A soap dispenser of your choice, a clean surface

- A permanent vinyl or a white or permanent vinyl, black

- A Sticky mat

- Scissors

- A transfer tape

- A weeder

- Some soap dispensers

- A permanent vinyl, white or a permanent vinyl, black

- A transfer tape

- A weeder

Steps:

1. Start by finding the font you like; then upload to the Design Space and spell out for your labels.

2. Arrange on the mat on your computer, attach the vinyl to the mat and load it into the Cricut.

3. Click the button 'MAKE IT' on the Design Space and follow the prompts to start the cutting process

4. Weed out any negative space, attach the transfer tape to the vinyl; then peel off with the use of the vinyl.

5. Line up; then center onto the soap dispenser and peel back the transfer tape.

Hologram Party Box Tumblers
Tools And Materials:

- Hologram stick-on vinyl

- Clear tumblers

- Green StandardGrip mat

- Cricut Fine-Point Blade

- Weeding tool

- Scraping tool or brayer tool

- Pair of scissors for cutting the material to size

Steps:

1. Open a new project in Design Space, select 'Square' from the 'Shapes' menu on the left-hand side menu.

2. Change the background color to grey.

3. Unlock the shape and change it to the width and height of the tumbler. The hologram will run from about 1" below the tumbler's lip to 1" above the base.

4. To accurately measure the hologram paper's width, wrap it around the tumbler and cut it.

5. Lay it flat on the cutting mat to get the hologram paper's dimensions.

6. Select 'Text' from the menu on the left-hand side, type in the person's name that the tumbler is for.

7. Select a nice chunky font that will work for the cutout, position the font onto the middle of the square on the screen and stretch it to fit across the square.

8. Select both the square and the text, right-click and choose 'Slice.'

9. Select the first layer of the name text, move it off to one side, then delete it.

10. Select the second layer of the name text, move it off to one side, then delete it.

11. You can add an image and repeat steps 13 to 16 for the shape or image if you like.

12. When the hologram image is ready, select 'Make it., make sure the fine-point blade is loaded.

13. Make sure the hologram vinyl is correctly stuck to the cutting mat.

14. Select the correct material and press 'Go' once the Cricut is ready to cut.

15. Once it has been cut, leave the vinyl on the cutting board and weed out the middle of the image and text.

16. Place the transfer sheet over the vinyl and use the scraper or brayer tool to smooth it out.

17. Remove the back sheet, carefully place the hologram paper around the tumbler.

18. Use the scraper to ensure it is on properly, remove the transfer sheet.

Paper Butterfly Bouquet
Tools And Materials:

- A Cricut® Explore Air 2™

- A Design Space®

- A 12-by-12-inch cardstock into dark pink (about 2 sheets),

- 2 light pink sheets, 2 yellow sheets; 2 orange sheets, 2 blue sheets and 4 green sheets

- A Cricut® 12-by-12-inch LightGrip

- An adhesive Cutting Mat

- A flower stem wire

- A floral wire

- A hot glue gun and some sticks

Steps:

1. Start by designing and cutting the bouquet and to do that, follow the project link to the Design Space®

2. If you want to alter your project, click the button "Customize," then use the tools you will feel into the Edit panel to make any changes, click the button "Continue" or the button "Make It."

3. Put the first piece of the cardstock onto the StandardGrip mat; then Follow these prompts to load your machine

4. Set the SmartSet Dial to the function "Cardstock."

5. Load the fine-point blade into the Clamp B; then load the mat and press the button "Load / Unload"

6. Press the flashing button that you see "Go"; then all you need to do is to cut

7. Unload your mat; then peel away any harmful material, and if needed, use your spatula from the basic tool set you have to lift each of the butterflies

8. Load the cutting mat with each of the new sheets of cardstock, then into the machine.

9. Assemble the bouquet; then arrange the butterfly pieces by design and color

10. Hot glue all the matching pieces of your butterflies to each other so that they are all double-sided

11. Glue each of the butterflies to one piece of the floral stem wire or the floral wire.

12. Arrange your floral wires into the grip of your hand, then place them into a vase.

Cactus Cricut Bag
Tools And Materials:

- A Cricut Maker or a cutting machine

- A Green Foil Iron-on Vinyl

- An EasyPress 2 small

- A Cricut Iron on a Protective sheet

- A cactus image on the Cricut Design Space

Steps:

1. Put the iron on the vinyl-colored side down on your mat; then set it to the function cut.

2. Cut about 14 cute little cactus; then weed out any excess of vinyl, cut all the cacti apart

3. Place the EasyPress mat right inside of the faux leather tote, line up the cactus in a way that the spaces look the same between each set of cactus and place the first on the three; then cover with the prepared protective sheet.

4. Set your EasyPress 2 to the setting you need for the faux leather

5. Set to a cooler heat at about 295°F for about 5 seconds at a time, then press again for about 5 additional seconds

6. Press firmly with the help of an EasyPress

7. Repeat the process for each cactus cluster, then allow the vinyl to cool fully before peeling off the plastic carrier sheet.

CRICUT MACHINE PROJECT IDEAS ADVANCED LEVEL

Heart Paper Envelope
Tools And Materials:

- A 12" x 12" cardstock

- A sticker

- A Cricut LightGrip or a StandardGrip cutting mat

- A Cricut Single Quick Swap Scoring Wheel

- A Cricut Scoring Stylus

- A Scraper tool

- Your Paper Heart Design

Steps:

1. Once the SVG cut file is uploaded to your Cricut Design Space, make sure to change the fold lines going across the shape of the heart from the button function "Cut" to "Score" into the menu Linetype; then select both of the layers and click the button 'Attach'.

2. Cut the easy heart envelope card from one piece of the double-sided cardstock

3. Place the cardstock onto a blue LightGrip or a green StandardGrip cutting mat

4. It is easier to place it outer side down on the mat for easier folding Load the mat into the Cricut, insert the fine-point blade and your scoring tool or scoring stylus into your Cricut machine, and press the flashing button to begin cutting, when the cutting process is done, make sure to flip the mat over

5. After finishing the process of cutting out the easy paper heart envelope card, fold all the score lines inward

6. Fold up the bottom

7. The last fold is the top, and you'll want to be sure to crease it good since it has extra layers:

8. Once the heart envelope is perfectly folded and creased, open it once more to write a message or to place anything inside, you can place a cute sticker to keep it closed

9. Here you are; it is all done now

Clear Personalized Labels
Tools And Materials:

- Cricut clear sticker paper

- High-gloss printer paper for the Inkjet printer

- Inkjet printer (check the ink cartridges)

- Spatula tool

Steps:

1. Create a new project in Design Space, choose the heart shape from the left-hand side 'Shapes' menu.

2. Select an image from the 'Images' menu on the left-hand side menu.

3. Choose a picture of a flower or search for M1525E.

4. Unlock the flower image, position it in the top left corner of the heart. Make sure it fits without any overhang.

5. Select the heart and the flower, then click on 'Weld' from the bottom right-hand menu. This ensures that the label is printed together as a unit and not in layers.

6. Once again, select the heart and flowers then click on 'Flatten' to ensure that only the heart's outline shape is cut out, choose 'Text' from the left-hand menu, choose a font, and type the text for your label. You can choose a color for your text and unlock and move the text into position in the middle of the label.

7. Adjust the size to fit comfortably.

8. Select the heart shape and the font, then click on 'Flatten' to ensure the label is cut as a whole and not layered.

9. To not waste sticker paper, you will want to print as many labels as you can per sheet.

10. Choose the square shape from the 'Shapes' menu.

11. Position it on the screen, unlock the shape, and set the measurements to a width of 6" and a height of 9".

12. Move the first label into place at the top left-hand corner of the screen, select the label and 'Duplicate it.'

13. Move the second label next to the first one. Give the labels a bit of room between each other and the edges.

14. Fit as many as you can on the sheet, then save your work, fill in each of the labels with the text you want.

15. If you have space left over when your labels are positioned, you can create smaller ones.

16. You can create all different sizes of labels, patterns, and designs, make sure that all the labels are for print and are flattened and delete the background rectangle.

17. Select all the labels and then click 'Attach' from the bottom right-hand menu.

18. Click 'Make it,' and check that the design and wording are correct before clicking 'Continue.'

19. Choose the high-gloss paper option and set it to the best quality, load the sticker paper into the Inkjet printer and press 'Send to printer.' And choose 'Sticker paper' for the Cricut materials.

20. Load the 'Stickers' into the Cricut and press 'Go' when ready to cut.

21. The Cricut will cut out the stickers so you can peel them off the backing sheet as and when you need them.

Wooden Airplane Décor
Tools And Materials:

- Two pieces of 1/32-inch thick balsa wood

- Dark stain

- Ivory adhesive vinyl

- Superglue or wood glue

Steps:

1. Using a strong grip cutting mat, lay your balsa wood pieces on and make sure to adjust your settings to "custom" on your machine. When you are ready, send your project to cut if the machine does not cut through the first time, repeat cutting without moving your mat three or four more times.

2. Gently remove the wood pieces from your mat. This is fragile wood, so be very careful in removing the pieces not to break them. Lay your pieces to the side for now.

3. Go back to Design Space and write out the name or message you want to appear on the side of the plane. Make sure the size is correct for the size of the plane. Add your vinyl to your StandardGrip cutting mat and tell your machine to cut the image. Follow the prompts on your computer.

4. Weed out your vinyl insides as necessary and remove the unnecessary exterior vinyl that is not part of your design. When it is ready, lay the design on your airplane and use the scraper tool to transfer the vinyl to the corresponding piece.

5. You can offer the plane pieces with instructions as a gift or assemble the plane yourself. If you are making it, use your super glue or wood glue to securely attach all the pieces and allow them to dry fully. Place this design somewhere people can enjoy your handiwork!

A Cricut Tulip
Tools And Materials:

- A Design Pattern of the petal and the stem/leaves

- A 12″ x12″ Cardstock

- A Cricut machine to cut the Vinyl

- A quilling tool

- A tacky Glue or a hot glue gun

Steps:

1. Cut out all of the petals and the stem/leaf pattern

2. Cut the chosen patterns with your Cricut machine; the petal pattern is about 8″ wide by about 9″ height; the stem/leaves is cut at about 8.5″ of width by 11″ height,n ow, it is time to shape the petals by curling it around the quilling tool and you can curl the tops down onto the six larger petals

3. Now, insert the loose end of the petal strip into the slot into the end of the quilling tool; then start rolling slowly towards you,

twirl all up until the strip is rolled and when you get right to the end; all you need o do is to remove the quilling tool; then crease the bottom circle

4. Fold-down the petals of the outer side and curl each of it at the base, trying to create the classic shape of a tulip

5. Glue the outer petals to the inner ones into place; make sure to slide those that are outer down a little bit

6. Make a small fold along the left side of the leaf and leaf pattern of about 1/8 inch

7. Keep folding until you will be able to roll the edge to keep it into place

8. Glue the top of the stem with the top circle to close it up, shape the leaves with the help of your quilling tool

9. Glue the base of the leaves; then keep rolling all the way, now, glue the base of the tulip petals with the top of the stem and let set

Cricut Stamps
Tools And Materials:

- A Cricut Explore machine

- Some Craft Foam Sheets

- Some Wooden Blocks

- A tacky Glue

Steps:

1. Gather all of your supplies

2. Add the select images to the Cricut Design Space; you can choose different images and choose the size of the images according to the wooden blocks you have

3. Set your machine to the cut Foam, with a heavy grip mat; place the foam sheets to cut on the Cricut machine.

4. Cut your images with the help of a Cricut Explore Machine with the use of a Deep Cut Blade to cut about 6 images in less than

about 5 minutes and use the Tacky glue to attach to the wooden blocks and let dry for overnight.

5. Use the negative part of the foam sheets to help draw the image onto the opposite side of the blocks

6. You can also cut the vinyl instead of the drawing but you can also simply draw the image over the blocks.

Woodland Drink Charms
Tools And Materials:

- 3 mm thick balsa wood

- inexpensive "silver" hoop earrings in the number of charms you

- want to make

- Variety of paints, such as brown, green, orange, etc.

Steps:

1. Open Design Space and insert various images you want to turn into wine charms. Keep the size smaller so that they will not interfere with someone holding the wine glass, but large enough to easily identify. Add a small circle to each shape that will be cut out and end up attaching the earring.

2. Trace the shapes onto the balsa wood and cut them out. It may be necessary to send it to cut several times to ensure that it has cut through your wood, remove the outside, additional wood, and weed out the circle from each form.

3. Paint or stain your forms in the colors of your choice. Allow them to totally dry.

4. Once dry, put one earring through the hole and get ready to adorn your next drink! For different occasions, consider adding initials, monograms, photos, and patterns to the wine charms.

Cricut Teapot
Tools And Materials:

- A Cricut Maker

- A Fine-Point Blade

- A Premium Vinyl in Something Blue

- A Premium Vinyl in Light Gray

- A Cricut LightGrip Mat

- A Cricut StrongGrip Transfer Tape

- A Teapot

- Scissors

- A teacup

- A tea saucer

Steps:

1. Start by opening up the text into the Cricut Design Space

2. Adjust all the measurements into the Canvas according to the size of the teapot you are using

3. Prepare the vinyl onto the LightGrip mat; you can use the Light Gray for the font and the Blue for the Snowflake, select the button "Make It"; then follow the directions.

4. Start by removing the vinyl from the mat; then weed out the small pieces into the font and after that use your Cricut Strong Grip Transfer tape to help you adhere to your Teapot

5. Follow the same steps for a teacup and for a tea saucer.

Christmas Ornaments
Tools And Materials:

- Adhesive vinyl

- Adhesive foil

- Cricut Pens

- Ornaments - plain or clear are good options

Steps:

1. In Design Space, upload your preferred design, image, or create your own with custom shapes.

2. To make a dimensional design, add various layers, and consider using different materials and colors to get a professional appearance.

3. If you want to cut words out and attach them to a strip of vinyl in another color, you can wrap that around your design. Or you could layer different vinyl, one solid and the other glitter.

4. Carefully lay out your vinyl where you want it to appear on your ornament and transfer the vinyl to the ornament. Transfer tape is best for this type of project. You can use a measuring tape or ruler and a marking pen to help you find the central location for the best results.

5. You can have vinyl and designs attached directly to the ornaments, or you can consider having pieces that hang on the outside or off of it as well. This can be a fun and personal gift, but the more you do it and practice working on a round surface, the better you will get at it!

Night Sky Pillow
Tools And Materials:

- Black, dark blue, or dark purple fabric

- Heat transfer vinyl in gold or silver

- Cutting mat

- Polyester batting

- Weeding tool or pick

- Cricut EasyPress

Steps:

1. Decide the shape you want for your pillow, and cut two matching shapes out of the fabric.

2. Create a new project, select the "Image" button in the lower left-hand corner and search "stars." And select the stars of your choice and click "Insert."

3. Place the iron-on material on the mat, send the design to the Cricut.

4. Use the weeding tool or pick to remove excess material, remove the material from the mat.

5. Place the iron-on material on the fabric, use the EasyPress to adhere it to the iron-on material.

6. Sew the two fabric pieces together, leaving allowance for a seam and a small space open.

7. Fill the pillow with polyester batting through the small open space, sew the pillow shut.

8. Cuddle up to your starry pillow!

Cricut Wall art
Tools And Materials:

- A Free Wall Art SVG file

- A Cricut Premium Adhesive Vinyl

- A photo Frame

- A 12x12 White Cardstock

- A Light Gripping Transfer Tape (I use this)

- A weeding Tool

- A Cutting Machine

- A Standard Grip Mat

- A Vinyl scraper

Steps:

1. Start by downloading the file, upload to the Cricut Design Space

2. Resize to the frame size, put the vinyl, the vinyl side up onto the Cricut mat

3. Load the image into the cutting machine

4. Click the button "make it" into the design space; try not to mirror; then click on the button 'continue'

5. Select your Cricut machine, now, adjust the setting of the cut Vinyl

6. Press the button 'go'; then remove the vinyl when you are done cutting

7. Remove the vinyl from the mat so that you can keep the vinyl from curling; then lay the mat onto a surface vinyl with the side down and while you are holding the vinyl; remove the mat, with the help of the weeding tool, remove the cut areas that you don't use

8. Cut one piece of transfer tape just the size of your design; place on top of your image

9. With the help Using the scraper, scrape both sides to help with the process of transferring to the transfer tape

10. Gently pull back your tape; then place the shared design over the card stock; then carefully transfer to your cardstock, put the image into your frame

11. Hang out the art onto the card stock and gently transfer to the cardstock

Easter banner

Every year when Easter rolls around you can see the Easter decor in stores and all around you. This Easter you can make your own Easter bunny banner using your Cricut machine.

You can do this Easter banner if you don't have a Cricut machine at home.

Tools And Materials:

- Cricut Maker cutting machine

- 4 Sheets of (12x12 in) of Cardstock (in various coordinating the colors)

- 1in White Pom poms

- A ribbon or a Twine to string up the bunting banner

- A bunny SVG Cut File

- A Cricut Explore Air 2

- A Standard Grip Mat

- A Fine Point Blade

- An Essential Tool Kit

- A Hot Glue Gun

Steps:

1. Download your Bunny SVG cut file for free

2. Now, upload the Bunny SVG into the Design Space; then insert the image into your design space Canvas

3. Size the Bunny to about 2.555 in Width x 5.194in Height

4. Add a Circle that is sized to about 167 inches; then duplicate it, position your circle at the top of the ears of the bunnies

5. Select the image of the bunny into the first circle; then click the button slice to cut the hole into your design.

6. Now, click the bunny image; then arrange to the back; and repeat the same process with the other circles

7. Duplicate the bunny for about 3 times, now duplicate the bunny for about 3 times: then make each bunny into a different color and select all the 4 bunnies; then copy them for about 7 times in each of the colors

8. Click the button 'Make it', set the Cricut to the Cardstock; then place your first sheet of cardstock onto your mat and start cutting

9. Once you have cut all of the bunnies out, Use the hot glue gun to attach the white pompoms onto each of the bunnies, string up the bunnies into a pattern; then tape it onto your wall.

Cricut Lamp
Tools And Materials:

- A Cricut Machine and a Cricut Design Space

- Some Swirls cut design

- A platinum-colored Glitter FX adhesive vinyl

- A cylinder vase style lamp

- A Transfer tape

Steps:

1. Start by cleaning the surface of the lamp very well

2. Make sure that the lamp is appropriately clean and dry before applying the vinyl to make sure the vinyl adheres very well, resize your design to make it fit the height of the lamp

3. Follow the on-screen instructions to cut your chosen design from the vinyl

4. Remember that there is no need to reverse the design when there are no words that are included.

5. Weed the entire design from the vinyl backing.

6. Using the transfer tape, carefully remove your finished design from the vinyl backing; then apply to the surface of your lamp, carefully rub the design so that it adheres the art to the surface of the lamp

Cricut Graduation or Wedding cards
Tools And Materials:

- A Cricut Maker/Cricut Explore

- A light Grip Cutting Mat

- An Essential Tools Set

- A Scoring wheel or a ruler

- 2 different colors of Cardstock of about (160gsm or more)

- A Glue Tape

- A Premium Fine Point Blade

- A Free SVG file

-

Steps:

1. Start by choosing the colors for your Graduation card

2. Upload the wedding card SVG file on your Design Space.

3. Next click on the button "Make it".

4. All you need to do is to choose the intricate cardstock from the list of materials you have, load the mat; then get everything cut; if you are usually using a glitter cardstock: make sure to place it with the right side up

5. To assemble the card, all you need to do is start off by applying the glue using the Glue Tape along all the edges of the card; you can also add some glue around the text and the swirls.

6. Stick the insert right to the backside; then fold the card along the edge of your insert and here you are!

Mason Jar Tags
Tools And Materials:

- Adhesive Vinyl in lighter colors like white or yellow

- Weeding Tool

- Transfer Tape

- Mason Jars

Steps:

1. Clean your jars well, especially the outside, where you want to place your label. Removing as much prior residue as possible will help your new labels stick better. This way, you know which jar label canvas you need to create.

2. In Design Space, open a new canvas based on your mason jar's size that you want to create the labels for. Typically, there is a pre-set canvas. If you do not find a canvas that is the right size, open the one closest to your measurements and adjust from there.

3. Upload the desired images to your canvas and add any words you want to appear on the label. This can include a special message or describe the contents of the jar, etc. Make sure to detach your images so it will appear properly on your labels.

4. After laying out your images and words, go back and attach all the pieces and send your file to cut.

5. After your labels are cut, weed out any unnecessary pieces and remove the excess vinyl you do not want to use. Remove the backing. Using the transfer tape, adhere the vinyl to the clean exterior of your mason jar. Smooth it with your scraper tool and then slowly peel back the tape.

Cricut Bookmark
Tools And Materials:

- A Cricut Maker

- A brown felt

- A faux suede (tan)

- A floral fabric

- A tassel

- A glue

- A needle and a thread (optional)

- A Peekaboo Flower Bookmark SVG

- A Peekaboo Flower Bookmark

Steps:

1. Start by downloading the Peekaboo Flower Bookmark SVG; then upload it to the Design Space.

2. There will be about three pieces; the flower cutouts are known as the faux suede, the rectangle one is known as the fabric; and the solid one is known as the scalloped piece is known as the felt.

3. Put the fabric over the felt, glue everything down very well; then glue the top of the bookmark onto the felt.

4. Add some of very simple stitching embellishment right around the flowers, but you don't need to do that to secure the bookmark, loop your tassel through the hole at the top of the bookmark and here you are done.

Clutch Purse
Supplies Needed

- Two fabrics

- fleece

- Fabric cutting mat

- D-ring

- Sew-on snap

- Lace

- Zipper

- Sewing machine

- Fabric scissors

- Keychain or charm of your choice

Steps:

1. Create a new project, select the "Image" button in the lower left-hand corner and search for "essential wallet." And select the essential wallet template and click "Insert."

2. Place the fabric on the mat, send the design to the Cricut and remove the fabric from the mat.

3. Attach the fusible fleecing to the wrong side of the exterior fabric, attach lace to the edges of the exterior fabric.

4. Assemble the D-ring strap and place the D-ring onto the strap and sew into place.

5. Fold the pocket pieces wrong side out over the top of the zipper, and sew it into place.

6. Fold the pocket's wrong side in and sew the sides, sew the snap onto the pocket.

7. Sew the lining piece to the zipper tape, fold the lining behind the pocket and iron in place and sew on the other side of the snap.

8. Trim the zipper so that it's not overhanging the edge, sew the two pocket layers to the exterior fabric across the bottom, sew around all of the layers and trim the edges with fabric scissors.

9. Turn the clutch almost completely inside out and sew the opening closed.

10. Turn the clutch inside out and press the corners into place, attach your charm or keychain to the zipper.

11. Carry your new clutch wherever you need it!

12.

Embroidery Hoop
Tools And Materials:

- A Cricut Maker

- A washable fabric pen

- A pink fabric mat

- A rotary blade

- A DMC 321, 823, 824, 3865, 4045

- A 9" embroidery hoop

- A Statue of Liberty Hoop design

- A fabric of your choice

- A Statue of Liberty Embroidery Hoop

Steps:

1. Start by loading your Cricut Maker with the help of a washable fabric pen eight on the left and the rotary blade on the right side

2. Put the piece of the fabric onto the mat; then to the Design Space link that is listed into the supplies; then let the Cricut Maker do its work

3. Use a simple backstitch for the hoop; the DMC 4045 is used for Lady Liberty, the 3865 for all the borders, the 321 and the 824 for the stars, and the 823 for all the words.

4. When you are done stitching; run the entire piece under a quantity of warm water; then lay it over a towel to dry it; he will remove any blue ink

5. Place it back into the hoop; then finish it how you want

Mini Christmas Trees
Tools And Materials:

- Spray adhesive

- Ruler

- Exacto or crafting knife

- Glitter tape or glitter paint

- Matching patterned fabric

- 3mm thick balsa wood

- The predesigned Christmas tree patterns in Design Space

Steps:

1. Open up the patterns in Design Space. Make sure to create both sizes for variety in height. Click "Make It" and follow the prompts. You may need to send it to print a few times to completely cut the image through the balsa wood. If you are making placeholders for your table, please write and add your names on your cuts now before cutting your images out.

2. You can write to them with a pen, although it can come out a little rough depending on your wood. Another option is to print the names in vinyl and apply them after cutting.

3. Use your Exacto knife to finish any cuts necessary. Remove the outside excess wood.

4. Spray one side of your tree pieces and lay them flat on your fabric, pressing down firmly to make sure the fabric adheres evenly to your design. Let the adhesive dry completely.

5. Working with your Exacto knife, trace around your tree shapes to cut away all the extra fabric. If you want to repeat steps 3 and 4 on the other side of the trees, you can have wholly decorated trees. If you do not, the trees' backside will be wooden while the fronts will have patterned, like the image above.

6. Using your Exacto knife, trim your glitter tape to 3mm, or purchase your tape 3mm wide. Wrap the tape around the edges of all the three pieces, pressing to secure it. If you are using glitter paint, carefully apply the paint to the edge of all the trees and dry.

7. Once all the pieces are designed and dry, slip the bottom cuts into the top, pressing down, so the "trunk" sits evenly on your flat surface. You are ready to decorate!

Baby Bandana Bib
Tools And Materials:

- ¼ yd of Fabric in your choice of pattern

- ¼ yd of Terrycloth fabric

- A Plastic snap

- A Thread in the corresponding color

- A snap tool

- A sewing Machine

- A Needle

- A Cricut Maker with Rotary Blade

Steps:

1. Start by downloading the free pattern, upload into the Cricut Design Space.

2. Place the patterned fabric onto the pink fabric grip mat, load into your machine.

3. Repeat the same process with the Terry cloth.

4. Now, face the right side of the patterned fabric down onto your white flannel; then pin or clip around all the edges.

Napkins
Tools And Materials:

- Cricut viable Infusible Ink Napkins

- Cricut Infusible Ink pens/markers

- Cricut EasyPress 2 with mat

- Cricut Maker or Explore

- heat safe tape

- Butcher paper and white cardstock

- laser paper

- project your napkins

Steps:

1. First, think of a theme or design that you will want to have on your napkin set! You can use the existing prints and designs from the Cricut gallery or make your own custom designs. If

you want to make these napkins personalized, you can design your own logos or brand names.

2. Perhaps there are endless ways to make use of the personalized napkin, depending on what you design and print on them.

3. For these napkins, we will use the Arial Font within the Cricut Design Space application. There are several script fonts, and you can try some others as well, but this one is suitable to draw and cut on the infusible ink transfer sheets.

4. Start by selecting the make-it options to cut the desired design on the transfer sheet and select the "mirror" option on the application interface's left-hand side.

5. Select the material as the "Infusible Ink Transfer Sheet", and if you want to use the Explore Air 2, then turn your machine dial to custom. Now it's time to cut the design. Your Cricut machine will now cut out the design automatically once you load this design and press the GO button. You can use the scissors to chop off the sections you need and separate them. Now use a weeding tool to peel away the portion of the design that you don't need. Now you will be left with the words on the sticky transfer sheet.

6. You can also try to make some circle or any other design to go with the napkin theme. Most designs are already present in the Cricut Design Space; if you search "napkin" in the image's gallery, you could choose from hundreds of options. For the next part, you will find your Easypress machine and the EasyPress mat. So, get ready for it.

7. Set the napkin over the mat. Now place your selected and cut design on top of the napkin, then use the heatproof tape to hold this design in place. Cover the transfer sheet with butter paper to protect it. Select 400 degrees F temperature to adjust the EasyPress heat settings for 60 seconds. Then hold the heat press over the napkin for the exact time, and remove it when it's done. The napkin will be very hot at this point, so wait for some time before touch it.

8. Repeat the same steps with more napkins and or cut patterns if you want to make more. Slowly remove the butter paper then the transfer sheet from the top, and you will see your selected design printed on your napkin permanently with infusible ink.

Wood farm sign
Tools And Materials:

- A 14" x 9" plank style sign
- A farmhouse-style home décor sign.
- About 2 stick-on arrow decals
- A thick rope
- A Spanish moss
- Some small flowers
- A Turquoise, black and white paint or paint colors of your choice
- Foam brushes
- A wire cutter
- A Ruler
- A Black permanent marker
- A E6000 glue
- A Glue Gun

Steps:

1. With the help of a ruler, mark about two holes, then equidistant from each other the edge of the very top side of the wood sign you will use

2. Poke some holes into those locations with the help of scissors into a piece of the wood farmhouse you choose

3. Now; paint the backside of the wood sign with the turquoise color; then let the paint dry completely

4. Dry the brushing paint onto a turquoise painted wood if you choose a metal farmhouse sign

5. Paint the arrows with the black color; then allow the paint to dry very well

6. With the help of wire cutters, carefully remove the metal sign from the wood backing; then trim the pins right from the back of the brads to make it sit flat, making sure brads are flat on one side for the metal farmhouse sign

7. Hot glue the beads onto the front part of the metal sign; then with the help of the craft glue, affix the metal sign right to the center of the turquoise painted sign

8. Roll about two handful-sized balls of Spanish moss; then hot glue them to either side of the metal sign.

9. Hot glue the little flowers that are peeking out from the Spanish moss; then hot glue the mini flowers to a farmhouse sign for decorating it

10. Affix the arrows above and the metal sign; then just thread the rope through the holes you have made into the sign and tie it up before hanging it on the wall

Cricut Wood Tray
Tools And Materials:

- A 1
- ×15 x 15″ Unfinished Wood Board
- A Minwax Wood Stain-Walnut
- A Liberty Handle Bar Pulls
- A Foam Brush
- A Cricut Vinyl – Midnight
- A stained board

Steps:

1. Start by staining the wood board with about 2 coats of stain; you can use walnut

2. Add in the Handles; then attach the large stainless bar pulls using the hardware that is included

3. Create your Monogram on the Cricut Design Space

4. Finally, remove or weed any of the vinyl that is around the monogram; then attach it to the wood board

Oven Mitt
Tools And Materials:

- A Tan Quilted Oven Mitt

- A Cricut Iron-On Vinyl

- A Cricut Easy Press or Iron

- A Cricut Explore Air 2

Steps:

1. Set to mirror image in a way that the words don't print out also backward

2. Lay the shiny side down; then get the handy weeding tool ready to remove any vinyl around your text

3. Lay the vinyl where you just want it to go on your oven mitt, whether in an angled way or straight

4. Lay one thin piece of the fabric over the vinyl; then use the easy press or you can use any iron

5. Hold the iron steady and try not to move it across

Ornaments

Rae Dunn products have been really popular over the years and these ornaments are so catchy out there. You can come up with the idea from Amber Simmons after you create some Rae Dunn-inspired pumpkins this past fall. These ornaments are easy to make. You don't need a Cricut machine or some sort of die-cutting machine to make these ornaments, just to know.

Tools And Materials:

- Cricut Explore Machine

- Clear Plastic Ornaments

- White Craft Paint

- Ribbon

Steps:

1. Fill the ornaments with white paint and gently tap until the inside is coated with white paint

2. Replace the top on the ornament, create and cut the Cricut Images

3. Weed the vinyl and attach contact paper and apply images to the ornaments, add ribbon and enjoy

Easy Lacey Dress

Easy Lacey Dress Lace dresses are adorable, but they can be hard to get ahold of and difficult to make. Fake it without anyone knowing better using your Cricut! The iron-on vinyl will look just like lace, and it will stand up to your child's activities much better than the real thing. Don't limit yourself to children's clothes; add some vinyl lace to your own as well! White vinyl will look like traditional lace the most, you can do this in any color that coordinates with the dress that you have. Use a Cricut EasyPress or iron to attach the vinyl to the fabric. You can use the Cricut Explore One, Cricut Explore Air 2, or Cricut Maker for this project.

Supplies Needed

- Dress of your choice

- White heat transfer vinyl

- Cricut EasyPress or iron

- Cutting mat

- Weeding tool or pick

Steps:

1. Create a new project.

2. Select the "Image" button in the lower left-hand corner and search "vintage lace border."

3. Choose your favorite lace border and click "Insert.", place your vinyl on the cutting mat.

4. Send the design to your Cricut, use a weeding tool or pick to remove the excess vinyl from the design.

5. Place the design along the hem of the dress with the plastic side up. Add lace wherever you like, such as along the collar or sleeves, carefully iron on the design.

6. After cooling, peel away the plastic by rolling it, dress your child up in her adorable lacey dress!

Leather handmade Ornaments
Tools And Materials:

- A Cricut Faux Woodgrain Leather

- A deco Art Patent Leather Paint in white color

- A Cricut machine (the Explore or the Maker will work here)

- A Cricut cut file

- A Tacky glue

- A twine

- A Paint brush

- A Paint Brush

- A faux Cricut leather and leather paint to make handmade ornaments.

Steps:

1. Start by accessing the Cricut cut file; then cut the shapes from the faux leather sheet with the help of your machine; you should place the leatherwood grain side up, remove the pieces from the mat

2. Each ornament will have a back and front piece, paint the back piece with the leather paint

3. Once everything is completely dried; you need to add the front piece right on top; then use the tacky glue all the way and around the edges

4. Put the two pieces altogether; then wipe away any excess of glue and place anything heavy over the top of the ornaments; then let dry

5. Add some of the twines for the hanging of your handmade ornaments on the tree.

6. Repeat the same steps for the handmade ornaments you want to make

Infusible Ink Handbag
Tools And Materials:

- White or plain Handbag

- Cricut Explore Air 2

- EasyPress 2

- EasyPress Mat

- Infusible Ink transfer sheet (multicolour)

- White cardstock

- Cricut Design Space File

Steps:

1. First think of a theme or design that you will want to have on your Handbag set! You can use the existing prints and designs from the Cricut gallery or make your custom designs. If you want to make these Handbags personalized, you can design your own logos or brand names.

2. Perhaps there are endless ways to use the personalized Handbag, depending on what you design and print on them.

3. Here I will be selecting the Mermaid theme text and the design to cut on my transfer sheets. You can select any other design as per your needs.

4. Starting by selecting the make-it options to cut the desired design on the transfer sheet, and select the "mirror" option on the left-hand side of the application interface.

5. Select the material as the "Infusible Ink Transfer Sheet", and if you want to use the Explore Air 2, then turn your machine dial to custom. Now it's time to cut the design. Your Cricut machine will now cut out the design automatically once you load this design and press the GO button. You can use the scissors to chop off the sections you need and separate them. Now use a weeding tool to peel away the portion of the design that you don't need. Now you will be left with the words on the

6. sticky transfer sheet.

7. You can also try to make some circles or any other design to go with the Handbag theme. Most designs are already present in the Cricut Design Space; if you search "Handbag" in the image's gallery, you could choose from hundreds of options. For the next part, you will find your Easypress machine and the EasyPress mat. So, get ready for it.

8. Set the Handbag over the mat. Now place your selected and cut design on top of the Handbag, then use the heatproof tape to hold this design in place. Cover the transfer sheet with butcher paper to protect it. Select 385 degrees F temperature to adjust the EasyPress heat settings for 55 seconds. Then hold the heat press over the Handbag for the exact time, and remove it when it's done.

9. The Handbag will be very hot at this point, so wait for some time before touch it. Repeat the same steps with more Handbags and or cut patterns if you want to make more. Slowly remove the butcher paper then the transfer sheet from the top, and you will see your selected design printed on

10. your Handbag permanently with infusible ink.

Cricut Necklace
Tools And Materials:

- A Cricut Explore® Air and Design Space software

- A Cricut Explore® Deep Cut Housing and Blad

- A Cricut® Strong Grip mat

- A Cricut® Transfer Tape

- A tooling leather

- An awl or a small hole punch

- Some gold or silver necklaces (buy the pre-made ones!)

- Wire cutters

- Jump rings

- A foam brush

- Pliers

- A Folk Art Paint

Steps:

1. Simply cut the image using the "Heavy option Leather" under the Custom setting "the Smart Set Dial

2. Once you have cut out your image, punch one hole into either side with the awl or a small hole

3. Paint; then add to the chain!

Easter eggs

If you have an Easter decor obsession, you will love these DIY Inspired Easter Eggs. These creations have been really popular over the years and totally have blown up on the craft marketplace. You need a Cricut machine or similar cutting machine to make these ornaments for this kind of project. The cut is super small and I would not recommend trying to cut these by hand.

Tools And Materials:

- Cricut Explore machine

- Vinyl

- Contact paper

- White Craft Eggs

Steps:

1. Download the free SVG, DXF, EPS, or PNG file and upload to Cricut Design Space or create one by your own.

2. Edit the free cut file in Design Space as needed and size the image accordingly.

3. Weed the cut images, apply contact paper and adhere to eggs.

4. Peel off the contact paper.

Cricut Card
Tools And Materials:

- A Cricut Maker locker card

- A 0.4 Tip Black Pen

- A LightGrip Machine Mat of about 12" x 12"

- A design Space File

- A picture of Choice

- A glue

- A gold Foil Cardstock

Steps:

1. Start by opening the Design Space file that is linked above; then cut out all of the shapes

2. The gold foil needs to be face-up during the cutting process for all of them except for the text with the white heart, for that one the gold foil should be face down on your mat so that the writing is placed on the white backing.

3. You can also edit the text, but you need to make sure it won't be cut off by the heart frame that will go over it

4. Cut out the chosen picture that you want to use so that it fits into the right heart frame

5. Glue to the heart frame; then glue the piece onto the right side of the card base

6. Glue the heart with the heart frame and the text together; then glue the piece on the left side of the card base

7. Let dry and that is all!

Cricut decorated Vases
Tools And Materials:

- A 12″ x 12″ 65 lb. or about 80 lb Cardstock or a poster board

- A Glue or just a tape runner

- A light Grip cutting mat

- An (Optional) Scraper

- A way to cut your paper vases, scissors, a craft knife

Steps:

1. Start by downloading the design you have chosen in a free printable PDF pattern

2. Cut the paper vase pieces and if you are going to cut this paper vase out by your hand, you can use the printable PDF to cut out the pattern; then trace it onto your paper, and then just cut it out.

3. If you are going to use a Cricut cutting machine to cut the paper vase, upload the free paper vase SVG into your Cricut Design Space, adjust the size if you want to make the vases smaller in size

4. You should also change the interior lines of each of the vases to score the lines; then ungroup the layers that have the interior lines; then select the underline type and change the cut to score

5. Once you have changed the cut lines to score, place the cardstock over the Cricut LightGrip cutting mat; then select the medium cardstock for your material.

6. Grab the cut vase pieces and the E-Z Runner Adhesive; you can also use the glue instead of the double-sided adhesive.

7. Now; start folding on each score line; then start applying the adhesive glue on the flaps, glue each of the tabs to the edge of the preceding flap.

Cricut Fairy House
Tools And Materials:

- A Cricut Midnight Vinyl

- A Cricut Iron-on Glitter, Green

- A Felt Green

- A felt Brown

- A Pipe Cleaner

- An Embroidery Floss; Flesh tone

- 1″ Bead

- Embroidery Floss – Brown

- Embroidery Floss – Gold

- Embroidery Floss – Green

- Brown Pom Poms

- Embroidery Floss – a Flesh Tone

Steps:

1. Start by cutting the pipe cleaner into about one of 4″ section and about one 8″ section; then use the 8″ section for the body and the legs; keep the 4″ section to use it for the arms, you can add a little quantity of glue to keep the arms into place.

2. Wrap the body with the flesh-colored embroidery floss, hot glue the body to the bead; then wrap the body into the embroidery floss to match.

3. Cut the fairy wings out of the felt; and make sure to choose the felt as the material when you start

4. Cut out the skirt as well, cut the glitter vinyl out and the weeding; then attach to the felt with the Easy Press help, you can add glitter iron on to both sides.

5. You can add hair by gluing some strands of embroidery floss to the top. You can also paint the hair color on if you want

Unicorn Wine Glass
Tools And Materials:

- Stemless wine glasses

- Outdoor vinyl

- Vinyl transfer tape

- Cutting mat

- Weeding tool or pick

- Extra fine glitter Mod Podge

Steps:

1. Create a new project, select the "Text" button in the Design Panel.

2. Type "It's not drinking alone if my unicorn is here, using the dropdown box, select your favorite font.

3. Adjust the positioning of the letters, rotating some to give a whimsical look.

4. Select the "Image" button on the Design Panel and search for "unicorn."

5. Select your favorite unicorn and click "Insert," then arrange your design how you want it on the glass.

6. Place your vinyl on the cutting mat, making sure it is smooth and making full contact.

7. Send the design to your Cricut, use a weeding tool or pick to remove the excess vinyl from the design. Use the Cricut BrightPad to help if you have one.

8.   Apply transfer tape to the design, pressing firmly and making sure there are no bubbles.

9.   Remove the paper backing and apply the words to the glass where you'd like them. Smooth down the design and carefully remove the transfer tape.

10. Coat the bottom of the glass in Mod Podge, wherever you would like glitter to be. Give the area a wavy edge, sprinkle glitter over the Mod Podge, working quickly before it dries.

11. Set it aside to dry.

12. Cover the glitter in a thick coat of Mod Podge, allow the glass to cure for at least 48 hours.

Cricut Floral Lantern
Tools And Materials:

- A Cricut cutting Machine

- Craft Scissors

- A High-Temp Hot Glue Gun

- A text Weight Frosted Paper – a star dream Metallic Crystal

- A Vellum Paper – Glama Natural Clear

- Some LED Tea Lights

- A ribbon or a twine

Steps:

1.   Download the pattern to the Cricut Design Space, print; cut; then score and fold all the sides to form you lantern shape and secure very well altogether with the glue dots; the double-sided tape or the hot glue

2.   Add one loop of ribbon to the top as you manage to glue the four points all together

Personalized socks

These colorful socks are amusing and make excellent cure presents. The phrase on the second sock may be changed to say whatever you wish. You may manufacture multiple pairs of these socks and sell them as a set in your business. You can make these socks in a matter of minutes and give them as gifts or wear them yourself. Winter is everyone's favorite season for spending time with family and friends over the holidays. Giving your guests some nice, monogrammed socks while sipping on a warm cup of coffee will make them feel comfy and festive during Christmas celebrations. This holiday season, curl up with a hot cup of coffee and some homemade socks.

Tools And Materials:

- Wool Socks

- Chosen image

- Printable Iron-On or paint

Steps:

1. Print the letters on sturdy cardstock and carefully cut them out with a knife to make a stencil, then paint on the socks.

2. Paint the bottom of each sock with an alphabet stencil.

3. Print the image on iron-on transfer paper and trim it to size.

4. Employ iron-on alphabet letters

5. Download the image and cut it out with a die-cutting machine to make an iron-on image.

Cricut Cosmetic bag
Tools And Materials:

- A Cricut Explore Air 2 or a Cricut Maker

- A Cricut EasyPress 2

- An Infusible Ink Transfer Sheet

- An easy Press Mat

- A Cutting Mat

- Some Weeding Tools

- Some Designs / SVG (

- A Cricut Blank Cosmetic Bag

- A heat Resistant Tape

- A White cardstock

- A Lint roller

Steps:

1. Start by uploading the design to the Cricut Design Space, you can resize the design to fit on your cosmetic bag.

2. Put an Infusible Ink transfer sheet on top of a StandardGrip Mat with the face up.

3. Place the iron-on vinyl on a StandardGrip Mat with the shiny side down.

4. Click the button MAKE IT; but you need to mirror the image for both the images

5. Choose the six for the infusible ink mat, and the iron-on vinyl for the other mat.

6. Load your mat, then press the button (cut) button on your machine.

7. When you are finished cutting, unload your machine; then take the Infusible Ink sheet off the mat.

8. Repeat both steps 7 and 8 for the iron-on vinyl; then remove the outside of your design from the cut so that your design is set left on the sheet.

Cricut Charm
Tools And Materials:

- Painters Tape

- Charms

- A strong Grip Mat

- A Cricut Maker

- An Engraving Tip

Steps:

1. Start by making "templates" of your charms, and type the words and he design, weld everything all together; then press to make it

2. On the next screen, put the design on the screen mat; then position the design on your on-screen mat

3. Press the button 'continue', grab the mat

4. Load into the machine, you can choose brass for your chosen material

5. Make sure that you have your Cricut engraving tip loaded, press the button 'cut'

6. Remove the charms; then you can optionally sand a little bit to smooth any rough edges, add to any necklace or bracelet

Paper Boat
Tools And Materials:

- A card stock paper or a wood-print paper and white vellum

- A 7-inch wood dowel or skewer

- A low-temp hot glue gun

- A paper curling tool

Steps:

1. Cut the pieces of the boat pieces from the card stock paper or the wood-print paper and the white vellum

2. Fold the base of the boat along the scoreline, fold about four tabs along the score lines.

3. With the use of a low-temp hot glue gun, glue the tabs on the boat's base

4. Glue; then assemble the sides of the boat, fold the boat seat along the score lines.

5. Glue the seat into the center of the boat, glue the small sail onto a wood dowel of wood of about 8 inches

6. Shape a large sail with a curling tool, glue the tip of the top and the bottom of the sail onto a smaller sail and a wood dowel and slide the dowel into the hole into seat and glue to the base of the boat

Cat mask
Tools And Materials:

- A Fabric for the adult size cut the fabric into 12 inches x 11 inches

- An iron-on Vinyl

- A Cutting Machine or scissors

- An Iron

- A sewing Machine

- An elastic 21 inches for the tied adjustable option

- About 10.5 inches for the sewn into elastic saving option

Steps:

1. If you have a Cricut Maker; cut everything you need with your Cricut machine; or you can use scissors

2. With the right sides; fold the fabric; then sew the edges all together with about ¼ seam allowance

3. Turn the right side out and the iron, iron the face of the kitty face right into the center top portion of your mask

4. Now, turn over; then mark the dark points with the help of a fabric marker or a pin on the underside of the mask and fold the fabric into a half lengthwise way, placing the vinyl towards the inside of your fold

5. Fold the fabric in a widthwise way; then fold one of the sides over again in a widthwise way and mark this will be the dart's point.

6. Mark the other end of the dart about halfway between the folded edge as well as the top edges when folded into half, sew the darts; then make sure to backstitch so that you can keep them nice and very well secure.

7. Fold all the side ends of the mask over about ½ inch; then sew into place with about 1/8 of the seam

8. allowance if you are using knit and if you are using a woven fabric; do the step with a zigzag stitch in a way that you make sure to go over the end edge of the fabric

9. Make sure to backstitch at both the ends and for the elastic saving option; just fold the side ends of your mask over about ½ inch; then sew into place with about a 1/8 seam of allowance if you are using a knit, making sure to tuck in all the edges of the elastic as you keep going and if you are using a woven fabric; do the step with a zigzag stitch making sure to go over the end edge of your fabric

10. Thread the elastic pieces through all the casings you have just made and for both the adult and the child; just cut the elastic to about 10.5 inches that allow making a knot

11. Once the knot is tied very well; carefully pull the elastic around to hide the knot into the casing

Cricut Poinsettia
Tools And Materials:

- A text-weight or a card stock paper

- Needle-nose pliers and wire cutters

- A pale green PanPastel Pigment and a brush

- An 18-gauge green floral wire

- A low-temp hot glue gun

Steps:

1. Start by cutting; then scoring the poinsettia with the help of a text-weight or a card stock paper.

2. Fold the petals as well as the leaves on the score lines.

3. With the help of the needle-nose pliers, carefully form a spiral at tip of 18-gauge floral wire and bend at about an angle of about 45 degrees, press the wire through the center of the first leaf piece; then slide to top.

4. Add the hot glue onto the wire spiral then place the second leaf piece onto the glue

5. Hold into place until it becomes cool, position; then glue the first set of the petals onto the leaf base.

6. Repeat with the second and the third set of the petals making sure to rotate so that all the petals become evenly spaced, roll the stamen into a spiral form

7. Fix tthe stamen into the center of the poinsettia using glue

8. Brush the pale green PanPastel Pigment right into the center of the poinsettia petals to add the layer of color.

Flower Garden Tote Bag

Flower Garden Tote Bag You can never have too many tote bags, whether you use them as reusable shopping bags, giant purses, or anything else. Create this cute flower garden bag to carry wherever you need to, and keep nature right by your side all day!

Choose your favorite flowers, and the more variety you have, the more interesting the bag will be to look at. Canvas bags are a nice neutral base that will last you years, but you can use this idea with a different type of tote as well. The white vinyl gives a silhouette effect, but you can use a different color or even make each flower its own color. You'll need a Cricut EasyPress or iron for the heat transfer vinyl. You can use the Cricut Explore One, Cricut Explore Air 2, or Cricut Maker for this project.

Supplies Needed

- Canvas tote bag

- White heat transfer vinyl

- Cricut EasyPress or iron

- Cutting mat

- Weeding tool or pick

Steps:

1. Create a new project, select the "Image" button in the lower left-hand corner and search "flowers" and choose your favorite flower and click "Insert."

2. Continue with a variety of flowers, lining them up together to form a straight edge at the bottom.

3. Place your vinyl on the cutting mat, send the design to your Cricut.

4. Use a weeding tool or pick to remove the excess vinyl from the design.

5. Place the design along the bottom of the tote bag with the plastic side up, carefully iron on the design.

6. After cooling, peel away the plastic by rolling it, carry around your new garden tote bag!

Cricut dish
Tools And Materials:

- A Glitter (optional)

- A Cricut Vinyl

- A few serving Trays

- A few dipping Dishes

- An epoxy

- A transfer Tape

- Tools

- Alcohol

- A Cricut Machine

- A weeding tool

Steps:

1. Gather all of your supplies

2. Clean your tray and your dish with the alcohol so that you can remove any oils or any dust particles on the spot that you will be applying the vinyl to measure the tray and the dish

3. Create the design; then resize so that they can fit, cut your design; then use the permanent or the removable vinyl.

4. Once you have your design cut, carefully transfer the image to the transfer paper and to the cleaned tray

5. Now measure the epoxy into equal parts according to the directions that you can find on the bottle, you only need a little bit, just enough to cover the bottom, mix very well, add the glitter directly to the epoxy

6. Pour over the epoxy, let the epoxy set for about at least 24 hours before using it

Laptop case

One of the best things about creating vinyl word art is being able to customize it. In this chapter, you can read a new idea about personalizing your laptop with a custom cut to create everyday vinyl word art design.

Tools And Materials:

- Free Create Everyday word art cut file

- Cricut Explore cutting machine

- Cricut Design Space account

- Adhesive glitter vinyl

- Transfer tape

- Chosen font

Steps:

1. Download the file and upload to your Cricut Design Space account, add the design to your canvas and size to fit your device, follow the on-screen instructions to cut the design.

2. Use transfer tape to remove the vinyl from its backing and then carefully apply it to the device surface.

Cricut Fruit card
Tools And Materials:

- A Cricut Joy machine

- A Computer

- An assorted cardstock paper

- A Cricut Joy card mat

- A ruler

- A Cricut portable trimmer

- A Cricut scoring pen

- A Card image svg file

Steps:

1. To download the SVG files to your Cricut Design Space, upload the image svg file into the design space or create your own, size of the image at about 4.25"x 5.2".

2. Contour the image base; then pre-cut the cardstock to about 5.5"x 8.5" and manually score into the center vertically down against a ruler, fold the cardstock into half like a card.

3. Insert the card into the Joy card Mat, cut with the help of the Joy and cut the cardstock inserts making sure to size them about 4"x 5".

Blossom letters
Tools And Materials:

- An iron-on VINYL

- A cutting-machine iron-on vinyl

- A weeding tool

- An iron and an ironing surface

- A smooth cotton cloth

- An ironing cloth

- A cutting-machine vinyl

- A vinyl transfer material

- Scissors

- A burnishing tool

Steps:

1. Cut the letters from the vinyl; then remove the excess, and use the weeding tool to remove the details from the design center, cut the transfer material the size you want of the letters; then place, and burnish.

2. Cut a strip of paper all the length of the letters; then tape the paper onto the wall using a level to ensure that it is straight, remove the backing paper from the letters.

3. Using paper on the wall as a baseline, place the vinyl onto the surface, use a burnishing tool to secure onto the wall, peel the transfer material off the wall at a quite sharp angle

4. Repeat the same with the remaining letters, using the burnishing tool to remove any bubbles.

Cricut Gift Box
Tools And Materials:

- A Cricut Maker

- A StandardGrip Mat

- A Kraftboard

- A foil Acetate

- A Scoring Wheel Combo Pack

- A clear tape

- A hot glue gun

- Some glue sticks

- A Cricut Cut File

Steps:

1. Start by opening the Cricut cut file

2. Start by making the base of the box which is made with Cricut kraft board

3. Now, add the kraft board to the StadardGrip mat you are using and load it into the Cricut Maker

4. You should use the Double Scoring Wheel in the clamp B; then, all you need to do is to switch over to the fine point blade after the kraft board is scored.

5. Then all you need is to make the sleeve acetate box; you will also need to use the Scoring Wheel; yet this time, you will use the single scoring wheel

6. To easily switch between the single and the double scoring wheel, just press down on the plunger to release; then attach, before adding the foil; acetate to the StandardGrip mat; then remove the clear backing

7. Place the acetate onto the mat with the foil side facing down and once again, the Cricut maker will score the acetate at the first place

8. Start with the Single Scoring Wheel; then switch the Scoring Wheel over to using the cutting blade into the clamp B without any need to remove the mat from the Cricut Maker.

9. Hit the button "go"; then cut the foil acetate.

10. For both your kraft board and the foil acetate; just fold along the scored lines and for your kraft board; just use a hot glue gun to hold all the double-folded sides of the box

11. To attach the flaps at each of the corners; all you need is to clear tape to attach the flap onto the foil acetate sleeve, the box is now ready to use it

Cricut bracelet

All you will really need to create your own DIY leather cuff is:

Tools And Materials:

- A Cricut Maker
- A Cricut mat
- A Cricut vinyl
- A Cricut Transfer Tape
- A Cricut Basic Tool Set
- Some patriotic slap bracelets
-

Steps and Instructions:

1. Measure the bracelets; then create the names into the Design Space to make it fit; then cut from the vinyl scraps and remove any excess of vinyl, weed excess of vinyl from the names using the Cricut weeding tool.

2. Add the transfer tape to the vinyl image.

3. Put on transfer tape; then use the Cricut scraper to burnish the vinyl on to the transfer tape.

4. Remove the backing from the name; then peel off the backing, center the name on the snap bracelet.

5. Burnish the name with the Cricut scraper; then remove the transfer tape.

Cricut Apron
Tools And Materials:

- A Cricut Explore or Maker
- A Green StandardGrip Mat
- A Weeding Tool
- An EasyPress Mini or Iron
- A Pressing Mat

- An iron-On Vinyl Pink, red, green, black

- An apron

Steps:

1. Upload the file and resize it, cut the pieces from the iron-on vinyl.

2. Weed the iron-on vinyl pieces, adhere the iron-on pieces to the apron with the help of the EasyPress Mini.

Monogram pillow

In this chapter, you can see a new crafting idea that you can enjoy in your home using the Cricut Explore Air. Haven't we all swooned over custom monogrammed pillows, but the price tag? You can use the Cricut Explore Air and some iron-on material to take things into my own hands and DIY a gorgeous pillow for my bedroom. Best of all, you don't need any crazy design skills or knowledge.

Tools And Materials:

- Cricut Explore Air machine

- Cricut Design Space account

- Cricut Iron-On in the color

- Cricut tools

- Iron

- Ironing board

- Scissors

- Ruler

- Pillow insert

- Pillow cover

Steps:

1. Begin by deciding on a design. I made a wreath monogram out of this lovely Pillow book font.

2. It came with several wreath freebies, so making the design was simple! Because it is so simple, you can do it in Photoshop or even Picmonkey.com.

3. Then, import your design into Cricut Design Space, resize it to your liking, and cut!

4. Check the iron on (reverse design) box and make sure the glossy side of the iron on vinyl is down.

Cricut Apron
Tools And Materials:

- Some laundry baskets
- A Cricut Vinyl

Steps:

1. Start by measuring the area of your laundry basket side to determine what size you need to cut the Cricut vinyl
2. Choose the color and the font; then get to cut
3. Use the transfer tape to apply the Cricut vinyl to the laundry basket
4. The transfer tape will make it very easy to keep the letters at their places
5. Remove the transfer tape
6. You will have a beautiful laundry basket

Live, Love, Laugh Glass Block
Supplies Needed

- Glass block
- Frost spray paint
- Clear enamel spray
- Holographic vinyl

- Vinyl transfer tape

- Cutting mat

- Weeding tool or pick

- Fairy lights

Steps:

1. Spray the entire glass block with frost spray paint, and let it dry, spray the glass block with a coat of clear enamel spray, and let it dry, open Cricut Design Space and create a new project.

2. Select the "Text" button in the Design Panel, type "Live Love Laugh" in the text box.

3. Use the dropdown box to select your favorite font, arrange the words to sit on top of each other.

4. Place your vinyl on the cutting mat, send the design to your Cricut.

5. Use a weeding tool or pick to remove the excess vinyl from the design.

6. Apply transfer tape to the design, remove the paper backing and apply the words to the glass block.

7. Smooth down the design and carefully remove the transfer tape.

8. Place fairy lights in the opening of the block, leaving the battery pack on the outside.

Cricut jeans
Tools And Materials:

- Fabric A: about 7"x 2.5", three of about 4.5"x 4.5", 4"x 4",

- two fabrics of 1.5"x 5.5", 2"x 9"

- A fabric B of about 4"x 4", 2"x 6"

- A Fabric C of about 3.5"x 2.5", one of about 7"x 3.5", about

- two of 1.5"x 5.5", 1.5"x 9"

- A fabric D: about three 4.5"x 4.5", 4"x 4", 2.5"x 5.5"

- A fabric E: of about 3.5"x 3.5", 4"x 4", 2"x 3.5"

- Rotary cutter

- Jeans

- A cutting board

- A ruler

- Pins

- A needle and thread

- An iron

Steps:

1. Cut; then sew together all the 5 patchwork pieces with the help of the attached patterns.

2. Use a seam of allowance of about 1/4"

3. When you are completed, square off the final pieces with the rotary cutter and the ruler

4. You should press as you go.

5. To hide your unfinished edges on each of the patchwork pieces, fold about 1/4" of the already unfinished edge to the back; then press

6. The edges will be hidden from unraveling as you start sewing them to the jeans

7. Place each of the pieces where you want it to sit on the jeans; then pin tightly in its place

8. Hand stitch around the edges of all of the 5 pieces while using an invisible stitch

Creative stenciled wood plank

Here you can find another great Cricut idea to make an amazing DIY project that you can make for your clients. It would be the perfect homemade gift for your friends.

Tools And Materials:

- Cricut Explore Air
- Adhesive cutting mat
- Vinyl
- Basic Cricut toolset
- Wood plank canvas
- White multi-surface paint
- Pouncer

Steps:

1. Connect your laptop to the Cricut and upload your stencil design photo.

2. Measure your stencil to fit nicely on your wood plank canvas, add a piece of vinyl to your cutting mat and smooth it out with the Cricut Scraper. Make sure your Cricut is set to cut vinyl and hit go!

3. Once your stencil is finished, use your Cricut Weeder to carefully remove the inside of all the letters and numbers, then gently peel the vinyl from the mat and you have your stencil.

4. Carefully unpeel the back from the vinyl then place on your canvas. Once you've centered the stencil place the rest of the details on that were left on the bottom of your vinyl piece. Press all edges to make sure the edges are sealed.

5. Use your pouncer and paint the entire stencil, then slowly peel it off and use the Cricut Tweezers to pull off the small stencil details.

6. Once dry, if desired, attach the needed hardware and display in your home!

Cricut Heart Shapes
Tools And Materials:

- A Cricut Joy cutting machine

- A Cricut Design Space account

- A World Heart cut design

- A Cricut Design Space Access

- A Jen Goode Adhesive-Backed Deluxe Paper

Steps:

1. Start by opening the Design Space; then Cut the File and size it to fit your door or window

2. Send the project to cut it and remember, with the Cricut Joy products, you don't need the use of a cutting mat

3. Repeat the same step until you get as many hearts as you need, weed any excess of adhesive-backed paper

4. Apply the adhesive hearts to the door or window

Cricut napkins
Tools And Materials:

- Some paper napkins

- Some Cricut Maker affiliate links

- A Cricut Easy Press

- An everyday iron-on vinyl (I used gold)

- A weeding Tool

- Scissors

- An SVG file (you can use whatever you like)

Steps:

1. Start by uploading the free SVG file into your Cricut Design Space or just create your own personalized design.

2. You can make the napkin by about 3.5 inches of width for your cocktail napkin

3. Copy and paste as many of the design as you want, using the attached tool Cricut; select the button "mirror" for the image,

select the button 'continue'; then choose the type of material to be used

4. You can use the everyday Iron-On vinyl into gold; then place a shiny side down on a mat.

5. Load the mat into a Cricut cutting machine, then start cutting, carefully remove the mat from the machine; then cut around the design

6. Remove the vinyl around the image with the weeding tool's help, which will make your work quick.

7. Weed the writing you want on the red napkin, put the image over the top of the napkin

8. Place the custom design right on top of the paper napkin

9. Set your Easy Press to about 120c (248f); then press the image onto the paper napkin for about 20 seconds.

Hanging
Tools And Materials:

- A quantity of purified water

- A vellum tracing paper (8.5" by 11" at the art supply store)

- About 4 pieces of long rope strands, some leather laces, a

- hemp twine of about (3–4 feet)

- A leather dye (optional) & gloves

- 1 square foot of veg-tanned tooling leather (12" by 12")

- Masking or a packing tape

- A dull pencil

- A carpet knife and/or an X-Acto knife

- A computer and a printer (for the printing template)

- Template

- A sponge for dyeing and wetting

Steps:

1. Print out the plant hanger pattern vellum paper of about 8.5" by 11"

2. Lay your pattern down onto the leather; then find the perfect placement so that you can transfer the pattern

3. Soften the leather; then wet the leather in an even way by dipping the sponge into the water; then blotting the water on your leather

4. Repeat the same step at least three times until the leather starts looking that it won't take any more water

5. Put the Vellum pattern down on the leather; then tape it into place

6. With the help of a dull pencil, draw right on top of the printed lines, pressing into every line with a medium weight, pull the pattern off your leather to reveal the different impressions that you have made on the surface

7. Cut every line even the outside; the perimeter line

8. Apply the desired dye; a water-based, that is low in VOC and that is meant for being used on natural veg-tanned leather; then Apply the dye with the help of a sponge while you are wearing the gloves

9. When the leather is drying; gently pull at the leather a little bit to expose those marks that you have made

10. Once the leather is dehydrated; punch four holes apart from each other

11. Tie one knot at each of the ropes so that the leather plant basket hangs in an even way

12. You can also use a leather lacing or twine

13. You Can add beads, tassels to decorate, you can also grab four strands; then tie it into a knot; you can also use the knot to hook it into the ceiling mounting hook or ring

Fabric bookmark

This is an excellent project for a novice or even a child. This year, my sons decided it would be fun to make some Christmas bookmarks and send them to their friends along with a nice Christmas book.**Supplies needed:**

- Cricut Maker cutting machine

- Two 7.5″ h x 2.5″ pieces of fabric

- 6.75″ h x 1.75″ medium/thick fusible interfacing or cardboard

You will need to cut two 2.5″x7.5″ fabrics per bookmark. You can use your Cricut Maker, of course. With the Cricut Maker you can cut a bunch super-fast using the new rotary blade feature that the Maker has.

You can make a few variations using different Christmas fabrics too, some with different fabrics on each side of the bookmark and some for both sides.

Fairy Garden
Tools And Materials:

- A Cricut Maker, a Cricut Explore Air 2, or a Cricut Joy

- A machine Mat

- A burnishing Tool

- A font

- A stencil Vinyl

- A transfer Tape

- A Painter's Tape

- A dark Spray Paint

Steps:

1. Start by measuring your container's width as well as the height of whatever you want your sign of being

2. Now, create the stencil into Design Space using your favorite font, cut the stencil out with the help of your Cricut machine, clean off the container.

3. Use the transfer to remove the stencil from the backing, carefully move the sticky part to the container and place it in position

4. Now, with the help of a burnishing tool; place some pressure onto the stencil; then remove the transfer tape

5. Cover any other spots with the painter's tape so that you can prevent any over quantity of spray

6. Spray on the paint following the instructions that you will find on the can; you can use one or two coats if needed, let dry for about 1 hour

Cricut decorated Stool
Tools And Materials:

- A Cricut machine (or scissors to hand cut the design)

- A Wood stool

- A Spray paint

- A Mylar (or vinyl)

- A Painter's tape

- An acrylic paint

- A Stencil brush

- A Polyurethane

Steps:

1. Before starting; paint the stool with white acrylic paint to give it a little bit of refresh

2. Start by finding a stencil design in the Design Space for the wood stool or you can just download the SVG if you don't have any machine and you still want to recreate the same pattern.

3. Don't forget to resize your design to fit the project

4. With the help of a Cricut Maker or a Cricut Explore machine, just cut the pattern with the right setting of the material you will use for the project

5. You can also use the Cricut Joy; lay the LightGrip mat; then cut it with a deep point blade using the "Mylar" setting; you can also cut the Mylar with the help of a fine point blade and depending on the sharpness of the blade, you may want to adjust the setting so that it will fit your project

6. Lay the stencil onto the surface of the project surface with the painter's tape

7. When the stencil design is secured to the surface of the project, being dabbing

8. Let the paint dry a little bit; then carefully remove the stencil

9. After the paint is completely dried, remove the stencil to check your design

10. Seal the stencil with the help of a polyurethane spray or an equivalent

Tea cupcake holder

For this project, you can see another unique idea called the tea party cupcake holder. The "Make it now" project is for mini cupcakes, so as prep for someone's child party, you can mess around with this project to see how you can resize it to fit a full-sized cupcake and how to find the exact right size.

If you want to create the project as a mini cupcake holder, you can find the "make it now" project idea easy. The great thing about the "make it now" project is it includes all the instructions for doing the project. You will want to go to this "make it now" project and read the instructions for both sized projects.

Tools And Materials:

- Cricut Maker

- Fine point blade

- Scoring stylus

- Light grip mat

- 12×12 cardstock in 2 different colors or prints

- Hot glue gun or double-sided tape

- "Cricut Maker" or "Cricut Explore", sticker paper and cutting mat.

Steps:

1. Login to "Design Space" using your "Cricut" ID and click on "New Project" to view a blank Canvas.

2. Click on the "Images" icon on the "Design Panel" and type in "recipe" in the search bar to narrow your search. Select all the images that you like and click on "Insert Images".

3. Your selected images will appear stacked up on the Canvas, as shown in the picture below. You can now edit your image as needed, for example, you could move the "recipe" image on top of the other image and click on "Color Sync" to change the color of the tab to match the color of the clover. Adjust the image's size as needed, a sticker should be between 2-4 inches wide.

4. Remember to move the design on top left corner of the canvas and then group the images together by clicking on "Group" on the right of the screen under "Layers panel".

5. Copy-paste the design multiple times, depending on how many stickers you need. You can either use your keyboard shortcut "Ctrl + C" and "Ctrl + V" or select the image and click on "Edit" from the "Edit bar" to view the dropdown option for "Copy" and "Paste".

6. Click on "Save" and give the desired name to the project, for example, "Recipe Stickers" and click "Save".

7. Now, your design is ready to be printed. Simply click on the "Make It" button on the top right corner of the screen. You will see the required mats and material displayed on the screen.

8. Click on 2 and 3 to view the mat instructions for your design's remaining objects, as shown in the pictures below.

9. Click "Continue" after loading your sticker paper to the "Cricut" machine and print the design onto the paper.

10. Note – If you are using images that are available for purchase, you would need to click on "Purchase" at the bottom right of

the screen to buy the images before you can print them. And once you have made the purchase the "Continue" button will be available to you.

11. Calibrate the machine with your device and use the "Vinyl" setting to cut the sticker paper. Place the sticker paper on top of the cutting mat and load it into the "Cricut Maker" by pushing against the rollers. The "Load/Unload" button will start flashing so just press it. Then press the "Go" button, which would already be flashing. Viola! You have your own customized recipe stickers.

Welcoming Home Card 'Hello'
Tools And Materials:

- A Cricut Maker or Cricut Explore

- A Cricut Cutting Mat

- A Scoring Wheel or a Scoring Stylus

- Your favorite color of the Cricut pen

- 3 pieces of cardstock or of a scrapbook paper for the card, one for the

- envelope liner you will use of about 12"X12"

- Some Glue dots

- Optional: Colored markers or pencils

Steps:

1. Log into the Cricut Design Space; then open the DIY Coloring Card Cut File and click the button "Make It"; then follow the prompts right on your computer screen.

2. Try to use the draw function on your Cricut so that it can help you create a beautiful, welcoming card

3. Fold the envelope and the envelope liner.

4. Use the draw function on the Cricut to create your card

5. Use the glue dots to adhere to your envelope's envelope liner, making sure to line up the scoreline for placement.

Plant Pots
Tools And Materials:

- Some terra Cotta Clay Pots
- A Vinyl- Creme
- A transfer Tape
- A Lace Flower Pots Art
- A Cricut Explore Air 2
- An essential Tool Set

Steps:

1. You need either to purchase or have access to Cricut Design Space
2. You can also search the "Lace Flower Pots" into the Cricut Access to find your project
3. Size the art to the size of your pots; then prepare the Vinyl and just follow the rest of the prompts that you will find on the Design Space so that you start cutting the Vinyl
4. After the process of cutting is over; all you need to do is to weed out the designs; then transfer the Vinyl to a Transfer paper
5. Apply the Vinyl to the pots and here you go

Paper basket
Tools And Materials:

- A Wild Whisper Home for the Holidays Paper
- Xyron Tape Runner
- Cricut
- Candies or Toffee
- A Cello Bag for the candy

Steps:

1. Start by opening the Design Space; then choose the best cut file for you, size it to fit the paper, and send it to your Cricut to cut, the Cricut will cut and at the same time will score the paper.

2. Fold the basket right on the score lines; then use the Xyron Tape Runner to apply the adhesive.

BOOK THREE: HOW TO DESIGN SPACE

INTRODUCTION

Cricut machines are fantastic gadgets to own because they do not only boost creativity and productivity; they can also be used to create crafts for business. With Design Space, crafters can make almost anything and even customize their products to bear their imprints.

All over the world, people use these machines to make gift items, t-shirts, interior décor, and many other crafts, to beautify their homes, share with friends and family during holidays, and even sell, etc.

The Cricut Explore and the Cricut Maker, and both machines are highly efficient in their rights, and experts in the crafting world use them to create a plethora of items, either as a hobby or for business.

Both machines are similar in many ways, i.e., the Cricut Maker and the Explore Air 2, but the Cricut Maker is somewhat of a more advanced machine because it comes with some advanced features, as compared to the Explore Air 2.

One distinct feature about the Maker that sets it apart from the Explore Air is the fact that it can cut thicker materials. The possibilities are limitless with the Maker, and crafters can embark on projects that were never possible with Cricut machines before releasing the Make.

Another feature that puts the Cricut Maker machine ahead of the Explore Air 2 is the 'Adaptive Tool System.' With this tool, the Cricut Maker has been empowered to remain relevant for many years to come because it will be compatible with new blades and other accessories that Cricut will release in the foreseeable future.

Although both machines have several dissimilarities, there are also areas where they completely inseparable. Take, for example, the designing of projects in Cricut Design Space.

As a crafter, without proper knowledge of Design Space, you're not only going to cut out poor products, you will also make little or no in-road in your quest to find success.

Understanding Design Space is important because it empowers crafters with enormous tools and materials to create generalized and custom products. It is a potent tool that just cannot be overlooked by anyone that intends to follow this path.

Thus, the understanding of Design Space is a MUST for people that intend to do a business out of Cricut machines or even utilize it as a hobby. With the software, crafters can create their designs from scratch or use already-made designs on the Cricut platform. Those who have an active subscription to Cricut Access have access to thousands of images, projects, and fonts. They can cut out their products using these images or projects, and they can also edit them to suit their style and taste before cutting.

WHAT TO KNOW TO DESIGN SPACE
The Essential About Cricut Design Space
Cricut Design Space is a web-based program used by Cricut machine to create, browse predesigned projects/images, and edit projects before cutting. You can use any compatible internet-enabled devices, including desktop, tablet, phone, or laptop.

The program was designed by Provo Craft to be user-friendly. However, the level of simplicity depends on your general knowledge of computers. If you are tech-savvy, then perhaps you can navigate design space with some effort. Otherwise, you will definitely require some help.

Over 50,000 images you can choose from in the library of Cricut Design Space, coupled with the 800+ predesigned projects, will ensure you never run out of design ideas.

The other fantastic and amazing feature of the Cricut Design Space is the ability to upload your own predesigned images and fonts to be used for the project you intend to execute.

The formats of the images used by Design Space software are the .jpg, .bmp, .gif, .png, .svg, and .dxf files.

You have the ability to assess the program from multiple computers and mobile devices. This is because the Cricut design space is a cloud-based program. You can also start and end on a different device as long as they are all connected to the internet.

Note that Cricut Design Space is not compatible with some devices, including computers running Unix/Linux OS and Chromebooks.

There are many tools, buttons, options that are displayed on the Canvas that makes the Cricut Design Space look difficult for first-time users. However, after reading through this guide book, you will master the Cricut design Space and obtain fair value for the money spent.

A Guide to the Cricut Design Space

Here is a brief overview of the Cricut Design Space to help you familiarize yourself with the functions and the tasks performed therein. Basically, there is the Design Panel, Header, and Zoom functions.

1. Design Panel

The first thing that you see when you open the Cricut Design Space is the home page, which is the Canvas area. It is the place where all the organization, modification of objects, and visualization of the final project are undertaken before the machine is instructed to cut. On the Design Panel, which is located on the left-hand side of the Canvas, are the following functions.

- *New*—used to create an entirely new project.

- *Templates*— this is used to help you to visualize finished projects with different templates.

- *Projects*—this is used to select, browse, and cut projects in the Project Tab.

- *Images*—this is used to browse, select, and insert pictures obtained from the Cricut Image Library as well as your uploaded images.

- *Text*—this is used to add letters, words, and phrases to the Canvas.

- *Shapes are* used to add basic shapes, including circles, triangles, squares, and even to score lines on the Canvas.

- *Upload*—this is used to upload supported images files for free including .jpg, .png, .bmp, .svg, .gif, and .dxf.

2. Header

The Header, which is the Top Panel, houses the editing area with many editing and arranging functions. You can select what type of font to use, change sizes, aligns objects, and many other functions as described below:

- *Menu (≡)*—this is used to explore the Cricut Design Space. When you click on this button, it opens a new menu that allows you to navigate to Home, Canvas, and many features of the Design space, including Link Cartridges, Settings, New Machine Setup, Sign Out and Help.

- You can calibrate your machine and blades from the menu, update the software, and manage your subscriptions.

- *Page Title*—this is used to inform you of the current page in Design Space where the work is being performed. It is also used to close any open tab.

- *Project Name*—this is where the name of the project appears. It will be labeled "Untitled" if the project is not yet saved. Note that you can only name your project after you have placed at least one image on the Canvas.

- *My Projects*—this is used to open any previously saved project that is in your library. With this, you can cut an already predesigned project saved in the personal library, and there will be no need to recreate it from scratch.

- *Save*—this is used to save the project to your account. It will make it accessible from iOS, Android, Windows, and Mac Operating Systems. You can use the Save As to rename your project. Ensure that you save your work at intervals, especially if you have no backup power where you are or incur browser crashes while working on it.

- *Make It*—this is used to prepare the mats and send your projects to the Cricut machine. Before clicking this button, ensure that you have uploaded your ready files for cutting.

Like the editing menu, the other menu will be discussed later in this guide book's subsequent section.

3. Zoom

- *Zoom In*—this is used to help you get a closer look at any project on the Canvas

- *Zoom Out*—this is used to get a better overview of your project.

4. Layers Panel

The layer to the right of the Canvas contains unique functions that increase your freedom when working with the Canvas. Some of the functions available on the Layers Panel are briefly described below:

- *Group/Ungroup-* this function allows you to group multiple images, layers, or text together. You can edit them together if they are grouped. The Ungroup function is the opposite of the Group function, which means that you can edit the images, text, or layers separately.

- *Duplicate-*this function is used to copy and paste the object(s) in order to create multiples of one object/image.

- *Delete-*use this function to remove any unwanted object on the Canvas.

- *Slice-*this function is to split two overlapping layers into separate items.

- *Weld-* use this function to join multiple layers together in order to create a single object.

- *Attach/Detach-* this is to hold an object in position so that the machine can cut it with precision. Use Detach to separate layers from each other.

- *Flatten/Unflatten-* use Flatten to turn an image into a printable object by merging selected layers into a single layer. Unflatten performs the opposite function.

- *Contour* is used to hide and unhide the contour's lines or cut paths on a layer.

- *Visible/Hidden layer-* Visible is depicted as an open eyeball icon to indicate that a particular layer is visible on the Canvas. When visible, a click on it will hide the layer. Therefore, you can toggle between clicks to hide or make an object visible.

- *Linetype-* this function indicates which action is to be undertaken by the machine to cut, draw, score, and print. This function will be discussed in more detail later.

Compatibility

It is practically impossible to develop any program that is compatible with every device on the planet. I do not know whether there are programs like that, but I know that every program has compatibility requirements, and the Cricut Design Space program is no exception.

There are minimum requirements for different platforms to enable efficient use of the Design Space for Cricut Machine as described in System Requirement below.

System Requirement

The minimum system requirement for Design Space software for Windows OS include

- Windows 8 or later;

- 4Gb RAM size;

- 50MB free disk space;

- available USB port or Bluetooth enabled;

- minimum display screen resolution of 1024px X 768px.

The minimum requirement for Mac OS includes

- Mac OS X10.12 or advanced;

- 50MB allowed disk space;

- 183GHz CPU;

- 4GB RAM size;

- the USB docks, Bluetooth connection, and resolution of the screen display keep on Windows similar.

- 2-3Mbps Download and 1-2Mbps Upload are required for internet connection.

Connection

One notable feature with the iOS devices, as stated above, is their ability to work in offline mode (without an internet connection) as well as in online mode. Secondly, memory usage varies as device usage while working offline.

To work in online mode is simpler compared to offline mode. All you need to do is connect to the internet with your device and log in to your Cricut account.

To work in offline mode, you will need to download the content to your device. Cricut Design Space will use the downloaded content to design and cut materials without connection to the internet. Isn't this wonderful? Yes, it is but this feature limited to only iOS devices.

Subscription

Cricut has a library with tens of thousands of images that have been optimized to cut with speed and accuracy. There are three sources of an image in the Cricut library, which are identified as Cricut images, Designer image, and Licensed images.

Cricut images are the original images developed by the Cricut crew; Designer images are images developed in partnership with top designers; and Licensed images are designs and characters from partner brands like Marvel, Disney, and Hello Kitty.

The visualization of these images is free, but you will require a subscription to use them for a project. It is an amazing marketing strategy to help their clients know the suitability of such images for their projects before purchasing them.

Cricut Access is the medium used for the subscription. It gives you access to the Cricut library with over 50,000 images, 370+ fonts, and over 1000 predesigned projects at no additional cost to you.

HOW TO DESIGN A PROJECT AND LAUNCH THE PLATFORM

When you see the finished product from a Cricut machine, you will definitely be blown away. The neatness and appealing look of a typical project done with the Cricut machine will take your breath away. However, only a few people understand the process involved in the creation of such amazing designs.

Curious to know how the Cricut machine can cut out materials effectively? You are reading the right book. There are three significant steps involved when using the Cricut machine:

Start from a Design

If you have a PC, you can access the Cricut Design Space to access the designs' library. The same platform to select a wide variety of designs. In case you don't have any of these two but possess an iPhone or iPad, you can use the Design Space for iOS.

If what you have is an android, you are covered as well. This is because you can take advantage of the Design Space for Android. These are online platforms where you can select any design that best suits your taste.

You can also customize a ready-made design to suit your need. For example, you can resize it or modify the shape. You can also add a text or image as you wish till you have the design just as you want it.

Set the Machine

Having selected the design you intend to cut out with the machine. You are ready for the next step. The machine needs to be prepared by turning it on. Once you switch on the machine, you don't need to do anything.

You don't have to press any button unless you are using the machine for the first time. In that case, the machine will give you instructions on what to do. It is that simple.

That is why both beginners and experts can make use of the Cricut machine without issues. Your computer or phone will have to be paired with the machine via Bluetooth for the first time. However, this will not be needed subsequently because the machine will remember the pairing.

Hence, once the machine is switched on, the pairing between the phone and the machine becomes automatic. The implication of this is that once the machine is switched on, the machine is ready. The next step is to send the design to the machine.

Send the Design to the Machine

This is the last stage of the process of cutting with the Cricut machine. Once the machine is powered on, you will see the Make It button at the screen's top right corner. This button is a big green button on the Cricut Design Space.

The first thing the software does is to preview the various mats you have. A mat represents a sheet of material; hence, having two different colors in your project implies two mats. There are times that your project can be a combination of fabric and paper.

During such occurrences, you will have a mat representing each material utilized for the project. Once you have prepared the machine, you need to decide the dimension with which the machine will do the cutting. If you intend to make two cards, the machine must be instructed to make two project copies.

Most of the materials you will be cutting will be cut at 12″ × 12″ size. It is because this is the standard size that is the most prominent on the Cricut machine.

However, if you prefer a different dimension, you can always alter it. The mirror switch has to be flipped to mirror the design you want if you want an iron-on design. This has to be done to guarantee that the finished project reflects the alteration.

Once you are set to send the design to the Cricut, you will click Continue. This option can be seen at the bottom right corner of the Cricut Design Space. It is easy to continue at this point because the software will prompt you to take you through what ought to be done.

Don't get what up about how to set up different projects of different materials and colors. The instructions you need will be displayed on the screen, and you can easily follow through. Once you follow the instructions presented to you by the machine, you are guaranteed top-quality cuttings.

This ease of use by simply following instructions is one of the principal reasons the machine is suitable for beginners. Mat no. 1 is where the machine begins. From there, it navigates to the others till it reaches the last one.

The machine will request that you pick the particular material you want to use for the first mat. Simply choose whether it is paper, vinyl, fabric, leather, or any other material. Once you do this, the machine will automatically adjust pressure, speed, and the brush blade as necessary.

Hence, just ensure you do your part of instructing the machine to do your bidding as desired. You can trust the Cricut machine from that point to do all that is needed for a perfect project. After the machine has adjusted itself to cut, you will put the material into the Cricut cutting mat.

At this point, you will then load the machine with the mat. What if I am using different materials for my project? That is also not an issue worth disturbing yourself.

This is because the software will take you through how to go about loading different materials. Once you are done loading the machine with the mat containing the material, you are good to go. It is because you will be prompted by the machine concerning setting the dial cutting, drawing, or scoring.

The machine will proceed to cut out the mat. The pieces that have been cut out can then be gathered by you and used as desired. This is how the Cricut machine works, and it is basically the same principle for every project.

It is apparent that you don't have to be a genius before you are qualified to use the machine. The instructions are simplified such that anyone who can understand basic English language can use it. Therefore, if you have thought that you might not be able to operate this machine, you are wrong. Basic Tools and Functions

All images, fonts, cartridges, and projects included in your Cricut Access membership are denoted by a little green flag, which permits ease of search for Cricut Access images.

Another benefit of the subscription is that the member is granted 10% off orders in Cricut Design Space and on cricut.com. Another amazing marketing strategy by Cricut.

The subscription to Cricut Access involves $95.80 per annum and $9.99 for a monthly subscription. Therefore, the choice is yours to make to have access to the benefits stated above. Do not let this be a limitation to the use of your Cricut Design Space or having unlimited access to images in the Cricut library.

SUGGESTIONS

Material Tearing or Not Cutting Completely Through

This is the biggest problem with most Cricut users. When this happens, the image is ruined, and you have wasted material. More machines have been returned or boxed up and put away due to this problem rather than any other.

But do not panic; if your paper is not cutting correctly, you can take several steps to correct the problem.

The most important thing is this: Anytime you work with the blade, TURN YOUR MACHINE OFF. I know it is easy to forget this because you are frustrated, and you are trying this and that to make it work correctly. But this is a necessary safety precaution that you should remember.

Make simple adjustments at first. Turn the pressure one number down. Did it help? If not, turn the blade one number down. Also, make sure the mat is free of debris, so the blade rides smoothly.

Usually, the thicker the material, the higher the pressure number should be set to cut through the paper. Do not forget to use the *'Multi-cut'* function if you have that option. It may take a little longer to cut 2, 3, or 4 times, but it should cut clean through by then.

For those of you using the smaller bugs that do not have that option, here is how to make your own multi-cut function. After the image has been cut, do not unload the mat; just hit load paper, repeat last, and cut. You can repeat this sequence 2, 3, or 4 times to ensure your image is completely cut out.

If you are using thinner paper and tearing, try reducing the pressure and slowing down the speed. When cutting intricate designs, you have to give the blade enough time to maneuver through the design. By slowing it down, it will be able to make cleaner cuts.

Clean the blade's edge to be sure no fuzz, glue, or scraps of paper are stuck to it.

Make sure the blade is installed correctly. Take it out and put it back, so it is seated firmly. The blade should be steady while it is making cuts. If it makes a shaky movement, there is a problem with the installation or a problem with the blade housing.

Be aware that there is a deep cutting blade for thicker material. You will want to switch to this blade when you are cutting heavy card stock. Cutting a lot of thick material will obviously wear your blade out quicker than the thinner material and cause you to change it more often.

Machine Freezing

Remember always to turn your machine off when you switch cartridges. When you switch cartridges, leaving the machine on, it is called 'hot swapping' and can sometimes cause the machine to freeze. It is more of an issue with the older models and does not seem to apply to Expression 2.

You know how quirky electronic gadgets can be, so give your machine rest for five or ten minutes every hour. If you work for several hours continuously, your machine might overheat and freeze up.

Turn the machine off and take a break. Restart it when you come back, and it should be fine. Then remember not to rush programming the machine and give it an occasional rest.

Do not press a long list of commands quickly. If you give it too much information too quickly, it will get confused in the same way a computer sometimes does and will simply freeze up. Instead of typing in one long phrase, try dividing up your words into several cuts.

If you are using special feature keys, make sure you press them first before selecting the letters.

Power Problems

If you turn your machine on and nothing happens, the power adapter may be at fault. Jiggle the power cord at the outlet and connect to the machine to make sure it is firmly connected. Ideally, you want to test the adapter before buying a new one. Swap cords with a friend and see if that fixed the problem. Replacement adapters can be found on *eBay* by searching for a Cricut adapter power supply.

The connection points inside the machine may also pose a problem; here is how to test that. Hold down the plug where it inserts into the back of the machine, and turn it on. If it powers up, then the problem is inside the machine, and the connection points will have to be soldered again.

If the machine powers up but will not cut, then try a hard reset. See the resource portion for step-by-step instructions on resetting your machine.

Here are a few tips, especially for Expression 2 users. Have you turned on your machine, you watch it light up and hear it gearing up, but when you try to cut, nothing happens? Or are you stuck on the welcome screen, or the LCD screen is unresponsive?

Well, here are two quick fixes to try. First, try a hard reset, sometimes called the 'Rainbow Screen Reset,' to recalibrate your die cutter.

To help cut down on errors, try to keep your machine updated. When an update is available, you should receive a message encouraging you to install the latest version.

For those of you using third party software that is no longer compatible with the Cricut, you probably already know that updating your machine may disable that software.

When you cut heavy paper and your Expression 2 shuts down, try switching to the normal paper setting, and use the multi-cut function.

Carriage Will Not Move

If the carriage assembly does not move, check to see if the belt has broken. It may also be possible that the car has fallen off the track. Provo Craft does not sell replacement parts, which is nuts, so try to find a compatible belt at a vacuum repair shop.

If the wheels have fallen off the track, remove the plastic cover, look for a tiny screw by the wheel, and unscrew it. You now should be able to move the wheel back on track.

Unresponsive Keyboard

If you are sure you are pressing the keys firmly, you have a cartridge inserted correctly, and a mat loaded ready to go, but the keypad is still not accepting your selection, the problem may be internal.

You will have to remove the keyboard and check if the display cable is connected to the keypad and the motherboard. If the connections are secure, you have a circuit board problem, and repairs are beyond this book's scope.

An important reminder, please do not attempt any repairs unless your machine is out of warranty.

Weird LCD Screen

The LCD screen is now showing strange symbols or is blank, after doing a firmware update; try rerunning the update, making sure your selections are correct.

When the image you choose is more significant than the mat or paper size you selected, the preview screen will look grayed out instead of showing the image. So, increase the paper and mat size, or decrease the size of your image.

Also, watch out for the gray box effect when using the center point feature. Move the start position down until you see the image appear. The same thing may happen when using the 'Fit to Length' feature. Try changing to landscape mode, and shorten the length size until the image appears.

Occasionally using the undo button will cause the preview screen to turn black. Your work will be lost, and you have to start again.

Cartridge Errors

Sometimes dust or debris accumulates in the cartridge port; gently blow out any paper fiber that may have collected in the opening.

With any electrical machine, overheating can be a problem. If you get a cartridge error after using your machine for a while, turn it off, and let it cool.

If this is the first time you are using the cartridge, and you get an error, I am sure you know the trick about turning the cartridge around and inserting it backward.

If you thought you could use your cartridges with your Expression 2, think again. You will get an error message because you can only use the art cartridges you can cut with; the colors and patterns cartridge are for printing.

Even brand-new items, fresh out of the box, can be defective. If you see a cartridge error 1, 2, 3, 4, 5, 6, 9, or 99, call customer service and tell them the name, serial number, and error message number, and they may replace the cartridge.

Trouble Connecting to Your Computer
All Cricut machines come with a USB cord that lets you connect to your computer and allows you to use the other products like the Cricut Design Studio software, Cricut Craft Room, or the Cricut Gypsy with your machines.

Double-check your USB connection and try another port.

Check to see if you may have a firewall or antivirus software that is blocking the connection.

You may need to update. Older machines update via firmware (Personal Cutter, Expression, Create, and Cake), while the newer (Expression 2, Imagine, and Gypsy) use the Sync program to update.

Glimmering Red Light
Check for a firmware update.

Strong red light:

Turn off the machine, and unplug for two or three minutes before connecting back and fueling on.

Check Machine for garbage and residue.

Move cartridge to and from multiple times in any event.

Check, and change the power source.

Call Cricut support if the issue endures.

My machine is not enlisting the print and cut imprints:
Make sure the machine is in the shade; brilliant daylight prevents the sensor from getting the lines. If this does not work, it may be that your room is excessively dull! Have a go at sparkling light onto the sensor.

The Explore Air Machines can just enroll white cardstock. The Maker, anyway, can identify 'Print and Cut Lines' on shaded and Kraft card.

Go over the dark lines with a dark sharpie to enable your machine to get the line.

My picture is not cutting with the Knife Blade:
Check the picture size; inside cuts ought to be no little than ¾ an inch.

Check the thickness of lines; this ought to be as thick as the standard pencil's finish.

Only utilize the knife-sharp edge when your machine is associated utilizing the USB link; never Bluetooth and check that you have a solid Wi-Fi association.

Ensure the material is taped down on every one of the four sides.

I am experiencing difficulty cutting chipboard:

Leave your chipboard out of its bundling, at any rate, for 24 hours before cutting.

Knife sharp edge is doing such a large number of goes and slicing through my tangle:

Pause undertaking, and check after a couple of spends; in some cases, the knife edge will have sliced through the material before it has completed the process of cutting. If this is the situation, first delay, then launch your venture.

Change the measure of passes.

BOOK FOUR: TIPS AND TRICKS

HOW TO GET THE BEST FROM A CRICUT MACHINE

There are a lot of things which you can achieve by making the correct use of your machine. However, it is not just enough to know these. You need to know easier and more improved ways to make use of the machine you have acquired. To make the most out of your newly-acquired machine, here are a few things you should do;

Test Out Your Machine First

It is a no-brainer, and you should do it as soon as the machine arrives. It is always a safe idea to start by testing your machine's components and double-checking to ensure that your device has all the promised accessories. Suppose you discover that your machine is missing a few things at this stage. In that case, you may want to immediately reach out to membership support and get the issues rectified.

Keep the Components of Your Machine (Especially the Cutting Mat) Clean

This is one of the parts of the machine that is continuously subjected to wear, tear, attack by dirt, and spoil. To make sure that your machine remains in the best of conditions, take out time to clean your mat frequently. Best practices when you are trying to get this done is to make use of a lint roller to wipe down the mat after every use and to also scan over the mat once you are done with it to make sure that you take out all the little pieces that may remain from the materials you just cut. Also, be sure to frequently replace the plastic protective sheet that came with the mat, and it is not entirely unheard of for you to wash the mat often. However, cleaning the mat can be a tricky business. Considering that the mat is meant to be specific, you need to make sure that you wash it so that you do not compromise the material's integrity from where the mat is made. For best practices, wash with lukewarm water and mild dish soap. With these, scrub gently in circular patterns, rinse and allow the mat to drip dry.

Cutting Certain Materials Require That Your Mat Be A Bit Sticky

So that it can hold the material you are looking to cut in place. Due to some factors like prolonged use, and continuous subjection to heavy work, there may be times that you would need to cut something that requires that the mat has a firm grip on the material. As a way around this, you can resort to using masking tape or painter's tape to hold the material you are looking to cut in place. However, take this as a cue to change mats because this option won't work forever.

Pattern on Storing Blades

To prevent the confusion that can come as a result of having to deal with many blades that you will need for your different projects, it can be safe to adopt the pattern of storing up your blades in such a way that you can tell almost instantly what blade is used to cut what material. In essence, you need to learn to separate your blades. Let there be blades that you use to cut vinyl, then the ones you use to cut paper, and wood, and all the rest of them. It will ensure that your blades last for much longer and that you don't use the wrong blades for the wrong projects, thereby creating troubles for your new machine. You can get started by finding small jars to hold the blades and then labelling each jar to signify which blades go into it.

Color of Vinyl

You do not always have to have the right color of vinyl to embark upon your projects. Let's assume that you are about to get started with a project, and you need some green vinyl, but all you have is pink-colored vinyl. You must not get dressed and go off to the mall to get the green-colored ones because there is a way around it. You need a different vinyl color, why not get some Rust-oleum Metallic Spray paint for the future. With this, you can give your un-cut vinyl some spraying and color-over without having to spend money every time. Just for a few bucks, you can get this over.

Recommendable Websites

Dafont and **1001freefonts** are amazing websites where you can find tons of fonts that you can make use of to create even more epic designs. If you have searched through the design space and you have not been able to see something that piques your interests, or you just need to try out something new, you may want to visit those platforms and see what they have in store for you. You will also find many support groups on Facebook, where you can find a lot of helpful information regarding your creative journey with the machine you have just acquired. Join these groups, and be sure to be an active member of them. You will see that some things may bother you that can be a walkover for another person.

Furthermore, these platforms serve as hosting sites for a ton of helpful tools that can even unclog your creativity even more. Find them as pinned documents, helpful DIY tips, post and comments threads, and in all other formats as they come. The goal is to make sure that you do not try to do this on your own.

Stenciling Tips

Want to do some stenciling, but you are not sure where and how you can get started?

There's no need for you to be confused when you can use freezer paper to create custom stencils for your projects.

Make Use of Tin Foils to Sharpen Your Blades

Notwithstanding how careful you are with the blades and how you do not mistake them for cutting different materials, it is not possible for your blades not to get to a point where they become blunt and weak. When your blades get blunt, a great way to get them up and running once again is by making use tin foils to sharpen them. By sharpening with tin foil, you can extend the life of your blade, almost by x3. Sharpening is very simple. Unclamp the blade and run the blade's tip through the tin foil between 10-15 times.

Using Pens Other Than the Cricut Pens to Write

Next to the Cricut pens, there are a ton of other brands that you can make use of, even with your machine. They include

- Uni-ball Signo UM-153.

- Tombow Duel brush pens.

- Sakura gelly roll.

- Bic marking and Bic crystal.

- Pilot Precise.

The list is endless. You can find them online for all these pens, and with just a few dollars, you can have them added to your bucket list of pens to work. However, to make use of these pens with your machine, you need a pen adapter. Pen adapters work for the Explore Air 2 or newer models of the Cricut machine. With these, you can connect any brand of Cricut pens and draw/write away.

Increase Your Image Options by Learning How to Make Your Own SVG Files Online

While the design space and the internet provide you with endless numbers of images, you will agree that there are those times when even the most intricately designed picture does not quite cut it; it does not do justice to what you want to create. Under these circumstances, you need to learn how to bring your inner genius to life.

Using Inkscape, you can create your own SVG files from scratch or convert your boring pictures to two-layered SVG files.

FAQ

Why does Design Space indicate that my Cricut machine is already in use when it is not?

To fix this, make sure you've finished your Cricut's New Machine Setup. Experiment with Design Space in a different browser. Google Chrome and Mozilla Firefox are the finest browsers to use; if one doesn't work, try the other. If this does not resolve the issue, try an alternative USB port and USB cable. Turn off the machine and disconnect it from the PC. Restart your computer while it is turned off. Connect the device and switch it on when your computer restarts. Wait a few seconds before attempting Design Space again. If you are still experiencing the same issue, please contact Cricut Member Care.

Why Doesn't My Cut Match the Preview in Design Space?

Test another image and see if the same thing happens. If it's only happening with the one project, create a new project and start over or try a different image. If it happens with a second project, and your machine is connected with Bluetooth, disconnect that and plug it in with a USB cable. Larger projects may sometimes have difficulty communicating the cuts over Bluetooth. If you can't connect with USB or the problem is still occurring, check that your computer matches or exceeds the running Design Space system requirements. If it doesn't, try the project on a different computer or mobile device that does. Suppose your computer does meet the requirements, open Design Space in a particular browser, and try again. Finally, if the issue still hasn't resolved, contact Cricut Member Care.

What Do I Do If I Need to Install USB Drivers for My Cricut Machine?

Typically, the Cricut drivers are automatically installed when you connect it with a USB cable. If Design Space doesn't see your machine, you can try this to troubleshoot the driver installation. First, open Device Manager on your computer. You'll need to have administrator rights. For Windows 7, click Start, right-click on Computer, and select Manage. For Windows 8 and up, right-click on the Start icon and click Computer Management. Within Computer Management, click Device Manager on the left-hand side. Find your Cricut machine on the list—it should be listed under Ports, but it might be under Other Devices or Universal Serial Bus Controllers. Select Update Driver Software. In the box that pops up, select Browse My Computer. In the box on the next screen, type in %APPDATA% and click Browse. Another box will pop up where you can search through folders. Find AppData and expand it. Click Roaming, then CricutDesignSpace, then Web, then Drivers, then CricutDrivers, and click OK. Click Next to install these drivers. Once it's finished, restart your computer. Once it's on, open Design Space again to see if it recognizes your machine.

Why Does My Cricut Maker Say the Blade Is Not Detected?

Ensure that the tool in Clamp B is the same one Design Space recommends in the Load Tools step of the Project Preview screen. If you don't have that recommended tool, unload your mat and select Edit Tools on the Project Preview screen. Here, you can select a different tool. If the tool and the selection already match, carefully remove the tool from Clamp B and clean the reflective band on the housing. Reinstall it in the clamp and press the Go button. If that doesn't resolve the problem, remove the tool again, and clean the machine's sensor. Reinstall the tool and press Go again. If the Maker still doesn't detect the blade, try a simple test project using a basic shape with one of the other tools. There may be something wrong with the drive housing of the original tool. If the problem continues with other tools or doesn't have another tool to test, try uninstalling and reinstalling Design Space and retry your project. If the issue persists, or if you've discovered it's an issue with the tool housing, contact Cricut Member Care.

Why Is My Cricut Machine Making A Grinding Noise?

If it's the carriage car making a loud noise after you press the cut button, and it sounds like the carriage might be hitting the side of the machine, record a short video of it and send it to Cricut Member Care. If the noise comes from a brand-new machine the first time you use it, contact Cricut Member Care. Otherwise, make sure that you're using the original power cord that came with your machine. If the machine isn't getting the correct voltage, it may produce a grinding sound. In another case, if you are using the machine's power cord, adjust your pressure settings. If it's too high, it might produce an unusual sound. Decrease it in increments of 2−4, and do some test cuts. If it's still making the issue even after decreasing the cutting pressure, contact Cricut Member Care

What If My Cricut Is Making A Different Loud Noise?

Make sure that you don't have Fast Mode engaged for cutting or writing. If it's not on, take a short video of the problem to send to Cricut Member Care.

Why Is My Mat Going into The Machine Crooked?

Check the roller bar to see if it's loose, damaged, or uneven. If it is, take a photo or video of it to send to Cricut Member Care. If the roller bar seems fine, make sure that you're using the machine's right mat size. Ensure the mat is correctly lined up with the guides and that the edge is underneath the roller bar when you prepare to load it. If it's still loading crookedly even when properly lined up with the guides, try applying gentle pressure to the mat to get it under the roller bar once it starts. If none of this works, contact Cricut Member Care.

Why Isn't the Smart Set Dial Changing the Material in Design Space?

Make sure that the USB cable between the computer and the Cricut Explore is appropriately connected. If so, disconnect the Explorer from the computer and turn it off. Restart your computer. Once it's on, turn on the Explore, plug it into the computer, and try the cut again. If it still isn't changing the material, connect the USB cable to a different computer port. If it's still not working, try Design Space in multiple web browsers and see if the problem replicates. If it does, try an entirely different USB cable. Check for Firmware Updates for the Explore. If you don't have another USB cable, the Firmware Update doesn't help, or there are no Firmware Updates, contact Cricut Member Care.

What Do I Do If My Cricut Maker Stopped Partway Through A Cut?

If the Knife Blade stops cutting and the Go button is flashing, the Maker has encountered some error. In Design Space, you'll get a notification that the blade is stuck. This might have been caused by the blade running into something. The possible causes are like a knot or a seam if too much dust.

It may also be because of debris built up in the cut area or if the blade got into a gouge in the mat from a previous cut. To resume your project, do not unload the mat. It will lose your place in the project, and it will be impossible to get it lined up again. Check the cut area for dust or debris, and gently clean it. If there's dust on top of Clamp B, brush it off with a clean, dry paintbrush. Do not remove the blade. Once the debris is gone, press the Go button. The machine will take a moment to sense the Knife Blade again, and then it will resume cutting.

Why Is My Fabric Getting Caught Under the Rollers?

Be sure to cut down any fabric to fit on your mat without going past the adhesive. If you have stuck the fabric and realize it's hanging past the adhesive, use a ruler and a sharp blade to trim it. Or, if it's the correct size but slightly askew, unstick it and reposition it

Why Would My Cricut Maker Continuously Turn Off During Cuts?

It can happen from a build-up of static electricity while cutting foil and metal sheets. Makers in dry areas are more susceptible to this. Spritzing water in the air will dissipate the build-up. Be careful not to spray any water directly on the Maker. If this doesn't seem to be what's causing the issue, contact Cricut Member Care.

What Do I Do About A Failing or Incomplete Firmware Update?

Be sure to use a computer to install the firmware update and that you're connected with a USB cable rather than Bluetooth. If your computer doesn't meet the minimum requirements, you'll need to use another computer that does. If it does and you're still having problems, disconnect the Cricut from your computer and turn it off. Restart the computer. Once it's back on, open Design Space and tries the firmware update again; if it still freezes up or doesn't complete, try the update using a different web browser. If that doesn't help or don't have another USB cable to try, contact Cricut Member Care.

What Do I Do If My Cricut Machine Has Power Issues?

If your Cricut Maker, Cricut Explore One, or Cricut Explore Air 2 is having power issues, these are the troubleshooting steps. If the machine doesn't have any power or only has it sometimes, make sure that the plug is completely plugged into the power port on the device, the power adapter, and the wall outlet. The cutting mat can sometimes knock the power cable loose as it goes through the machine. Make sure the excess cord isn't bundled up behind the machine. If everything is securely plugged in, make sure that you're using the genuine Cricut power cable that came with your device and that the green light on the adapter is lit up. If you're not using the Cricut power cable, you can buy one or contact Cricut Member Care. Or try using a different wall outlet. If it's still having problems, try another Cricut power cable. If the issues continue even after this, take a short video of the issue happening and forward it to Cricut Member Care.

What Do I Do If I Have Issues with The Machine's Door?

If the door won't open or won't stay open, take a short video to forward to Cricut Member Care. If the door won't close or won't stay closed, make sure there aren't any accessories loaded into the accessory clamp. If there aren't, take a photo or short video to forward to the Cricut Member Care team.

CONCLUSION

It's time to get crafting! Enjoy your new knowledge of your amazing machine and give a new project a try. The beauty of the Cricut is the versatility of functions and user-friendly format. Use this to make your life and home and those of your friends and family more exciting and beautiful!

At this stage, we can both settle that Cricut bids a whole lot more than it entails. Do not give up trying to absorb how to cut on Cricut machines. Even though it might be slightly frustrating getting designs right sometimes, keep striving to attain perfection. You'll become professional in no time and probably start teaching other people how to use it.

Cricut machines are being paid more widespread every day. A lot of individuals have a partiality for Cricut machines for numerous motives. User-friendliness is one of the primary motives that people pick Cricut machines to ensure their cutting job. It is laid-back to use and also easy to learn if you have the right resources. Almost anybody can set up a Cricut machine since it is not too complicated.

There are so many amazing things that you can do with a Cricut machine. This book is only the beginning of what your creativity can do if you work with the Cricut machine. There are only new and better updates to the machine, so now is the best time to get one and get in the door to understand what it can do for you.

You can use reference the book or visit the Cricut website for help. Understanding and studying the foundations of your Cricut is wise to make sure you are building on your skills with a solid foundation of knowledge. From there, your creativity can blossom, and the sky is the limit for what you can create.

I hope that you enjoyed this book and learned a lot! If you did, I would love to see your opinion and review it on Amazon! Please mention at the end of the book the following sentence:

If you enjoyed this book, don't forget to check out the other books of the series on our page. Learn tips, tricks, and techniques to master your Cricut today!

If you find this book helpful, please take a minute to leave us a review and show your support.

BOOK FIVE: AMAZING CRICUT MACHINE PROJECT IDEAS

INTRODUCTION

In the Cricut collection, there are pre-designed cutouts for you to use for your project. Some of these already include what you may need: cardstock, transfer tape, paper trimmer and cutting machine. If your card is to be handmade, then you will have to consider things like whether or not the recipient will be able to read it. Does the recipient have visual impairment?

Get the right design. A Cricut design can be very simple or it could be very complicated. You just have to decide on what is appropriate for your project. If you are sending a greeting card that will hang as an ornament, then a simple design would do as compared to if you are giving a gift card, then a more elaborate and complicated design would do better.

Think about the font size before cutting. You might think you can do a larger font size and have it still be readable, but this is not true. When using the Cricut machine, the font size for each separate design will be different. Therefore, you want to make sure that the font size is appropriate for your type of project.

Use multiple fonts when creating your card. The Cricut print feature does not allow you to use more than one font at a time or combine lettering from two or more fonts into one design. It has to be one or the other. So, if you have multiple fonts, use them all for your project card.

Use color to make the card more readable. Just like in printmaking, color is very helpful for making the font easier to read. You can also use color to help with readability of a design that has a lot of intricate lines that may cause it to be a little hard to figure out what is going on in it.

Don't use a lot of color on each line. When using the Cricut machine, you will notice that you have the option of a lot of colors. This can help make your project unique and attractive. But it also has to be legible.

When making your card, think about how you can personalize it for your recipient as well as making sure that the font and color are easy for them to read. When creating the card, try to think about how you can take extra steps for those who have a visual impairment. This will make sure that your card will be the most effective for its intended use.

VINYL CRAFT PROJECTS
Personalized Pillowcase

What would you say to make a personalized pillowcase without actually sewing anything? The best yet is that the Cricut machine will do all the needed cutting. Once again, you are going to be using vinyl to make a lovely personalized item for decorating your home, as a gift for someone you care, or to take a nap! You will find everything you need to start making your personalized pillowcase below.

Materials:

- Iron-on Vinyl

- Pillowcase

- Weeding tool

- Cricut Machine

- Easy Press or iron

Instructions:

1. Upload your preferred design or choose one from the Design Space image library. You can also make your own design. Make sure to adjust the size of the image to the size of the pillow – you don't want the image to be too small, but you don't also want it to go over the entire surface of the pillow. You can also create a mock-up statement or a witty citation by using a font of your choice. When your design is ready, you can proceed to "Make it" – there you will specify iron-on vinyl as your material of choice. Make sure to use "Mirror" on your design as you will be attaching the image to the pillow. Before you start cutting the image with the machine, set up your cutting mat and arrange the material. Proceed to cut.

2. Your design is cut and now it's the time for weeding. Take your weeding tool and start removing all the excess vinyl from your design until only the image you want on the pillow is left. Remove all vinyl scraps from the working surface and prepare your Easy Press or regular iron. Heat your Easy Press – you can set the timer on. The heating up will take 5 seconds. Afterward, you will heat the pillow surface for 30 seconds before attaching the design to the pillow. Place the vinyl on the pillow where you

want the image to be, and then use the Press again. Make sure to apply mild pressure onto the Press and hold for 15 seconds.

3. Let the vinyl piece cool a bit before you remove it from the pillow and reveal your new design. At this moment, the vinyl is too hot and it can burn your fingers. Once the vinyl piece cools down, you can remove it and enjoy your design.

Giant Vinyl Stencils

Vinyl stencils are a good thing to create, too, but they can be hard. Big vinyl stencils make for an excellent Cricut project, and you can use them in various places, including bedrooms for kids.

You only need the explore Air 2, the vinyl that works for it, a pallet, sander, and of course, paint and brushes. The first step is preparing the pallet for painting, or whatever surface you plan on using this for.

From here, you create the mermaid tail (or any other large image) in Design Space. Now, you will learn immediately that big pieces are hard to cut and impossible to do all at once in Design Space.

You can add square shapes to the image, slicing it into pieces so that it can be cut on a cutting mat that fits.

At this point, you cut out the design by pressing 'Make It'

From here, you put it on the surface that you are using; piecing this together with each line. You should have one image, after piecing it all together. Then, draw out the line on vinyl, and then paint the initial design. For the second set of stencils, you can simply trace the first one, and then paint the inside of them. At this point, you should have the design finished. When done, remove it very carefully.

And there you have it! Bigger stencils can be a bit of a project, since it involves trying to use multiple designs all at once; but with the right care and the right designs, you will be able to create whatever it is you need to in Design Space, so you can get the results you are looking for.

Cricut Quilts

Quilts are a bit hard to do for many people, but did you know that you can use Cricut to make it easier? Here, you will learn an awesome project that will help you do this. To begin, you start with the Cricut Design Space. Here, you can add different designs that work for your project. For example, if you are making a baby blanket, or quilt with animals on it, you can add little fonts with the names of the animals, or different pictures of them too. From here, you want to make sure you choose the option to reverse the design. That way, you will have it printed on correctly. At this point, make your quilt. Do various designs and sew the quilt as you want to.

From here, you should cut it on the iron-on heat transfer vinyl. You can choose that, and then press 'Cut'. The image will then cut into the piece.

At this point, it will cut itself out, and you can proceed to transfer this with some parchment paper. Use an EasyPress for best results and push it down. There you go, an easy addition that will definitely enhance the way your blankets look.

Cricut Unicorn Backpack

If you are making a present for a child, why not give them some cool unicorns? Here is a lovely unicorn backpack you can try to make. To make this, you need ¾ yards of a woven fabric – something that is strong, since it will help with stabilizing the backpack. You will also need half a yard of quilting cotton for the lining. The coordinating fabric should be around about an eighth of a yard. You will need: about a yard of fusible interfacing, some strap adjuster rings, a zipper that is about 14 inches and does not separate, and some stuffing for the horn.

To start, you will want to cut the main fabric; you should use straps, the loops, a handle, some gussets for a zipper, and the bottom and side gussets.

The lining should be done too, and you should make sure you have the interfacing. You can use fusible flex foam, to help make it a little bit bulkier.

From here, cut everything and then apply the interfacing to the backside. The flex foam should be adjusted to achieve the bulkiness you are looking for. You can trim this, too. The interfacing should be on the backside; then add the flex foam to the main fabric. The adhesive side of this will be on the right-hand side of the interfacing.

Fold the strap pieces in half and push one down, on each backside. Halve it, and then press it again; stitch these closer to every edge, and also along the short-pressed edge, as well.

From here, do the same thing with the other side, but add the ring for adjustment, and stitch the bottom of these to the main part of the back piece.

Then add them both to the bottom.

At this point, you have the earpieces that should have the backside facing out. Stitch, then flip out, and add the pieces.

Add these inner pieces to the outer ear, and then stitch these together.

At this point, you make the unicorn face in the Design Space. You will notice immediately when you use this program everything will be black, but you can change this by adjusting the desired layers to each color. You can also just use a template that fits, but you should always mirror this before you cut it.

Choose vinyl, and then insert the material onto the cutting mat. From there, cut it and remove the iron-on slowly.

You will need to do this in pieces, which is fine because it allows you to use different colors. Remember to insert the right color for each cut. At this point, add the zipper, and there you go!

20 Custom Back to School Supplies

Materials needed:

- Vinyl

- Standard Grip Mat

- White Paper

- Markers (including black)

- Pencil Case

- 3 Ring Binder

- IPad Pro (optional)

- Apple Pencil

- Cricut Design Space App

- Drawing app (e.g. ProCreate)

- ProCreate Brushes

Instructions:

1. Convert your kid's drawing into an SVG file that the Cricut Design Space recognizes. This will be done by tracing it in the ProCreate app.

2. Get your child's design – it should not be too complex, to minimize weeding.

3. Open the Procreate app on your iPad.

4. Create a new canvas on ProCreate. Click on the 'Wrench' icon and select 'Image'.

5. , click 'Take a Photo'. Take a picture of the design. Click 'Use It'.

6. On the Layer Panel (the two squares icon), add a new layer by clicking the 'plus' sign.

7. Select the layer containing the picture and click the 'N'. Also, reduce the layer's opacity so that you can easily see your draw lines.

8. From your imported brushes, select the 'Marker' brush. To avoid the need to import a brush, choose the inking brush. You can resize the brush in the brush settings under the 'General' option.

9. On the new layer, trace over the drawing.

10. Click on the 'Wrench' icon, click 'Share', then 'PNG'.

11. , 'Save' the image to your device.

12. Alternately, use your black marker and trace the drawing on a blank piece of paper, then take a picture of it.

13. The stage is to cut the design out in Cricut Design Space

14. Open the Cricut Design Space app on your iPad.

15. Create a 'New Project'.

16. Select 'Upload' (located at the screen's bottom). Select 'Select from Camera Roll' and select the PNG image you created in ProCreate, or the image you traced out.

17. Save the design as a cut file and insert it into the canvas. Here, you can resize the design or add other designs.

18. , click 'Make It' to send it to your Cricut.

19. Choose 'Vinyl' as the material.

20. Place the vinyl on the mat and use the Cricut to cut it.

21. Now, you can place the vinyl cutouts on the back, to make your child stand out!

FABRIC CRAFTS

Customized Makeup Bag

Materials:

- Pink fabric makeup bag

- Purple heat transfer vinyl

- Cricut EasyPress, or iron

- Cutting mat

- Weeding tool, or pick

- Keychain, or charm of your choice

Instructions:

1. Open Cricut Design Space and create a 'New Project'.

2. Measure the space on your makeup bag where you want the design and create a box that size.

3. Select the 'Image' button in the lower left-hand corner and search 'Monogram'.

4. Choose your favorite monogram and click 'Insert'.

5. Place your vinyl on the cutting mat.

6. Send the design to your Cricut.

7. Use a weeding tool or pick to remove the excess vinyl from the design.

8. Place the design on the bag with the plastic side up.

9. Carefully iron on the design.

10. After cooling, peel away the plastic by rolling it.

11. Hang your charm or keychain off the zipper.

12. Stash your makeup in your customized bag!

Stickers with Your Cricut

Materials:

- Cricut Explore Air

- Printable sticker paper by Cricut

- Instructions:

- Log in to your Cricut Design Space account.

In the Cricut Design Space, you will need to click on Starting a New Project. Then, select the image that you would love to use for your stickers. You can use the search bar on the right-hand side at the top to locate the image that you want to use.

, click on the image and click Insert Image so that the image is selected.

Click on each one of the files that are in the image file, and click the **Flatten** button at the lower-right part of the screen. This will turn the individual pieces into one whole piece. This prevents the cut file from being individual pieces for the image.

Now, you want to resize the image, so that it is the size that you wish it to be. This can be any size from within the recommended space for the size of the canvas.

If you want duplicates of the image for sticker sheets, you should **Select All**, then edit the image, and then click **Copy**. This will allow you to copy the whole row that you have selected. Once you have copied, you can then edit and paste the multiple images to make a sheet. This is the easiest way to copy and paste the image over and over again.

At this time, you are ready to start printing your stickers. Click the **Save** button to save the project, and chose the option **Save as Print** and then

Cut Image. Once done, you can click the green button that says **Make It**. This will be located to the right of the screen.

Verify that everything is how it needs to be, and click **Continue**. This will give you a prompt to print the image onto your paper. Make sure you have used the sticker paper for the stickers; otherwise, it will not work.

Print out the image with your printer. If the Cricut sticker paper is too thick for your printer, using a thinner sticker paper is fine.

After the design is printed, adjust the Smart Set Dial to the appropriate setting. Place the paper onto the cutting mat, and load it into the Cricut machine by pushing against the rollers. Press your Load and Unload button that is flashing.

Press Go, and this will begin to cut your stickers. Since the stickers are small and intricate, you will need to be patient.

A tip for getting a good cut is to not touch the mat. Once the first cut is done, repress the flashing button to re-cut the stickers on the same lines that were earlier cut.

Tooth Fairy Pouch

Materials:

- Array of Pens

- Tons of products, such as the Sports Flex iron-on vinyl

- Weeding tool

- Embossed foil paper

- Holographic sparkle XL scraper

Instructions

1. Begin by opening a blank canvas in the Design Space.

2. Kindly go to Images in the left Design panel and search for the word 'tooth.' It is the middle tooth in the screenshot below. Then click on the face and white tooth spots in the Layers panel, and delete them, leaving the gray piece. We will cut the tooth in iron-on white vinyl, but using the gray layer makes it simpler to see what we are doing.

3. Then, using the Design panel text tool, type your child's name.

4. Then, we want to make this a Cricut font with a description. To do this, go to the font drop-down menu, right-click Filter and select Multi-Layer. This will narrow your decisions down to more than one layer of fonts.

5. Then, pick the one you like. I chose *Piper's Alphalicious Short Stack, Miles ' Cherry Limeade*. Change letter spacing, if you think letters are too distant. Copy and paste a second name copy.

6. In the Layers Panel, visualize the outline layer by pressing the eye icon.

7. Then delete the primary font layer, leaving the outline.

8. Then choose both name and tooth, and click on Slice at the bottom of the Layers panel. Slice the tooth and name.

9. Delete the purple letters (there will be two— the portion of the letters outside the tooth, and the portion of the letters inside the tooth). Then, delete the gray messages, leaving an overview of the letters. Insert the other name you recorded earlier on top of the tooth, to make sure everything fits together.

10. Having your two parts adhered to, you are done. I enjoyed this project because Cricut Design Space is readily customizable— no additional files needed.

DIY Coloring Gift Wrap

Materials:

- White craft paper or a big sheet of white paper

- Cricut Explore or Maker

- Cricut Pens

- Mat

Instructions

1. Pick your design, to begin with. I searched for 'draw Christmas' and chosen these adorable woodland creatures, ideal for drawing with pens.

2. After duplicating the images multiple times, I rotated and resized some of them to create the desired design. I then added the holly design (from my fantastic pal Jen Goode, to fill some of the larger animal rooms.) Delete the colored layers and use the doodled holly.

3. Finally, I connected the whole design to maintain it all together. Then came changing the holly's color to red or green. Check your readings before sending the design to your device.

Calfskin Hair Bow

Materials:

- Cricut Investigate

- Faux calfskin or cowhide

- Transfer tape

- Strong grasp Cricut tangle

- Bow Cricut configuration space document

- French barrette clasps

- Binding clasps

Instructions:

1. Line your artificial softened cowhide or calfskin with your exchange tape. This will give something for the texture to clutch, as opposed to leaving fluff everywhere on your tangle and essentially demolishing it. This was an immense help and I will never return to staying the texture ideal on the solid hold tangle again.

2. When you pick the artificial cowhide setting on your Keen Dial, it will slice through the item twice. At the point when your pictures are excessively near one another, occasionally it will catch and draw the item. To stay away from this, move your pictures promote separated when you are seeing your tangle. This will spare item over the long haul, and spare a great deal of cerebral pains. Try not to be hesitant to utilize some scissors in the event that you have one nick in the calfskin.

3. Begin with every one of your pieces laid out. You will need to overlay the longest piece with the goal that the finishes compromise. Secure that with the E6000 stick and a coupling cut.

4. You will assume the back, and position the E6000 stick in the center. Take your bow piece and hold fast it to that, safe with a coupling cut. Enable it to dry only a couple of minutes in the middle of each progression.

5. , put some E6000 on the barrette and lay the back piece to it. Take your little center piece and apply paste to that. Overlay it over the bow in the center and around the back of the barrette. Secure that with a coupling cut. I would permit these too dry for a couple of hours before you stick them in their hair, to make sure they do not get any paste on them.

HEAT VINYL CRAFT

Chipboard Tree Ornaments

Personalized Christmas ornaments are filled with history and memories for a family. With the Cricut, you can make all sorts of Christmas tree ornaments.

Materials

- Cricut glitter adhesive vinyl — red or a selection of colors

- Cricut chipboard

- Green Standard Grip mat

- Purple Strong Grip map

- Cricut Fine-Point Blade

- Cricut Knife Blade

- Weeding tool

- Spatula

- Pair of scissors for cutting the material to size

- Ribbon — red or white

- White matte finish paint

- Builder's tape

Instructions:

1. Open a new project in Design Space.

2. Select 'Diamond' from the 'Shapes' menu on the left-hand side.

3. Leave the color as the default color.

4. Unlock the shape and change it to 1.969" wide and 3.416" long.

5. Select 'Octagon' from the 'Shapes' menu on the left-hand side.

6. Leave the color as the default color.

7. Leave the shape as the default 3.111" wide and 3.111" long.

8. Select 'Star' from the 'Shapes' menu on the left-hand side.

9. Leave the color as the default color.

10. Leave the shape as the default 3.271" wide and 3.111" long.

11. Select 'Heart' from the 'Shapes' menu on the left-hand side.

12. Leave the color as the default color.

13. Select 'Text' from the menu on the left-hand side.

14. Leave the color as the default color.

15. Choose a nice Christmas font. Balega STD Regular is used as an example for this project. The font size is set to 44.2.

16. Type "Peace" and move the text to the middle of the octagon. Leave some space on either side of the text box.

17. Duplicate the text and move the duplicate text to one side out of the way.

18. Highlight the text and octagon, right-click, and select 'Slice.'

19. Remove the top 2 slices and delete them.

20. Repeat steps 17 to 20 for each shape.

21. Type "Love" for the heart shape

22. Type "Joy" for the star shape

23. Type "Hope" for the diamond shape

24. Select 'Circle' from the 'Shapes' menu on the left-hand side.

25. Leave the color as the default color.

26. Leave the shape as the default 0.306" wide and 0.306" long.

27. Make four duplicates of the small circle.

28. Position one circle on the left round part of the heart shape.

29. Select the circle and the heart, right-click, and select 'Slice.'

30. Remove and delete the top 2 slices.

31. Repeat steps 26 to 28 for the right round part of the heart shape.

32. Position one circle on the top point of the star shape.

33. Select the circle and the star, right-click, and select 'Slice.'

34. Remove and delete the top 2 slices.

35. Repeat steps 30 to 32 for the rest of the shapes, positioning the circle at the top in the middle of each.

36. You can fit at least 2 of each shape onto one board.

37. Set 'Project copies' to 2 and click 'Apply.'

38. Position the objects on the page so they are not touching.

39. Set the Cricut blade to the fine-point blade and print out the glitter vinyl copies first.

40. Each ornament will need two vinyl overlays, one for each side. It is suggested to have one side in red glitter vinyl and the other side in green glitter vinyl.

41. Once the glitter vinyl copies have finished cutting, set the Cricut blade to the knife blade and use the purple mat.

42. Remember to stick the chipboard down with builder's tape to keep it steady.

43. While the chipboard is being cut, weed the vinyl overlays and get them ready.

44. When the chipboard has finished being cut, remove the ornaments from the mat.

45. Clean the shapes and text.

46. Paint them on both sides and the edges with the white matte or chalk finish paint.

47. Leave the ornaments to completely dry.

48. When the ornaments are dry, carefully transfer the glitter vinyl onto them.

49. Cut pieces of ribbon and tie it through the little holes on the top of the ornaments.

50. They are ready to hang on the tree.

Easter Basket Fun

Christmas is not the only time for decorations! Here's a great suggestion for how to liven up the Easter holidays.

Materials

- Pink Cricut cardstock

- Blue Cricut cardstock

- Pink Cricut glitter tape

- Clear Cricut sticker paper

- Green Standard Grip mat

- Cricut Fine-Point Blade

- Stylus scoring pen or wheel

- Weeding tool

- Scraping tool or brayer tool

- Pair of scissors for cutting the material to size

- Inkjet printer

- Glue dots or hot glue gun

Instructions

1. Open a new project in Design Space.

2. Select 'Pentagon' from the 'Shapes' menu on the left-hand side.

3. Change the background color to blue.

4. Leave the shape as the default size.

5. Select 'Square' from the 'Shapes' menu on the left-hand side.

6. Leave the background color as the default color.

7. Unlock the shape and change it to 3.375" wide and 3.139" long.

8. Move the pentagon to the following position on the screen: x = 1.986 and y = 1.833

9. Move the square over the top point of the pentagon in the following position on the screen: x = 1.972 and y = 0

10. Select the square and the pentagon. To not disturb the slice, select the objects from the 'Layers' panel on the right-hand side of the screen keyboard, then selecting the pentagon. Right-click and select 'Slice.'

11. Remove all the slices and delete them.

12. Remove the 2 triangle objects but do not delete them; instead, move them out of the way.

13. Change the sliced pentagon to the following size: width = 5.75" and height = 2.724".

14. Select 'Square' from the 'Shapes' menu on the left-hand side.

15. Change the background color to blue.

16. Unlock the shape and change it to 3.111" wide and 2.724" long.

17. Create a duplicate of the square.

18. Unlock the duplicate square and change it to 4.724" wide and 4.724" long.

19. Move the larger square to the following position on the screen: x = 4.306 and y = 3.361

20. Move the pentagon to the following position on the screen: x = 2.955 and y = 0.611

21. Move the smaller square to the following position on the screen: x = 5.917 and y = 0.611

22. Select the pentagon shape and the smaller square shape, right-click, and select 'Weld.' This is the box's side.

23. Select 'Score Line' from the 'Shapes' menu on the left-hand side.

24. Unlock the shape and change the height to 2.724".

25. Move the score line to the following position on the screen: x = 4.333 and y = 0.847

26. Create a duplicate of the score line and move over to the side.

27. Swivel the score line so it runs horizontally.

28. Unlock the shape and change it to 3.111" width.

29. Move the score line to the following position on the screen: x = 4.306 and y = 3.361.

30. Select the box side and the 2 score lines, right-click, and select 'Attach.'

31. Create 3 duplicates of the box side with score lines.

32. Rotate each of the box sides and fit them together around the square.

33. When all the sides are attached to the square, it will resemble a flattened box.

34. Select 'Square' from the 'Shapes' menu on the left-hand side.

35. Change the background color to pink.

36. Unlock the shape and change it to 3.111" width and 2.724" length.

37. Select 'Images' from the menu on the left-hand side.

38. Change the background color to pink.

39. Find an image of bunny ears. This project uses #M8620AE4 as an example.

40. Unlock the shape and change it to 1.276" wide and 1.168" long.

41. Create a duplicate of the bunny ears.

42. Move the one bunny ears over the top of the pink square.

43. Flip the duplicate of the bunny ears vertically and attach the image to the bottom of the pink rectangle.

44. Select the pink square and both bunny ear images, right-click, and select 'Attach.'

45. Select 'Score Line' from the 'Shapes' menu on the left-hand side.

46. Unlock the shape and change the height to 0.847".

47. Swivel the score line so it runs horizontally.

48. Create a duplicate of the score line and move it over to the side.

49. Move the one score line to just below the bunny ears on the top of the pink rectangle. It must fit perfectly into the pink square.

50. Do the same for the second score line at the bottom of the pink rectangle.

51. Select the pink rectangle and the score lines, right-click, and select 'Attach.'

52. Make sure the scoring stylus is loaded into the Cricut.

53. Set the Cricut dial to cardstock.

54. In Design Space, click 'Make it.'

55. Position the box on the mat so it fits with enough bleed around the edges of the cutting board.

56. Make sure the bunny handle is not flush against the side of the pink cutting board.

57. Load the appropriate color material, which is going to be blue cardstock for the basket and pink cardstock for the bunny handle.

58. When the basket and handle have printed, use the glue dots to glue the basket sides together.

59. Where each side of the box folds into the other, you will need to make a small snip at the bottom to free the fold.

60. When the basket is assembled, stick the pink Cricut glitter ribbon around it.

61. Fold the bunny ears on the bottom of the handle up against the rectangle and glue them into position.

62. Where the bunny ears fold up onto the handle will be where you will stick the hand onto the basket.

63. Fill with Easter goodies.

Customized Doormat

Materials

- Cricut Machine
- Scrap cardstock (The color does not matter)
- Coir mat (18" x 30")
- Outdoor acrylic paint
- Vinyl stencil
- Transfer tape

- Flat round paintbrush

- Cutting mat (12" x 24")

Instruction:

1. Create your design in Cricut Design Space. You can also download an SVG design of your choice and import into Cricut Design Space. Make sure that your design is the right size; resize it to ensure that this is so.

2. , you are to cut the stencil. You do this by clicking "Make it" in Cricut Design Space when you are done with the design. After this, you select "Cardstock" as the material. Then, you press the "Cut" button on the Cricut machine.

3. When this is done, remove the stencil from the machine and weed.

4. The step is to mask the parts of the doormat which you do not want to paint on. You can do this using painters' plastic.

5. Now, it's time to spray-paint your stencil on the doormat. Keeping the paint can about 5 inches away from the doormat, spray up and down, keeping the can pointed straight through the stencil. If it is at an angle, the paint will get under the stencil and ruin your design. Spray the entire stencil 2-3 times to make sure that you do not miss any part and that the paint is even.

6. You're just about done! Now, remove the masking plastic and the stencil and leave the doormat for about one hour to get dry.

Tips and Tricks

Vinyl stencils are a good thing to create, too, but they can be hard. Big vinyl stencils make for an excellent Cricut project, and you can use them in various places, including bedrooms for kids.

You only need the explore Air 2, the vinyl that works for it, a pallet, sander and, of course, paint and brushes. The first step is preparing the pallet for painting, or whatever surface you plan on using this for.

And there you have it! Bigger stencils can be a bit of a project since it involves trying to use multiple designs all at once. Still, with the right care and the right designs, you'll be able to create whatever it is you need to in Design Space so you can get the results you're looking for.

DIY PAPER CRAFTS

3d Paper flowers
Materials

- Cricut Machine

- Cricut mat

- Colored scrapbook paper

- Hot glue gun and glue sticks

Instruction

1. To make flowers, you need an appropriate shape for the petals. To make such a shape, you can combine three ovals of equal size. To create an oval, select the circle tool, then create a circle. Unlock and reshape the circle to form an oval.

2. Duplicate this oval twice and rotate each duplicate a little, keeping the bottom at the same point, as shown in the picture.

3. Select all three ovals and weld them together to get your custom petal shape. For each large flower, you need 12 petals – each one about 3 inches long, while for each small flower, you need 8 petals – each one about 2 inches long. For each flower, you also need a circle shape for the base of about the same width as each petal. Arrange the petals and base circle shape in Cricut Design Studio.

4. After you cut out the petals, remove them and cut a slit about half an inch long in the bottom of each one. Place a bit of glue on the left side and glue the right side over the glue for each petal.

5. The thing to do is to place the petals on the circle base. For large flowers, you need three circles of four petals each. For small flowers, you need five circles on the outside and three on the inside. Glue the petal and add to the circle as described above.

6. For the center of the flowers, search Cricut Access for "flower" and chose shapes with several small petals. Cut these out using

a different color of cardstock and glue to the center of the flowers.

Luminaries

Materials

- Luminary Graphic (From a Cricut Project)

- Sugar Skull (SVG File)

- Cricut Explore Air or Cricut Maker

- Cardstock Sampler

- Scoring Stylus

- Glue Stick

- Battery-Operated Tea Light

Instruction

1. The first step is to open your Luminary graphic on the Design Space.

2. Then go ahead to upload the SVG file of your Sugar Skull and adjust its size to around 3.25" high. After doing that, move the Sugar Skull to the bigger part of the Luminary graphic (in the middle of the two score lines) and center-align it.

3. Select the Sugar Skull and the Luminary Graphic and then go ahead and click on "Weld".

4. Try selecting every graphic on the design space and click on "Attach." Then copy and paste the selected graphics on the same page (duplication).

5. Select "Light Cardstock" under the "Materials" menu, and then start loading the Mat and Cut. Also ensure that your Scoring Stylus is in Clamp A. This will automatically change your machine settings from scoring to cutting.

6. When the cut-out is done, fold it along the Score lines. Then start gluing the small Flap to the interior part of the lantern's back.

7. Switch on the Battery-Operated Tea Light, and then place your lantern on top of it.

Valentine's Day Classroom Cards

Materials

- Cricut Maker

- Card Designs (Write Stuff Coloring)

- Cricut Design Space

- Dual Scoring Wheel

- Pens

- Cardstock

- Crayons

- Shimmer Paper

Instruction

1. Open the Card Designs (Write Stuff Coloring) on the Design Space, and then click on "Make it" or "Customize" to make edits.

2. When all the changes have been done, Cricut will request you to select a material. Select Cardstock for the Cards and Shimmer Paper for the Envelopes.

3. Cricut will send you a notification when you need to change the pen colors while creating the Card. Then it will start carving the Card out automatically.

4. You will be prompted to change the blade because of the Double Scoring Wheel. It is advisable to use the Double Scoring Wheel with Shimmer Paper; they both work best together.

5. When the scoring has been finished, replace the Scoring Wheel.

6. After that, fold the flaps at the Score lines in the direction of the paper's white side, and then attach the Side Tabs to the Bottom Tab's exterior by gluing them together.

7. You may now write "From:" and "To:" before placing the Crayons into the Slots.

8. Place the Cards inside the Envelopes and tag it with a sharp object.

Clutch purse

Materials

- Two fabrics
- Fusible fleece
- Fabric cutting mat
- D-ring
- Sew-on snap
- Lace
- Zipper
- Sewing machine
- Fabric scissors
- Keychain or charm of your choice Instructions

Instruction:

1. Create a new project.

2. Select the "Image" button and search for "essential wallet."

3. Select the essential wallet template and click "Insert."

4. Place the fabric on the mat.

5. Send the design to the Cricut.

6. Remove the fabric from the mat.

7. Attach the fusible fleecing to the wrong side of the exterior fabric.

8. Attach lace to the edges of the exterior fabric.

9. Assemble the D-ring strap.

10. Place the D-ring onto the strap and sew into place.

11. Fold the pocket pieces wrong side out over the top of the zipper, and sew it into place.

12. Fold the pocket's wrong side in and sew the sides.

13. Sew the snap onto the pocket.

14. Sew the lining piece to the zipper tape.

15. Fold the lining behind the pocket and iron in place.

16. Sew on the other side of the snap.

17. Trim the zipper so that it's not overhanging the edge.

18. Sew the two pocket layers to the exterior fabric across the bottom.

19. Sew around all of the layers.

20. Trim the edges with fabric scissors.

21. Turn the clutch almost completely inside out and sew the opening closed.

22. Turn the clutch all the way inside out and press the corners into place.

23. Attach your charm or keychain to the zipper.

24. Carry your new clutch wherever you need it!

Framed Succulents Made from Paper

Materials:

- Foam brush

- Standard grip cutting mat

- DecoArt acrylic paint for the frame

- Scissors to curl the succulent petals

- A piece of chipboard, cardstock, or cardboard

- 'X' cardstock in assorted green colors

- Glue gun

Instructions

1. Start with painting the picture frame that you wish to use. Unless you wish to leave it rustic and old, like I would.

2. Place your chipboard or cardboard to the inside of the frame. This is for placing the succulents on. Glue it in the frame properly.

3. , find the image of the file that you wish to use.

4. Press Go to cut out the succulents.

5. Once all the pieces have been cut from the paper, then you can begin to assemble the pieces to make your succulent.

6. Once the succulents are created, you can begin to glue them to a board.

Wooden Gift Tags

Dress up your gifts with special wooden tags! Balsa wood is light and easy to cut. The wood tags with gold names will give all of your gifts a shabby chic charm. Change up the color of the vinyl as you see fit; you can even use different colors for different gift recipients. People will be able to keep these tags and use them for something else, as well. An alternative to balsa wood is chipboard, though it won't have the same look. The Cricut Explore One and Cricut Explore Air 2 can get by using the Deep Cut Blade.

Materials:

- Balsa wood

- Gold vinyl

- Vinyl transfer tape

- Cutting mat

- Weeding tool or pick

Instructions

1. Secure your small balsa wood pieces to the cutting mat, then tape the edges with masking tape for additional strength.

2. Create a new project.

3. Select the shape you would like for your tags and set the Cricut to cut wood, then send the design to the Cricut.

4. Remove your wood tags from the Cricut and remove any excess wood.

5. In Cricut Design Space, select the "Text" button in the lower left-hand corner.

6. Choose your favorite font, and type the names you want to place on your gift tags.

7. Place your vinyl on the cutting mat.

8. Send the design to your Cricut.

9. Use a weeding tool or pick to remove the excess vinyl from the text.

10. Apply transfer tape to the quote.

11. Remove the paper backing from the tape.

12. Place the names on the wood tags.

13. Rub the tape to transfer the vinyl to the wood, making sure there are no bubbles. Carefully peel the tape away.

14. Thread twine or string through the holes, and decorate your gifts!

Pet Mug

Show your love for your pet every morning when you have your coffee! A cute silhouette of a cat or dog with some paw prints is a simple but classy design. You're not limited to those two animals, either. Use a bird with bird footprints, a fish with water drops, or whatever pet you might have! You can add your pet's name or a quote to the design as well. You have the freedom here to arrange the aspects of the design however you'd like. You could put the animal in the center surrounded by the paw prints, scatter the prints all around the mug, place the animal to its name and paw prints along the top, or whatever else you can imagine. Think of this as a tribute to your favorite pet or dedication to your favorite animal, and decorate accordingly. You can use the Cricut Explore One, Cricut Explore Air 2, or Cricut Maker for this project.

Materials:

- Plain white mug

- Glitter vinyl

- Vinyl transfer tape

- Cutting mat

- Weeding tool or pick

Instructions

1. Create a new project.

2. Select the "Image" button and search for "cat," "dog," or any other pet of your choice.

3. Choose your favorite image and click "Insert."

4. Search images again for paw prints, and insert into your design.

5. Arrange the pet and paw prints how you'd like them on the mug.

6. Place your vinyl on the cutting mat.

7. Send the design to your Cricut.

8. Use a weeding tool or pick to remove the excess vinyl from the design.

9. Apply transfer tape to the design.

10. Remove the paper backing, and apply the design to the mug.

11. Rub the tape to transfer the vinyl to the mug, making sure there are no bubbles. Carefully peel the tape away.

12. Enjoy your custom pet mug!

DIY WOOD IDEAS

Organized Toy Bins

How much of a mess is your kids' room? We already know the answer to that. Grab some plastic bins and label them with different toy categories, and teach your child to sort! You can use the type of bins that suit your child or their room best. Many people like to use the ones that look like giant buckets with handles on the sides. There are also more simple square ones. You could even use cheaper laundry baskets or plastic totes with or without the lids. You can add images to the designs as well—whatever will make your child like them best! You can use the Cricut Explore One, Cricut Explore Air 2, or Cricut Maker for this project.

Materials:

- Plastic toy bins in colors of your choice

- White vinyl

- Vinyl transfer tape

- Cutting mat

- Weeding tool or pick

Instructions

1. Create a new project.

2. Select the "Text" button in the lower left-hand corner.

3. Choose your favorite font and type the labels for each toy bin. See below for some possibilities.

4. Legos

5. Dolls

6.   Cars

7.   Stuffed animals

8.   Outside Toys

9.   Place your vinyl on the cutting mat.

10. Send the design to your Cricut.

11. Use a weeding tool or pick to remove the excess vinyl from the text.

12. Apply transfer tape to the words.

13. Remove the paper backing and apply the design to the bin.

14. Rub the tape to transfer the vinyl to the bin, making sure there are no bubbles. Carefully peel the tape away.

15. Organize your kid's toys in your new bins!

Froggy Rain Gear

Decorate a raincoat and rain boots with a cute froggy design that will have kids asking to wear them! A simple raincoat and boots that you can find at any store for a reasonable price become custom pieces with this project. The outdoor vinyl is made to withstand the elements and last for ages. You can customize this even more by adding your child's name or change up the theme completely with different images. You can use the Cricut Explore One, Cricut Explore Air 2, or Cricut Maker for this project.

Materials:

- Matching green raincoat and rain boots

- White outdoor vinyl

- Vinyl transfer tape

- Cutting mat

- Weeding tool or pick

Instructions

1.   Create a new project.

2. Select the "Image" button and search for "frog."

3. Choose your favorite frog and click "Insert."

4. Copy the frog and resize. You will need three frogs, a larger one for the coat and two smaller ones for each boot.

5. Place your vinyl on the cutting mat.

6. Send the design to your Cricut.

7. Use a weeding tool or pick to remove the excess vinyl from the design.

8. Apply transfer tape to the design.

9. Remove the paper backing and apply the design to the coat or boot.

10. Rub the tape to transfer the vinyl to the rain gear, making sure there are no bubbles. Carefully peel the tape away.

11. Dress your kid up to play in the rain!

Snowy Wreath

Wreaths are a popular decoration year-round. This one is perfect for winter. You can buy premade grapevine wreaths at almost any store, or you can get really crafty and assemble one yourself. The berry stems can be found in the floral parts of craft stores. Silver will fit the snowy theme well, but you could also use red for a holiday-themed look or an entirely different color. You can also change up the whole project to theme it toward your winter holiday of choice. You can use the Cricut Explore One, Cricut Explore Air 2, or Cricut Maker for this project.

Materials:

- Grapevine wreath

- Silver berry stems

- Spray adhesive

- Silver and white glitter

- Piece of wood to fit across the center of the wreath

- Wood stain, if desired

- Drill and a small bit

- Twine

- White vinyl

- Vinyl transfer tape

- Cutting mat

- Weeding tool or pick

Instructions

1. Thread the silver berry stems throughout the grapevine wreath.

2. Use the spray adhesive and glitter to create patches of "snow" on the wreath.

3. If you want to stain your wood, do so now and set it aside to dry.

4. Create a new project.

5. Select the "Text" button in the lower left-hand corner.

6. Choose your favorite font and type, "Let it snow."

7. Place your vinyl on the cutting mat.

8. Send the design to your Cricut.

9. Use a weeding tool or pick to remove the excess vinyl from the text.

10. Apply transfer tape to the words.

11. Remove the paper backing and apply the design to the wood piece.

12. Rub the tape to transfer the vinyl to the wood, making sure there are no bubbles. Carefully peel the tape away.

13. Drill two small holes in the corner of the wood and thread the twine through.

14. Hang your wreath and sign for the winter season!

Antiqued Kitchen Sign

Aged wooden signs are easy but effective décor, and they are very chic right now. Spray paint is easy to use. It would create the aged look by not laying down an even coat. Use it in short, sweeping bursts to avoid getting too much in one spot. There are also different stains and finishes you can use. Take a look at crackle paint for a really aged look. Use the vinyl to spell out one of the phrases below, or use one of your own that represents your home best. You can use the Cricut Explore One, Cricut Explore Air 2, or Cricut Maker for this project.

Materials:

- Wooden sign of the desired size

- Black and white spray paint

- Vinyl

- Vinyl transfer tape

- Cutting mat

- Weeding tool or pick

Instructions

1. Paint the sign black and set it aside to dry.

2. Create a new project.

3. Select the "Text" button in the lower left-hand corner.

4. Choose your favorite font and type a phrase for your kitchen sign. See below for some possibilities.

5. Eat Here

6. Marketplace

7. Family

8. Gather Here

9. Diner

10. Place your vinyl on the cutting mat. Send the design to your Cricut.

11. Use a weeding tool or pick to remove the excess vinyl from the text.

12. Apply transfer tape to the words.

13. Remove the paper backing and apply the design to the sign.

14. Rub the tape to transfer the vinyl to the wood, making sure there are no bubbles. Carefully peel the tape away.

15. Use white spray paint on the whole sign. Do so messily, leaving some spots of black for the aged appearance. Set aside to dry.

16. After drying, peel away the vinyl letters.

17. Hang your sign and enjoy!

DIY Resin Monogram Necklace with Vinyl

Make a beautiful monogram collar in only a couple of minutes, with DIY Resin Monogram Vinyl necklace. Perfect handmade gift to a lover. If you are new to use resin, this collar will be easy to create and a great project. Jewellery resin is great to addict-you're going to love it!

Materials:

- Scrapbook Paper

- Scissors or circle punch

- Chain ETI Jewelry Resin

- Screening Pad or Sealer

- Black Vinyl

Instructions

1. Cut the paper in size with a scissors or a punch inside of the bezel.

2. Put the transmission tape inside the scrapbook paper and then paint the paper Mod Podge on the top of the paper too.

3. Now read the instructions for a resin.

4. This bezel doesn't need much or, but the pads are made with the vinyl maker.

5. Use the cricuter to cut some vinyl of the size of your pendant bezel, about 3/4 "tall.

6. Use transmission tape to obtain the vinyl monogram from the scraps book paper.

Easter Baskets DIY holographic vinyl tote bag

Easter baskets aren't my stuff, have you seen that there are whole aisles full of old baskets in the thrift shops? With that big plastic grass that goes all over... and big jelly beans. The sparkling holographic iron, cut into adorable origami animals, makes this bag unique and unique-and can also be used for church bags, book bags in the library and carry-alls.

Shiny iridescent vinyl holographic iron with the most remote Easter basket maker.

Here's the funny Easter baskets. Put the Lego set, books, toys, sandwiches and plenty of paper on those Easter totes.

To cut the vinyl into origami and press it onto the tote sacks using the EasyPress 2 use the Cricut producer.

Materials:

- Cricut EasyPress 2

- Cricut tote bag

- Weeding tools

Full iron added to the vinyl tote bags, the ideal alternative to Easter bags

These bags are all great to wear! They are fairly large: 12.5 X 13.5 X 6.5 centimeters. Great enough for big items such as books or even books... but great for water bottles and a beach towel. I love Tote Bag Factory bags, which is great for mass events such as summer camp. Great colors too, and the delivery is quick! If before 1 p.m. you order. (PST) the same day it's going to ship out! At all price points, Tote bag Factory has so many different types of bags. They print customized for meetings, enterprises or camps. They have a great team of staff, I love working with them too.

Make vinyl and cricut maker custom totes of iron.

Instruction:

1. Make custom tote bags with Cricut Maker and Cricut EasyPress.

2. Cut back pictures with the iron's brilliant plastic side, on the tacky side of the mat. Use the hook tool after cutting to wear the vinyl surplus iron.

3. Cut origami paper crane, whale and bunny images out of iron into vinyl using the Cricut Maker.

4. They are polyester bags now, which can melt if they are not properly handled. Start by inside the sac with an EasyPress Mat. This avoids the tote melting of the indoor layers.

5. On another EasyPress mat, place the bag. For 30 seconds, set the EasyPress 2 to 330*. Five seconds warm up the tote. Put the vinyl on top of the bag.

6. Cut off the tote bag from melting with a protective plate and press for 30 seconds.

7. Cool the bag somewhat and remove the EasyPress mat inside. Make sure you don't hold up the inside lining. Then repeat with the other bags of the tote. Once the vinyl is cooled, remove the sheet of plastic from the top of the tote.

8. Tote bags are made, ideal to use year-round instead of just seasonally instead of Easter baskets.

9. That it is! Stuff your sacks with goodies, books, toys, dolls, drinks, LEGO boxes, or anything you do for Easter–perhaps even a bottle of water filled. You're so sweet.

10. Perfect way of celebrating Easter with a gift! The beauty of this tote bag is that it is not Easter, so it is perfect for any reason to bring a tote around all year.

DIY HALLOWEEN IDEAS
Rae Dunn Succulent Planter DIY Inspired Terracotta

Do you want the simplicity and decoration of Rae Dunn? This project is fun and very fast, and you can DIY it in about 15 minutes or less!

This belongs to the Terracotta Pots series: Craft Lightning!

Materials:

- Terracotta Pot

- Black Vinyl

- Explore the Air 2 machine

Instruction

1. Download free font, Skinny, design your own Rae Dunn and save the nice little GROW png file.

2. Upload and choose to cut a file in the Cricut Design Space. Or type your new font on CDS for easy letters to cut.

3. I only used a small vinyl scrap for it.

4. Keep these scraps! Keep these scraps!

5. Click the' cut' button to place the mat on the Cricut Explore Air 2 machine!

6. Remove the mat vinyl and weed the hook tool on excess vinyl.

7. Use the scraping tool to place a small transfer tape right above and smooth.

8. Remove the vinyl backrest and position on the pot of clay. With the scraping tool roll the letters down.

9. Peel the transfer rubber gently and finish the planter!

10. Simply add soil and succulent in home decoration!

Snowflakes

Materials:

- White Iron Glitter-on Vinyl

- Vinyl Holographic Iron-On

- Iron squeezing

- Cricut

- Twine

- Felt Blue

- A folder of snowflake SVG that you submit to the design space

Instructions

1. The Ornamentation

2. Modify the form to a diameter of around 4 inches; erase all drawing a distinction & Layers

3. Plan the backdrop that the felt sheet would be mounted on.

4. Create the upper layer on which the holographic vinyl iron lies.

5. Schedule the presentation of the green color to be positioned on the vinyl white shimmer iron.

6. Proceed with the on-screen prompts to cut the built layers.

7. Arrange a 12-inch twine and place it near the spot of the twine on the felt.

8. Snowflake.

9. Press the holographic iron-on vinyl to guarantee that the twine is properly positioned in the middle of the vinyl and that the blue felt is added to the pressing iron as the pressure is applied.

10. Place the iron-on vinyl with white glitter on it and iron it.

11. With the twine in its place right on the snowflake, make an exquisite little bow.

12. Manage a card as well as an envelope.

13. Get the silver glitter vinyl that suits the form of the card exactly.

14. Place on the card with the split vinyl.

15. Put a hole on the card with a paper punch.

16. Get and tie the ready decoration to the front of the card, make use of the rope, and lock it securely in place. To keep it, then you can also make use of an adhesive.

Spider Web Halloween

Materials:

- Bits of paper with a parchment
- Machine to Cricut
- Adhesive
- Black paper
- Web SVG Spider File

Instructions

1. Put the SVG file in the Template Space and begin cutting through various spaces. Web Lengths.

2. Put the parchment papers in the workspace.

3. Arrange the spider's web on the work piece exactly as you'd like it.

4. Once the web has been arranged, go on to connect the edges of the web with the adhesive. To guarantee that you just have the edges linked around, you have to be patient here.

5. Dry appropriately.

6. Hang it along with the door, and you've got your great spider for Halloween Constructing the Web!

DIY GIFT IDEAS
Anchors for Walls which are Herringbone Themed

Materials:

- Machine to Cricut
- The Vinyl

- Board oak (12" width)

- Hooks

- Wax

- Brushes of foam

- Paint finishing

- Screws

- Drill

Instructions

1. The sand, the wooden floor, and place your favorite colors on a coat. Using foam, then using a bush with a cloth to apply it uniformly.

2. Just get the herringbone layout in your design space. It is more probable that this design is usable on your stencil.

3. Template the model to match your pine board width as well as probably if you like it to fill the whole surface or perhaps the length of the board, just midway, or whatever length you choose.

4. Click the GO" button on the GUI when you're finished.

5. You will then continue to the window display.

6. Go for the prompts coming up.

7. The vinyl as well as the pad load up.

8. Make sure that perhaps the vinyl is set on the unit.

9. On the GO icon, click.

10. Strip the cut content from the cutting material just after the slicing process is finished, and afterward, put it on a board of pine.

11. Cover the cut of your selection of paint on the board and leave it to dry.

12. Strip the cut of the vinyl and instead of sand that one a bit.

13. Wax the sheet, enable it to dry and afterward dust it up with a lint-free cloth.

14. Have some anchors and position them on the panel in the pre-drilled holes before putting them on the wall.

Toppers for Cricut Cake

There is a little bit of additional complexity for Cricut cake toppers since they need some specific scoring. The builder of the Cricut is definitely the right piece of equipment for the work, and we'll tell you how to do it here. Your best choice is the scoring method since this would also make different shapes much simpler. You may want to make sure that, along with a fine-point blade for cutting, you have cardstock as well as the cutting pad. The tape for these, too, is handy.

, go to Space Modeling and pick the rosettes that you like. The press generates it from there and executes the prompts. Then you'll be asked if you want a single or double roller. Scoring shells are intended to build products with extra-deep score lines to get the optimal fold. The single wheel will make one crease, and a parallel wheel that will crease will make the double wheel ideal for specialty pieces. More, a double wheel is thicker, so folding is simpler.

You remove everything and swap the scoring wheel with the fine-point blade until you score it all. You literally fold anything from here and just follow the thread. This can render the rosette, and to form a pleasant backdrop, you can also use contrasting centers to create more of these.

Tassels

Tassels have benefits that are almost infinite. These are extremely quick to produce and to make; it can be tailored to suit any reason you choose. Attach them to the edges of pillows or covers, use one as a keychain or zipper pick, hang them from a cord to make a flag, and a million other items! For a classier look, you can even try making these with leather or imitation leather. Tassels are lovely on almost all.

Materials:

- Rectangles of 12" x 18" fabric

- Mat of fabric

- The Glue Gun

Instructions

1. Open the Design Space at Cricut and build a new project.

2. In the bottom left corner, select the 'Image' button and check for 'tassel.'

3. Choose a rectangular image with lines on either side and then press "Insert."

4. On the cutting mat, position the cloth.

5. Give the template to Cricut.

6. Remove the cloth from the mat, and the extra square will be saved.

7. Place the fabric face down and start tightly rolling, beginning on the uncut side. As required, untangle the edge.

8. To attach the tassel at the tip, get some of the leftover fabric and a silicone adhesive stick.

9. With your new tassels, adorn what you want!

Monogrammed Drawstring Bag

There are simple and easy to use drawstring bags. They are just as quick to produce!

This involves instructions for stitching together the pieces, so if you're not handy with a needle and thread, you might also use fabric glue. For any friend or relative, you can hold these bags convenient to pick and go as desired.

Materials:

- Two matching cloth rectangles

- Needle and floss

- Ribbon

- Vinyl heat exchange

- Easy Press Cricut or Iron

- Mat cutting

- Tool for weeding or selecting

Instructions

1. Open the Design Space at Cricut and build a new project.

2. In the lower left-hand corner, select the 'Image' button and check for "the monogram."

3. Pick your preference of monogram and press "Insert."

4. Set the light liner side of the iron-on substance flat on the cutting mat.

5. Give the layout to Cricut.

6. To extract extra fabric, just use a weeding instrument or pick.

7. From the mat, remove the monogram.

8. Focus the monogram on your cloth, and transfer it down a couple of inches because when the ribbon is drawn, it will not fold up.

9. Iron the pattern onto the cloth.

10. Put the two rectangles along with the fabric's external side facing inward.

11. Sew along with the corners, leaving the allowance for a seam. Let the top open and leave the top open and Stop a few inches from the top down.

12. Fold back the majority of the bag till it hits the stitches.

13. Sew the folded edge around the rim, leaving open the edges.

14. Switch out the pocket on the right side.

15. Connect the ribbon around the top of the bag through the loop.

16. To bring what you need, use your new drawstring pack!

17.

Paw Print Socks

The ultimate comfortable thing is socks. No warm pajamas, without a pair, are full! With very little paw prints, apply a cool, secret touch to the bottom of your or your child's socks. In demonstrating off your love for your pet or animals any time you snuggle up! With almost every tiny style, you can do this and even use text to apply a quote to the bottom of your feet.

Materials:

- Socks
- Vinyl heat exchange
- Mat cutting
- Cardboard Scrap
- Tool for weeding or selecting
- Easy Press Cricut or Iron

Instructions

1. Opening the Design Space at Cricut and build a new project.
2. In the bottom left corner, click the "Image" button and check for "paw" prints.
3. Find your option of paw prints and click "Insert."
4. On the mat, put the iron-on stuff.
5. Give the layout to Cricut.
6. To extract extra fabric, use the weeding instrument or pick.
7. Withdraw the stuff from the mat.
8. Place the cardboard scrap within the socks.
9. Put the iron-on stuff.
10. To mount it to the iron-on stuff, use Easy Press.
11. Strip the cardboard from the socks after cooling.

12. Dress your cute socks for paw print!

HEAT PRINTED CRAFTS
Night Sky Pillow

The night sky is a majestic sight, and on a warm pillow, you'll enjoy seeing a piece of it. Personalize this or link constellations, asteroids, galaxies, and more of the stars you love most! Kids and adults alike may enjoy these elegant pillows. A sewing machine is going to make this project

You should tie the wind together or use a needle and thread. Using fabric glue to close the pillow when you're not good at sewing. Choose a comfortable fabric you enjoy so you can use this cushion for cuddling up. You're going to need your

Cricut Easy Press or iron for mounting the vinyl heat exchange.

Materials:

- Fabric in tan, dark blue, or dark purple

- Gold or silver heat-transfer vinyl

- Mat cutting

- Batting polyester

- Tool for weeding or picking

- Easy Press Cricut

Instructions

1. Choose the shape you like for your cushion, then cut the fabric into two similar designs.

2. Opening the Design Space at Cricut and build a new project.

3. In the bottom left corner, click the "Image" button, and check for "stars."

4. Pick the stars that you want and press "Insert."

5. On the mat, put the iron-on stuff.

6. Give the layout to Cricut.

7. To extract extra fabric, just use a weeding tool or pick.

8. Withdraw the substance from the mat.

9. On the cloth, put the iron-on stuff.

10. To mount it to the iron-on stuff, use Easy Press.

11. Sew the two cloth bits together, allowing a gap and a nice narrow space.

12. Cover the pillow through a little open space of polyester filling.

13. Sew shut the pillow.

14. Snuggle your starry pillow with you!

Custom Graphic T-shirt

First, you will need to determine what you want your shirt to say. It is best to stick with just one color when you start. But as you get better at creating with your Cricut, you can move to more color options in one design. is to pick which shirt you would like to use. This can be a preexisting shirt from your closet or it could be one that you purchased specifically for this project. The shirt needs to be a material that can be ironed. Collect the items that you will need to create your shirt.

Materials:

- Cricut machine

- Vinyl for the letters

- Your Cricut tools kit

Instructions:

1. Choose the image you want to use. This can be done in Photoshop or you can place your text directly into the Design Space.

2. , open the Cricut Design Space. Choose the canvas that you wish to use by clicking the Canvas icon on the dashboard that

is located on the left-hand side. Select the canvas that you will be using for your vinyl letters. This can be anything within the categories they offer.

3. Then, select the size of the shirt for the canvas. This is located on the right-hand side of the options.

4. Now, click Upload for uploading your image, which is located on the left-hand side. Select the image you are using by browsing the list of images in your file library. Then, select the type of image that you have picked. For most projects, especially iron-on ones, you will select the Simple Cut option.

5. Click on the white space that you want to be removed by cutting out. Remember to cut the insides of every letter.

6. , be super diligent and press Cut Image instead of Print first. You do not want to print the image; you cut it as well.

7. Place the image on your chosen canvas and adjust the sizing of the image.

8. Place your iron-on image with the vinyl side facing down on the mat and then turn the dial to the setting for iron-on.

9. , you will want to click the Mirror Image setting for the image prior to hitting go.

10. Once you have cut the image, you should remove the excess vinyl from the edges around the lettering or image. Then use the tool for weeding out the inner pieces of the letters.

11. Now you will be placing the vinyl on the shirt.

12. And now, the fun part begins. You will get to iron the image on the shirt. Using the cotton setting, you will need to use the hottest setting that you can get your iron, too. There should not be any steam.

13. You want to warm the shirt by placing the iron on the shirt portion that will hold the image. This should be warmed up for 15 seconds.

14. , lay the vinyl out exactly where you want it to be placed. A pressing cloth will prevent the plastic on the shirt from melting.

15. Place your iron onto the pressing cloth for around 30 seconds. Flip the shirt and place the pressing cloth and iron on the backside of the vinyl.

16. Flip your shirt back over and begin to peel off the sticky part of the vinyl that you have been overlaying on the shirt. This will separate the vinyl from the plastic backing. This should be done while the plastic and vinyl are hot. Place the iron back on the part that is being difficult. Then proceed to pull up and it should come off nicely.

17. This should remove the plastic from the vinyl that is now on the shirt. Place the pressing cloth on top of the vinyl once again and heat it to ensure that the vinyl is good and stuck.

18. Although there are tons of steps, it is still an amazingly simple process.

Quilted Blanket

Quilts are a wonderful sentimental gift or keepsake. Sometimes people use them every day, while others keep them as mementos. Designing a quilt does not need to be just for children. A quilt is great to signify any occasion.

Materials:

- Iron

- Iron-on fabric

- Cotton fabrics or a plain blanket

Instructions

1. In Design Space, upload or design the words or numbers you want to appear on your blanket. Select the negative spaces of the images or text and make sure to mirror your plan.

2. When you are choosing what to put on your project, think of things like a date, picture, or phrase.

3. Send your file to cut onto the iron-on fabric. Once it is cut, it is ready to be used. Place the image or words on your blanket

where you want it to appear and then follow the instructions on your iron-on fabric and attach it with your iron.

4. The important part of this project is to make sure you are working on a level surface with a folded towel under the blanket. This allows a little movement to the fabric as you are working on it. This is how the edges of the iron-on fabric will adhere properly.

5. In addition, make sure your iron hears up to a minimum of 305°F (150°C). Set your iron over the fabric and let it sit for 30 seconds before lifting and moving it to adhere to another area.

Matching Family Disney Shirts

Maybe you are planning on going on a family vacation or planning a family photo-shoot. Have you started looking at matching outfits yet? Have you freaked out over the cost of trying to get you all to look great together? As a Cricut owner, you do not need to suck it up and pay the cost. Buy an inexpensive sweatshirt or t-shirt for every member of your family and design what you want for a fraction of the cost. For this project, you can make the Disney themed shirts or any other image of your choosing.

Materials:

- Cotton shirts for each member of your family or for each person you are making them for Iron-on vinyl in red and black

- Any additional embellishments you desire, like ribbon or glitter, etc.

Instructions:

1. In Design Space, find the image of Mickey Mouse and aviator sunglasses. For the Minnie Mouse heads, add a bow shape to it.

2. When you have your designs and words laid out for each shirt, send the file to cut. Make sure the heads and sunglasses are cut together from black iron-on and the bows are cut from red.

3. Most likely, you will need to use your weeder tool to remove parts of the design you do not want and then peel back the rest of the negative iron-on you do not want to show up. Use the tips

listed earlier in this chapter to help ensure your transfer is most successful. Test your transfer before peeling the backing off completely. Apply more heat as necessary to make sure the transfer is complete. When the iron-on has completely attached, peel off the plastic backing. Make sure to repeat the process for every shirt and design you made.

Table Runner

For the holiday coming up, grab a simple set of placemats, a tablecloth or table runner, and some iron-on vinyl to set the table from the magazines. You can choose phrases, images, or shapes to correspond to any occasion or holiday. The following instructions are to help you design the image above.

Materials:

- Black iron-on vinyl

- Tan table runner

- Iron

Instructions:

1. In Design Space, upload two different "Day of the Dead" skulls and one rose outline. If the skulls you find do not have frames around them, also find and upload frames to places around the skulls. Center the rose design in the middle and space the skulls and frames equally on each side.

2. Send your files to cut and weed out the inside of the image that you do not want as part of your design. Remove the excess iron-on as well. Place your designs on your table runner in the locations you want them to appear and iron them on.

3. When the images are transferred to your runner, gently peel back the backing of the iron-on and pass your iron quickly over your designs before decorating your table.

CREATIVE WOOD IDEAS

Decorative Birdhouse

This birdhouse project is a beautiful one. This birdhouse project is included in the free Design Space projects. This is a ready-made project with all the settings and measurements in place. You must select this project and click "Make it." This is an advanced project. For this birdhouse, more than two different materials are used in the making. The base materials will be chipboard. Three different cutting tools are also used. This birdhouse can be kept for yourself as decoration. It is also ideal for gifting.

(A decorative birdhouse)

Materials

- Cricut Machine
- Easy Press 2 (Cricut)
- Hooked weeding tool
- White glue
- Damask patterned chipboard
- Glittered vinyl (Silver)
- Cricut chipboard
- Fusible fabric (red)
- Premium permanent vinyl in pink and red
- Adhesive foil (red)
- Knife blade
- Fine point blade
- Rotary blade

Instructions:

1. For every project, it is most important to first have a clean, clutter-free space.

2. Then collect all the materials, supplies, and all the different blades you will require.

3. Once all of this is done, turn on your laptop or device with design space and start. As this project is already present in the Design Space, you will not have to design in this project.

4. Just go to the projects and choose the Birdhouse Design and click 'Make It."

5. Now as simple as it seems, to complete the whole project will take some time and expertise.

6. When you click the Make its option, the cutting process can be started.

7. The software will give you instructions regarding the materials and blades to be used.

8. According to the instructions, this project will be cut into 20 mats.

9. First, you install the Knife blade and cut the Demask Patterned chipboard as Mat one.

10. Now for mats 2 and 3, you will use the chipboard. The design space will also instruct for multiple passes for compete cutting. You can follow the instruction to fully complete the cutting for each material sheet or Mat.

11. After cutting the chipboards, the blade will be changed to a fine point blade. With this blade, the three types of Sheet will be cut:

12. Adhesive foil

13. Premium permanent vinyl both sheets

14. Glitter vinyl sheet

15. The standard cutting mat will be used for these cuttings.

16. , the blade must be changed to the rotary blade. With these, the fusible fabric cutouts will be easily cut.

17. This step will end the cutting process. You can now put away the Cricut maker. And start weeding with the hooked weeding tool.

18. When all the wedding is done, you will start assembling the project. The instructions for that are given in the project file.

19. First, you will transfer all the vinyl cuttings appropriately to the chipboard cuttings.

20. Transfer the fusible fabric to the rooftop cuttings with the help of the Cricut Press 2. Heat the easy press to 300 degrees Fahrenheit and keep the cupboard and fabric under the press for 30 seconds. Let it cool down before use.

21. When all the projects are ready, join them together with the help of white glue.

Wooden Earrings

Jewelry is every girl's weakness. There are very few girls who do not wear jewelry or do not like jewelry. Customized jewelry is a creative way to express yourself. With the Cricut Maker, you can cut and shape several different materials. The main difference with the Cricut Explore is its ability to cut thicker and heavier materials. It would help if you had a ticker and more sturdy material to create jewelry. So, the Cricut Maker is ideal for jewelry creation. You can design all kinds of pieces, like necklaces, chunky rings, earrings, bracelets, anklets, etc., with the Cricut Maker. Personalized and handmade jewelry make for unique gifts. You can gift your loved one's pieces according to their unique personalities. And with Cricut Maker, you can create jewelry with more than 100 materials. In this tutorial, we discuss a specific pinecone earring made from wood veneer, which is wood, sliced into very thin layers and then adhered together with strong glues to make it stronger and more durable. This is an easy-to-follow step by step tutorial to create beautiful earrings.

Materials:

- Cricut Maker

- Earring hooks

- Jump rings

- Jewelry pliers

- Deep cut blade

- Cricut Wood Veneer (light brown)

- Cricut Wood Veneer (dark brown)

- Strong Grip Mat

- Cricut Scraper

- Cricut Tweezers

- Cricut Brayer

Instructions:

1. Declutter the working space. Collect all the materials required to complete the project

2. Turn on the Design Space. For this project, you will have to make a Cricut Access purchase. If you are a subscribed member, this will be available for you for free.

3. Select the Pinecone Earring Svg and pay for the design.

4. Upload the design.

5. A reasonable size for such earrings will be 2.5 inches tall.

6. When you are done editing, click 'Make It.'

7. When you enter the Prepare Screen, you will see that this project will be cut on two mats. It means that this project has two layers or two parts. Do not make any changes on the Prepare screen.

8. On the Make screen, select your custom material to be a wood veneer.

9. , check the blade in your machine; it should be a deep cut blade.

10. Prepare your material. Place the veneer on the Strong Grip mat. Use a brayer for the proper adhesion. If it is needed, you can fix it with tape.

11. Now let the first layer cut.

12. , prepare the other Sheet to be cut in the same way.

13. When both sheets are ready, peel off the wood from the Mat.

14. Weed out the cuttings from the wood.

15. Now assemble your earrings. Align the two layers, darker at the back and lighter in the front.

16. Connect them with a jump ring and close it with the pliers. Now connect with the fishhooks, taking care that you attach the fishhook in the correct direction.

17. Your beautiful earrings are ready to wear. Felt Bows

This is also a ready-made project. We will make these creative and beautiful bows together. These bows are easy and straightforward to cut as the whole project with instruction is being used. The assembly process is time-consuming and will require more concentration. During the assembly of these bows, you must be very careful. The glue will stick the bow together, and it takes a while for the fabric to fully attach with glue. If you do not work with patience, this assembly may become very messy. And messy projects   do   not   give   a   good   impression. The bows you will create are usually used for decoration. You can sow or glue a felt boy to a baby hairband.

These bows can be glues to blank pins to create beautiful hair embellishments for little girls. They can even be glued to scrunches to create decorative hair ties. With step-by-step instructions, the project is relatively easy to follow.

Materials:

- Cricut Maker

- Rotary blade for fabric

- Hot glue gun

- Strong Grip Mat

- Cricut Felt material of different colors

- Scissors

Instructions:

1. Clear up the working space. Turn on your laptop or device with a design space.

2. Start a new project.

3. For this project also you will need to purchase an image from Cricut Access.

4. Choose the Felt Bow SVG.

5. , upload the template on the Design Space. It will appear on the Canvas.

6. Resize and change the color of each bow on the template.

7. This is ready to make the project, so remember not to unlock it. The individual bows are already attached.

8. If you want to cut the entire project with the same color and same material, you can unlock the design. Then attach all the components and cut on the same piece of felt. However, in this tutorial, we are making each bow on a separate piece of felt.

9. When you are satisfied with your design, click the 'Make It' button.

10. Comes the Prepare screen. Each bow appears on a separate mat.

11. On the Make screen, choose the correct material. Since we are using the Cricut Felt, the Mat's size will not have to be adjusted.

12. Check that the rotary blade has been installed in the Cricut Maker. This blade is especially for fabric and is exclusive to the Cricut Maker.

13. , prepare the felt on the Strong Grip Mat.

14. Install the Mat into the machine and let the cutting be done.

15. Remove the felt from the Cricut Mat. It will leave behind all the components of the bow.

16. Repeat the same procedure with other felt sheets.

17. Separate all the cut pieces for the bows.

18. Now when you have got all the cutouts, assemble the bows.

19. Take the first cut out, fold one side to the center, and stick it with the glue. Repeat the same with the other side. You will have the basic bow shape.

20. Turn over the bow and stick it to the larger bow cut out with the glue gun.

21. Now wrap around the thin cutout in the middle tightly and secure it at the back.

22. The other bow is also assembled similarly by stacking and sticking the pieces from bigger to smaller. Then secure them with the center cutout.

23. The bow is cut in a way that it has four corners. Each corner must be brought into the middle and glued in the center.

24. , you will wrap around the center cutout and glue it securely. At the back, you will attach the ribbon cutout.

25. You can also mix and match these bows or can make them in solid colors.

26. These bows can be used for decorations for kids and holiday gift packaging. These bows will be most useful to glue on little girls' headbands, hairclips, and hair ties.

STYLISH PAPER CRAFT

Cricut Gift Boxes

What is the fun of creating crafts without gifting them to others – once we are at gift shops, we might wish to share some patterns for easy making of various sets of boxes with your Cricut machine. You can also design your own box patterns when you get more conversant in Design Space tools – nothing makes one's skill better than practice. Let's see how you can start making your own gift boxes today.

Materials:

- Glitter cardstock or another sort of cardstock

- Glue

- Scoring Wheel

- Cricut machine

Instructions:

1. You can start by designing your box pattern or by uploading SVG files for box patterns – there are numerous designs for boxes found online while you can also make your own designs if you are good with creating patterns that ought to be assembled.

2. Once you access your Design Space, click on "New Project" and upload the patterns you have found and downloaded. Alternatively, start making your own patterns for boxes. You can start from the pillowcase box as perhaps the simplest to make for a beginner. Size your patterns to suit the intended size of the box by using the top editing panel in Design Space. Just in case you are making more than one box (perhaps you are making smaller gift boxes), make sure to press "Ungroup" to separate designs that ought to be cut and used separately for assembling. Make sure to change the line type to "Score" for parts of the design that ought to be folded before sending your design to cutting. once you are finished with scoring the lines that require to be folded, select the whole design and click on "Attach", finish the sizing if needed from this point, then proceed to click on "Make it".

3. Choose cardstock as your preferred material when specifying cutting settings under "Make it". Once you have prepared the material and the cutting mat, you can proceed to cut. After this step, you'll assemble your box/boxes. Just in case you have chosen light materials like paper or regular cardstock, you won't need to glue the box to keep the parts together. However, just in case you are using glitter cardstock and similar materials, you will need to secure the parts of the box with glue – except the part that is supposed to seal (close) the box.

4. Start assembling your box and glue the parts that need to be secured as you go. The best thing is to use tacky glue or glue gun to make things faster and more efficient. And, your box is ready!

Cupcake Wrappers

Are you planning a themed party, must make goodies for an upcoming event, or want to do something special with your family? Then this is the project for you! It creates a great visual and message for the family, friends, and guests.

Materials:

- Paper or cardstock—that's it!

Instructions:

1. Open Design Space and search the library for cupcake liners or wrappers. There is a selection on the website, or you can develop your own. Set the canvas to your cardstock or paper size and make as many wrappers as you can. You do not need to make a minimal number of wrappers because you can always use them again in the future! Keep in mind that a standard cupcake needs a wrapper that is about nine inches long.

2. When you have your design set, place your paper, or cardstock on the mat and send the file to cut. Finish cutting the designs.

3. Remove any small pieces that did not come out while cutting. If your design did not call for it, add a small cut on the top on one side and the bottom on the other. This cut should extend about halfway up the wrapper. If you used a pre-set cupcake wrapper, it probably already included it. This means when you wrap your cupcake with the wrapper, you will slide the top into the bottom to close the wrapper.

4. If you do not want to make a slice in your design, use a few glue dots to glue the design together instead.

A Bookmark

It may seem a little archaic to have or give a custom bookmark, but it is still practical and very personal. Plus, it is a simple project you can do fast!

Materials:

- Vinyl

- Paper of cardstock

Instructions:

1. Bookmarks can be just about any size and shape you desire, so when you open Design Space, create a shape you prefer. In this example, the bookmark is about two inches wide and six inches tall. These include text cut out from the bookmark, so choose any word or phrase you want to appear and adjust the size and font to your liking. You can always add a picture or other details if you wish.

2. To cut the vinyl out of the vinyl of the bookmark, make sure to select your text and tell the software to set the text as a separate layer and then select "Attach."

3. Send the file to cut and follow the prompts on your screen. Once the bookmarks are cut and assembled, if you have a laminator, consider laminating them to help them last even longer and bring an even more professional appearance to your project.

GLITTER HOLLOW IDEAS
Napkin Holders

Make your dinner party stand out with personal and custom napkin holders. You can make them in any design you like to match your dinner party theme or season. You can also make it as simple as possible, with just a few images or words, or more complicated with multiple materials and pieces.

Choose a version based on your comfort and preference level. Also, you can also decide how you want to attach your holders. You could also add small holes on either side of the holder and lace ribbon or string through it.

Materials:

- Colored or glitter cardstock

- Vinyl, if preferred

- Your closure method of choice: glue dots, double-stick tape, etc.

Instructions:

1. In Design Space, design the text or names that you want to appear on your napkin wraps. Make sure it is adjusted so that the words will appear appropriately on your wrap width. This is also the time to develop a layer with the flourishing details, like the olive branch and your napkin wrap shape. Also, think about images and different shapes you could include on your napkin holders.

2. With your napkin wrap base designed, repeat your patterns and words on the number you need for your place settings. This

is what will tell your Cricut to cut multiple pieces and allows you the opportunity to customize each one if you desire. If you will be closing the wraps with ribbon and need holes or want to slide the ends together with slits, make sure to add those in now.

3. Once you have your designs laid out, send the file to cut. Weed out any small items you do not want in your design. Assemble your napkin wrap pieces and wrap your napkins or silverware for your big event! Make sure to attach them securely according to the method you have chosen.

Magnetic Flowers

Adding a few bright flowers to your fridge can take your kitchen from average to extraordinary. It can help it go from a place you "have" to be to a place you "want" to be! They are also awesome gifts!

Materials:

- Cardstock in a variety of colors or patterns

- Hot glue gun

- Magnets

Instructions:

1. Open Design Space and develop the shape of your petals. These look good as half circles or oval shapes. You can also create bumped petal shapes by stacking oval over one another. Repeat the petal shapes to make enough flower magnets that you want. A large flower typically has about 12 petals, while a medium one has about eight. Medium petals are about two inches long, while large petals are usually about three inches. Measure the size of your magnet base and develop a circular flower base. You can add a small, ½ inch long slit at the end of every petal for easiest construction if you want to.

2. Once you have your petals designed and duplicated, load the cardstock on your cutting mat and get it ready to cut. Send the file to cut. If you did not add the slit in Design Space, use a crafting knife at the bottom of each petal. Once all the petals

have a cut, add a dot of glue and glue one side to the other, making them into the petal shape. Do this to all the petals.

3. Place your magnets down on the table, gather all the base circles, and glue them to the magnets' tops. Begin gluing the petals to the circle bases, starting on the outside and working your way in. Continue adding petals until it looks full. Large flowers will have about three or more layers, while medium may only have two. Keep playing with your petals until you have a shape and set up that looks best to you.

4. Go back to Design Space and create smaller petals. These are designed to add to your flowers' center, so adjust them according to what you want. Add the slits to the petals again or wait until they are cut to add the slits with an Exacto knife. When you are ready, send the file to cut. Create the petal shapes with a little bit of glue.

5. Add glue to the flower design's interior and begin adding the smaller petals to the inside of your flowers. Gently pinch your flowers' edges for a more geometric appearance or gently curve them inside for something more natural. You can add as many petal layers as you like.

Hologram Party Box Tumblers

Instead of party goody boxes, why not try hologram personalized party tumblers stuffed with the goodies? The kids get their party treats inside an awesome tumbler to take home for use.

Materials:

- Hologram stick-on vinyl

- Clear tumblers

- Green Standard Grip mat

- Cricut Fine-Point Blade

- Weeding tool

- Scraping tool or brayer tool

- Pair of scissors for cutting the material to size

Instructions

1. Open a new project in Design Space.

2. Select 'Square' from the 'Shapes' menu on the left-hand side menu.

3. Change the background color to grey.

4. Unlock the shape and change it to the width and height of the tumbler. The hologram will run from about 1" below the tumbler's lip to 1" above the base.

5. To accurately measure the hologram paper's width, wrap it around the tumbler and cut it.

6. Lay it flat on the cutting mat to get the hologram paper's dimensions.

7. Select 'Text' from the menu on the left-hand side.

8. Type in the person's name that the tumbler is for.

9. Select a nice chunky font that will work for the cutout.

10. Position the font onto the middle of the square on the screen.

11. Stretch it to fit across the square.

12. Select both the square and the text.

13. Right-click and choose 'Slice.'

14. Select the first layer of the name text, move it off to one side, then delete it.

15. Select the second layer of the name text, move it off to one side, then delete it.

16. If you like, you can add an image and repeat steps 13 to 16 for the shape or image.

17. When the hologram image is ready, select 'Make it.'

18. Make sure the fine-point blade is loaded.

19. Make sure the hologram vinyl is correctly stuck to the cutting mat.

20. Select the correct material and press 'Go' once the Cricut is ready to cut.

21. Once it has cut, leave the vinyl on the cutting board and weed out the middle of the image and text.

22. Place the transfer sheet over the vinyl and use the scraper or brayer tool to smooth it out.

23. Remove the back sheet.

24. Carefully place the hologram paper around the tumbler.

25. Use the scraper to ensure it is on properly.

26. Remove the transfer sheet.

GARDEN IDEAS

Spinning Heart Card

Spinner cards offer a variety of fun messages that you can send. An example is a "love" theme with a glittering heart, but you can change the message, colors, and spinning shape to be anything you want. Think of spinning images like boats, people, airplanes, flowers, etc.

Materials:

- Two pennies

- Foam dots or circles

- Glue

- Pink and white cardstock

- Grey faux-leather cardstock or material

- Blue craft foam

Instructions:

1. Open the Spinner Card design file in Design Space. Cut the cardstock as instructed, following the prompts.

2. Using glue, add the grey, faux-leather cardstock to the pink card base, aligning it in the center of the card's front side.

3. Add the foam to the back of the white cut cardstock. On the front of the white part, add words or images that align with your card's theme. Do not put anything that pops out from the card close to the cut put track as it will interfere with your spinning object.

4. Lay one penny on the table and then place the white cardstock on top with the blue foam facing down to the table, lining up the penny's middle in the visible track. Glue the small blue foam circle on the penny in the middle of the track. Carefully glue the second penny on top of the first that now has the foam dot attached. Allow drying completely before moving.

5. Glue the white circle of cardstock on the top of the penny on the design side of your white cardstock front, not on the side with the blue foam. Glue your spinning image on top of the white circle. Allow drying completely before moving again.

6. Once your glue is dry, and your spinning image is secure, glue the white part to the pink and grey card base, aligning the white in the center of the grey faux-leather background. Allow to dry completely and then test your spinner!

Cottage Wood Sign

You can create anything as lovely as the others you've seen with a little effort and support from your Cricut. This sign for the cottage restroom brings to your environment the perfect amount of beauty. Plus, as presents, you would love to send away cottage log signatures too. You can see how easy it is until you put up your own Woodworking cottage symbol for your restroom.

You will make somebody really happy if you send one of the wooden signs that look as nice as a present. They're going to totally love it, and you're going to realize the key is that it was super simple to create. Don't think about selling them at design shows as well! When people go for something that's a farmhouse or rustic, people go. All recognize that the primary thing you are shopping for if you go to a frame shop is home decor.

Materials:

- Pick up two black wire baskets at the local dollar store.
- Resources for weeding
- Unfinished sign in wood with six slats
- Vinyl Cricut, any color, not permanent

- 12"x 24 "mat.
- Only Cricut
- Cricut paper for vinyl transfer
- Paint in black
- Four tiny black screws (it is important to weigh these so that they do not go through the board)
- Light brown (for lettering) design
- Wash with foam
- Big brush with color
- Measurement or governor of tape
- Screw Driver or Screw Pistol
- Mod Podge for
- Hanging Wire Photo Package
- There are some decorative and useful things that, with your farmhouse bathroom sign, would look lovely. They're not necessary, but they look amazing.
- Washing laundry
- Goat Cleaner

- Ware of Enamel

- Bowls of Wood

- Linens Farmhouse

- Candle of the Farmhouse

Instructions:

1. Collect supplies. In your Cricut software, upload the farmhouse signature SVG.

2. To suit the size sign, you have, expand or decrease the size of the SVG.

3. Apply a 12"x24 "pad with vinyl and load it into the Cricut unit. Cricut Vinyl Cutting System

4. Place aside the split vinyl.

5. Two beige coats of paint board slats where the sentences are going to be. Give time to dry.

6. Peel off the sheet of vinyl softly, leaving only the words. * Cut each row of terms into different strips for a faster transition.

7. To "pick up" the line of terms, use move document. For longer lines, two strips of transfer paper can need to be held together.

8. When centering the line of terms, weigh the top board lattice from top to bottom and left to right.

Note: Use a craft knife short lines where you want the terms on either hand to be put. It is also beneficial to keep the letters above the region when taking measurements. Take the time to double-check the dimensions. In the long run, the marker lines would be replaced with black ink, but do not think about them.

Click the term 'farmhouse' on the monitor. To smooth the terms out, use the Cricut Scraper. Lift the transferring paper away from the acrylic letters cautiously, keeping the letters on the board in place.

Repeat the method of weighing each board slat and adding the words on it.

Over every single word, use a tiny paintbrush and brush mod podge, coating the edges right over the letters. Enable many hours or overnight to dry entirely.

Paint black on the whole surface. Around the margins, and right above any phrase of vinyl. Only paint two paints. Enable it to dry.

Using the weeding method, Cricut to raise the vinyl letters carefully. * I also used this cool script technique, and it turned out to be really good. Use a really small paintbrush to fix it up with the right color if you notice a place where the paint spilled under due to losing a place of mod podge.

We should seal it since the dark wood sign would be in a humid part of the house. Wipe modified podge all over the black paint with the foam cleaner. It'll be bright and dry. Enable it to dry.

"To connect d-rings and string to the rear of the wooden sign 2" from the highest point, one on either side, use a photo hanging pack. If the image hanging kit * as seen here is not accessible, simply run a small screw in the board and loop the string over it to protect the wire. Then, finish locking the board with the screw.

Your black wire baskets are weighed and focused. Protect the baskets by using four tiny black screws. On either end of the bucket where the upper links to the frame, screw-in 2. * You can color them very well with a brush if you do not have black screws.

Camp out in your farmhouse toilet. Add additional decor to the farmhouse, such as those mentioned above.

DIY GLASS IDEAS

Monogrammed Drawstring Bag

Drawstring bags are quick and easy to use. They're just as easy to make! This includes steps for sewing the pieces together, but you could even use fabric glue. You can keep these bags handy for every member of your family to grab and go as needed

Materials:

- Two matching rectangles of fabric
- Needle and thread
- Ribbon
- Heat transfer vinyl
- Cricut EasyPress or iron
- Cutting mat
- Weeding tool or pick

Instructions:

1. Create a new project.
2. Select the "Image" button and search "monogram."
3. Select the monogram of your choice and click "Insert."
4. Place the iron-on material shiny liner side down on the cutting mat.
5. Send the design to the Cricut.
6. Use the weeding tool or pick to remove excess material.
7. Remove the monogram from the mat.
8. Center the monogram on your fabric, then move it a couple of inches down so that it won't be folded up when the ribbon is drawn.
9. Iron the design onto the fabric.
10. Place the two rectangles together, with the outer side of the fabric facing inward. Sew around the edges, leaving a seam allowance. Leave the top open and stop a couple of inches down from the top.
11. Fold the top of the bag down until you reach your stitches.
12. Sew along the folded edge, leaving the sides open.
13. Turn the bag right side out.
14. Thread the ribbon through the loop around the top of the bag.
15. Use your new drawstring bag to carry what you need!

Etched Monogrammed Glass

Glasses are one of the most-used things in your kitchen, and it's impossible to have too many of them. It's quite easy to customize them with etching, and it will look as if a professional did it. Simply use glass etching cream that you can find at any craft store! Be sure to read the instructions and warning labels carefully before you begin. The vinyl will act as a stencil, protecting the parts of the glass that you don't want to etch. Be sure to take your time to get the vinyl smooth against the glass, especially where there are small bits. You don't want any of the cream to get under the edge of the vinyl. You can use the Cricut Explore One, Cricut Explore Air 2, or Cricut Maker for this project. Materials:

- A glass of your choice – make sure that the spot you want to monogram is smooth

- Vinyl

- Cutting mat

- Weeding tool or pick

- Glass etching cream

Instructions:

1. Create a new project.

2. Select the "Image" button in the Design Panel and search for "monogram."

3. Choose your favorite monogram and click "Insert."

4. Place your vinyl on the cutting mat.

5. Send the design to your Cricut.

6. Use a weeding tool or pick to remove the monogram, leaving the vinyl around it.

7. Remove the vinyl from the mat.

8. Carefully apply the vinyl around your glass, making it as smooth as possible, particularly around the monogram.

9. If you have any letters with holes in your monogram, carefully reposition those cutouts in their proper place.

10. Apply it to your monogram.

11. Remove the cream and then the vinyl.

12. Give your glass a good wash.

13. Enjoy drinking out of your etched glass!

Live, Love, Laugh Glass Block

Glass blocks are an inexpensive yet surprisingly versatile craft material. You can find them at both craft and hardware stores. They typically have a hole with a lid so that you can fill the blocks with the items of your choice. This project uses tiny fairy lights for a glowing quote block, but you can fill it however you'd like. The frost spray paint adds a bit of elegance to the glass and diffuses the light for a softer glow, hiding the string of the fairy lights. Holographic vinyl will add to the magical look, but you can use whatever colors you'd like. This features a classic quote that's great to have around your house, but you can change it. You can use the Cricut Explore One, Cricut Explore Air 2, or Cricut Maker for this project.

Materials:

- Glass block

- Frost spray paint

- Clear enamel spray

- Holographic vinyl

- Vinyl transfer tape

- Cutting mat

- Weeding tool or pick

- Fairy lights

Instructions:

1. Spray the entire glass block with frost spray paint, and let it dry.

2. Spray the glass block with a coat of clear enamel spray, and let it dry.

3. Create a new project.

4. Select the "Text" button in the Design Panel.

5. Type "Live Love Laugh" in the text box.

6. Use the dropdown box to select your favorite font.

7. Arrange the words to sit on top of each other.

8. Place your vinyl on the cutting mat.

9. Send the design to your Cricut.

10. Use a weeding tool or pick to remove the excess vinyl from the design. Apply transfer tape to the design.

11. Remove the paper backing and apply the words to the glass block.

12. Smooth down the design and carefully remove the transfer tape.

13. Place fairy lights in the opening of the block, leaving the battery pack on the outside.

14. Enjoy your decorative quote!

Unicorn Wine Glass

Consider using these for a party and letting the guests take them home as favors! You can use the Cricut Explore One, Cricut Explore Air 2, or Cricut Maker for this project.

Materials:

- Stemless wine glasses

- Outdoor vinyl

- Vinyl transfer tape

- Cutting mat

- Weeding tool or pick

- Extra fine glitter

- Mod Podge

Instructions:

1. Create a new project.

2. Select the "Text" button in the Design Panel.

3. Type "It's not drinking alone if my unicorn is here."

4. Using the dropdown box, select your favorite font.

5. Adjust the positioning of the letters, rotating some to give a whimsical look. Select the "Image" button on the Design Panel and search for "unicorn."

6. Select your favorite unicorn and click "Insert," then arrange your design how you want it on the glass.

7. Place your vinyl on the cutting mat, making sure it is smooth and making full contact. Send the design to your Cricut.

8. Use a weeding tool or pick to remove the excess vinyl from the design. Use the Cricut

9. Apply transfer tape to the design, pressing firmly, and making sure there are no bubbles.

10. Remove the paper backing and apply the words to the glass where you'd like them. Smooth down the design and carefully remove the transfer tape.

11. Coat the bottom of the glass in Mod Podge, wherever you would like glitter to be. Give the area a wavy edge.

12. Sprinkle glitter over the Mod Podge, working quickly before it dries.

13. Add another layer of Mod Podge and glitter and set it aside to dry.

14. Allow the glass to cure for at least 48 hours. Enjoy drinking from your unicorn wine glass!

Cowhide Notebook

Materials:

- Cricut Maker

- Blade

- Scoring Wheel

- Cricut Metallic Leather
- Foil Poster board
- White cardstock
- Regular Iron-on in white
- Material Paper
- Specialty blade
- Needle
- String
- Scissors
- Wedding apparatuses (discretionary)
- Cricut EasyPress
- Simple Press tangle
- Speedy dry glue
- Cricut Cut File

Instructions:

1. Calfskin spread – cuts incredible with the blade sharp edge. Make certain to move the star wheels right to one side before cutting.

2. Iron-on applique – make sure to reflect your picture before cutting. Cut with your fine point cutting edge and remove abundance parcels with your weeding instruments.

3. White card stock – cut nine pieces every that are scored down the middle. The single scoring wheel works extraordinary for ordinary card stock. The machine will score your material first, at that point stop and request the cutting sharp edge.

4. Foil cardstock – the scoring wheel is an absolute necessity for this sort of material! Utilize the twofold wheel to guarantee an incredible overlap line with insignificant breaking.

5. Utilize the Easy Press for most extreme achievement.

6. Put the weeded bit of iron-on straightforwardly on the calfskin with the transporter sheet despite everything joined.

7. Spread the whole thing with material paper to secure your surface.

8. Follow the authority Cricut Easy Press rules for time and temperature.

9. Expel the transporter sheet while still warm.

10. At that point, utilize a speedy dry cement to put the foil banner board within your scratchpad as demonstrated as follows. Line up the folds with the little cuts in the cowhide.

11. When dry, utilize an art blade to move those slice cuts to the foil piece.

12. Proceed through every one of the three arrangements of three until the entirety of your paper has been sewn into the calfskin scratchpad.

13. Bunch off your string and you have finished your undertaking! In any case, how would you keep your new calfskin diary shut? Well, that is simple!

14. Simply pull up on the circle you made in the calfskin and afterward get it through the rectangular opening. Include a pen and this is one charming DIY cowhide diary!

15. You can compose the entirety of your profound contemplations or simply write down certain notes!

Coffee Sleeves

Espresso sleeves make an extremely extraordinary and cheap gift.

Materials:

- Felt (I utilized the Cricut felt sheets)

- Iron-on Vinyl (I utilized the sparkle vinyl in silver)

- Cricut Cutting Machine

- Weeding instruments (discretionary)

- Cricut Easy-Press (discretionary however suggested – see underneath for subtleties)

- Velcro

- Texture paste or sewing machine

- Cut document

Instructions:

1. Start by cutting your pieces. Cut the words from sparkle iron-on vinyl utilizing you're fine point cutting edge. Make sure to reflect the cuts on the iron-on vinyl and spot it glossy side down on your tangle. Cut the sleeve itself from felt.

2. Start by featuring your first tangle with a sleeve. At that point click on the sleeve itself.

3. , snap the second tangle that has a sleeve. Snap the sleeve itself and snap the three dabs. At that point pick "move to another tangle".

4. Pick the tangle with the principal sleeve.

5. Presently you simply need to turn it and move the position, so it isn't covering the first. You would now be able to cut two sleeves from one sheet of felt.

6. Expel all overabundance from your vinyl pattern including the focuses of your letters.

CONCLUSION

We have a lot of ideas for various projects. Cricut project ideas are an excellent method to broaden your knowledge and abilities. You may broaden your creative horizons and improve your capacity to produce by exploring a number of different topics or approaches. We provide tips and methods for a wide variety of tasks. If you want further assistance, consult the project ideas book. You'll find a plethora of tasks that you can do with your kit.

Browse through our library for ideas, or use our simple search function to discover your project. This book will help you in exploring your imagination and producing some fantastic projects. Look through our book for a project that will get your creative juices flowing! We know that you want to create a unique project for everyone to enjoy. That is why we have thousands of projects already prepared for you to choose from. The idea you want to try out is the perfect one! We also understand that sometimes you may want to start your own project from scratch. If you're looking for some project ideas, browse our easy to use catalog and order your tool today!

This is a fantastic way to save money while still having fun. Nobody knows how this concept will come out, which is half the fun! So choose one today and have fun building something with your 1/64th CNC machine. We understand that building your own projects might be difficult. That is why we have prepared user-friendly guidelines for you. We can help you produce the ideal present or the perfect family treasure, whether you're an expert Cricut user or just starting out with your first project. Cricut offers a limitless supply of project ideas and accessories to help you along the way.

We have some fantastic project ideas. We offer intermediate and family projects that will teach you all you need to know about Cricut software. We also offer ideas for family and gift crafts that are ideal for creating personalized gifts for any occasion.

Do you want to make a family calendar for the entire year? What about a teacher's appreciation gift? Or perhaps you require a birthday card for each member of the family!

There are some excellent intermediate project ideas, as well as some excellent beginner project ideas, to get you started. Get ideas for your next project by visiting our project ideas page!

BOOK SIX: CRICUT ACCESSORIES

So, you have a Cricut cutting machine in which now you are entirely hooked on cutting, attracting, as well as making all the important things!

There are so many incredibly awesome devices that support your machine that isn't purely required; however, they sure are enjoyable!! Right here is the need to have Cricut accessories that you can't (do not wish to) do without!

I enjoy my Cricut Manufacturer, and also it has remarkably transformed the method I stitch.

There are numerous unique things that it can do, and also I am discovering brand-new pointers as well as tricks for using it day-to-day. I have created a list of all the fun devices that I like and utilize with my Cricut.

Infusible Ink
Infusible ink is an enjoyable new Cricut classification. It is the Circuits' take on sublimation.

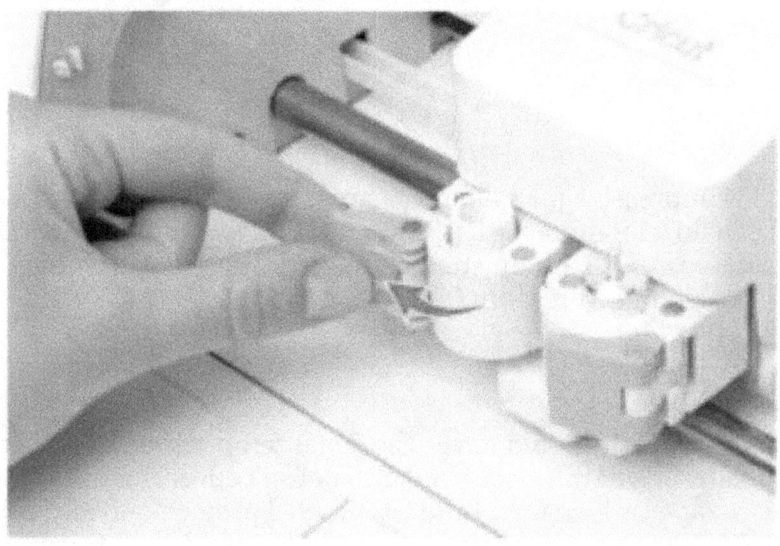

Wavy Blade

The wavy blade is fantastic for usage with material and felt.The jagged edge is one of the newest blades for the Cricut Maker as well as cannot make use of with the Explore line of machines.

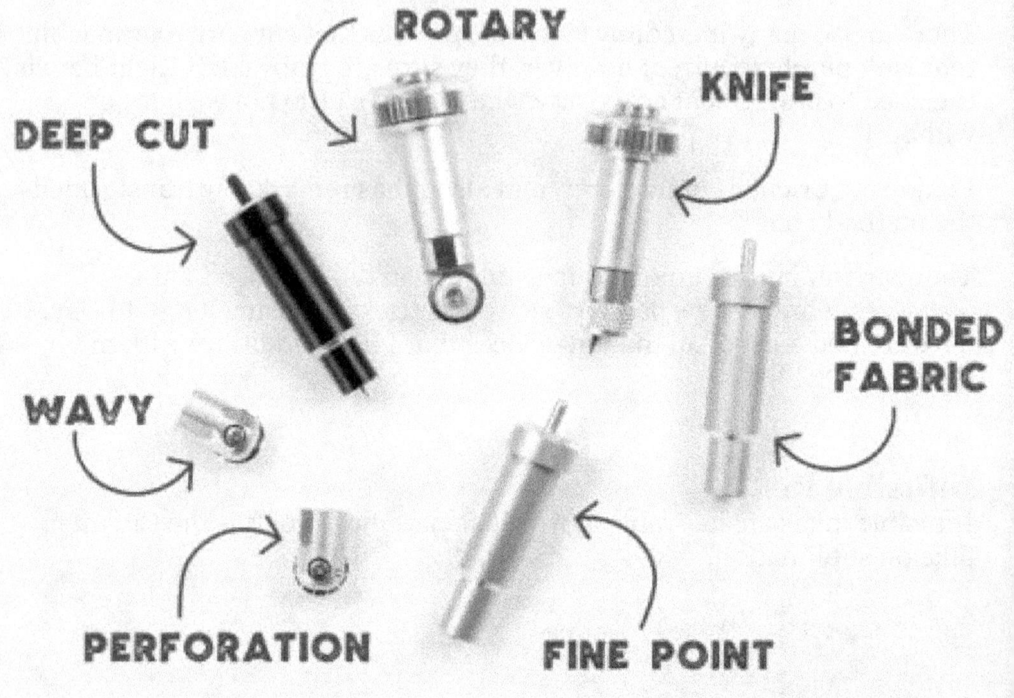

Brightpad

The BrightPad is impressive for so many factors. It is terrific for weeding vinyl, yet you can do a lot more with it! I use it for paper stitching. It is beautiful for tracing as well as adjusting patterns. It is seriously among my preferred tools in the craft room.

XL Scraper

This enormous scrape is a should have. The small scraper is excellent, and all; however, really, it is hard to hold and also doesn't cover many locations. This scraper is best for a little larger vinyl project, and also it is friendly and robust, which assists get all the bubbles out. It functions excellent with transfer tape as well as adhesive vinyl also.

Easy Press

I will certainly be sincere before I had the EasyPress; I prevented iron-on or heat transfer vinyl like the torment. It never stayed and always left me very irritated. This maker is fantastic for affixing iron on. It functions great, it warms up quickly, and also it is easy to use. A consistent temperature level is crucial for sticking iron-on and keeps a steady temperature while again using stress. I certainly recommend this if you do any kind of iron-on. It also functions terrific with Warm N Bond for appliqués and including Deco Foil; make sure to let the aluminum foil cool before peeling because the glue demands to cool a bit to transfer the aluminum foil. See my reduced stitch napkins for a fun EasyPress tutorial. Currently, you can likewise get the EasyPress 2, which comes in several dimensions.

The huge perk of the 2 is that it bears in mind the last temperature level you set, so if you use the very same temp each time, you won't need to click with a bunch of times to get to that same temperature. They both work equally terrific. However, EasyPress 2 has a couple of extra rewards that make it unique. The weblink will undoubtedly take you to all the alternatives on the Cricut website, so whether you are shopping on a budget plan or searching for the perfect size with a few additional rewards, you can locate journalism that is right for you!

Pen Set

I love these pens! The colors are so beautiful, and they are excellent for all of your Cricut attracting projects. I such as to claim I have scribbling skills by viewing my Cricut do the scribbling for me! Make use of these to resolve your envelopes or sign your cards with gorgeous script handwriting. There are seriously so many fun choices! Do not utilize them on material because only textile markers work well on material! (See my fake cross stitch gift tags to see just how I use these markers).

Craft and Machine Tote

If you don't have a table or counter area for your equipment after that, you should have a great place to store it. Grab a tote to keep every one of your Cricut devices as well as your equipment. The material is lovely as well as it merely yells for some customization with iron-on! Right? It finds in numerous colors, so you can order whichever one fits your fancy!

Weeder

This simple weeder is fantastic if you do not do too much amount of weeding. It is a basic weeder with a lengthy side that permits you to get under the vinyl and easily remove it. If you do even more weeding or more elaborate designs abilities, this one and also see the weeding collection listed below.

Weeding Tool Set

If you do a great deal of weeding, this is a great device set for you. There are several terrific weeding tools that you will undoubtedly want to have a look at. One has a long straight point that is excellent for minimal weeding, pierces the vinyl, and pulls it directly with this device. There's also a weeder with the conventional curve; however, it contours once again just at the factor. It is fantastic for a pulling movement when weeding. This tool functions excellent for a more significant area of weeding. Obtain under the vinyl and afterward maintain hold of it with the pointed end as you pull away. This collection additionally consists of two sets of tweezers as well as the typical weeder revealed above

All Function Mat Set

Cricut has four various shades of mats today. The pink carpet (not noted or imagined) creates for cutting textiles. Heaven mat is the light grip mat that you will utilize with paper and other lightweight materials like crepe paper. This mat has much less adhesive and allows you to reduce materials that formerly would have stuck to a typical mat. The trick for utilizing heaven mat is to turn the floor covering over and peel off the floor, covering far from the paper instead of peeling off the paper away from the floor covering. The environment-friendly mat is your standard floor covering that functions well with vinyl, iron-on, and I likewise utilize it for really felt. The purple mat is the strong mat that you will use for thicker products like timber veneer and various other heavy-duty materials. The added ling floor coverings are great for making multiples or larger designs. This package is a great deal and also an excellent way to stockpile on floor coverings.

CRICUT TOOLS AND HOW TO USE THEM

Cricut Design Space is a free software included with your Cricut machine that allows you to do everything from uploading images to editing designs to scoring and finalizing your project. You should make yourself familiar with Design Space and all it has to offer before you start using your Cricut machine. Design Space features project ideas, SVG files you can print on your products, and other helpful tips for your DIY Cricut projects.

In addition to your Cricut cutter and all that is included with it, you can also buy a Cricut Machine Beginner Set, which includes the following Cricut tools:

The Cricut Weeder Tools

The weeder tool, which looks similar to a dental pick, is used for removing negative space from a vinyl project. This weeder tool is a must when doing any type of project that involves vinyl. Trying to get rid of access vinyl is nearly impossible without a weeder, especially with materials like glitter iron-on. A weeder is a useful tool for any type of project using adhesives. Instead of picking up the adhesive with your fingertips, use the weeder

tool and keep your fingers sticky, mess-free!

The Cricut Scraper and XL Scraper

The Circuit Scraper tool is essential (and a lifesaver!) when you need to rid your cutting mat of excess negative bits. This tool typically works best with paper, such as cardstock, but other materials can easily be scraped up as well. Use the mat's flexibility to your advantage as you scrap the bits off the mat to ensure you are not scraping up the adhesive on the mat as well. You can also use the Cricut Scraper as a score line holder, which allows you to fold over the scoreline with a nice crisp edge. It can also be used as a burnishing tool for Cricut transfer tape. It will allow seamless separation of the transfer tape from the backing.

The Cricut Spatula

A spatula is a must-have tool for a crafter who works with a lot of paper.

Pulling the paper off of a Cricut cut mat can result in a lot of tearing and paper curling if you are not diligent and mindful when removing it. The spatula is thinly designed to slip right under the paper, allowing you to ease it off the mat carefully.

Be sure to clean it often, as it is likely to get the adhesive built upon it after multiple uses. You can use it as a scraper if your scraper tool is not readily available!

The Cricut Tweezers

They're super helpful if you don't have tweezers yet. I like to carry two types, one for vinyl and one for picking up small items.

All right, this isn't a Cricut tool, but it's too good not to share! The Pazzles Needle Point Tweezers are the tweezers I like for weeding. These tweezers are sharp and excellent for vinyl. These points are intelligent enough to collect vinyl right from the center without using the edges. It can also order the smallest scrap!

The other tweets that I like are mainly for collecting and holding items. The Cricut Tweezers did not sell separately anymore. The EK tools Craft Tweezers are vital if you're still looking for a good pair! They are ideal for collecting rhinestones and other enhancements with reverse action. The opposite is excellent, so you don't get sore hands.

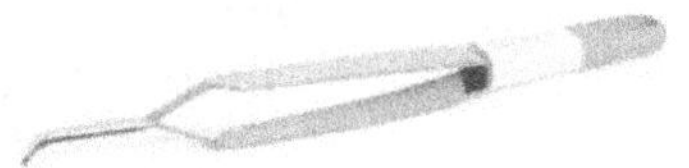

The Cricut Scrissors, Shears, and Snips

The right scissors can make a difference in the world for the job—the Cricut Scissors made of hardened stainless-steel blades, which even cut while remaining lasting. The scissors are rather sharp and come with a microtip blade, making it easier and cleaner to work on smaller areas' fine details. Keep a pair of sharp scissors with you. Sharp enough to cut cards, ribbons, and papers. Must buy a cover for scissors. Place it above the reach of children and in a place where humidity does not affect it. Neat paper or card cutting affects your decorative work.

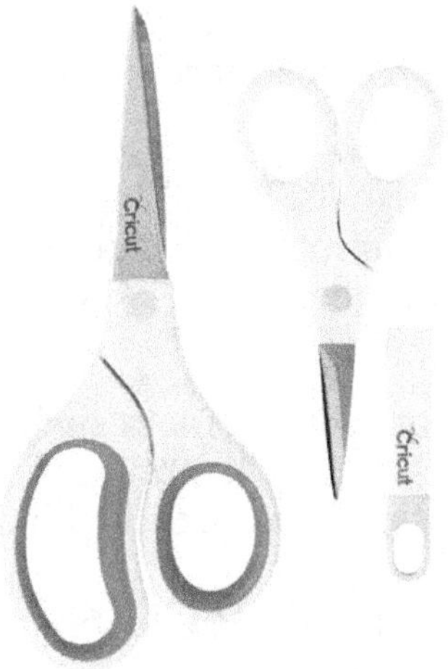

The Cricut Scoring Tool

Add a scoring stylus to your cart as soon as possible if you are a paper crafter. The tool is excellent for making paper baskets and boxes. It gives the products the professional, store-bought finish and makes them so easy to fold as the stylus already creates the grooves for folding your paper projects.

The Cricut Trimmer

Blades and trimmers are essential things; it helps in cutting papers very neatly and in the desired shape without putting additional effort to create a neat effect.

The stock of paper and cards Card is comparatively thicker than paper. They are different things. Buying a stock makes you tension-free; either you do test cuttings or throw it in, making unusual shapes for the trail. They should be enough until your whole tasks get complete.

The Cricut True Control Knife

At the point when Cricut discharged their marked art blade, it was incredulous. It does not sell on requiring another specialty blade—it believes in working fine and dandy. However, once you begin utilizing it, it discovers that Cricut honestly solved a couple of issues. Cricut True Control Knife can be used to cut a wide range of materials. As cardstock, vinyl, acetic acid derivation, fabric, and the sky is the limit from there.

Initially, it has a decent vibe when I'm holding it. The blade's body is thicker than some other specialty blade utilizes, and it feels great to hold. The hold is delicate, however firm and has a sense of safety in hand. The other art blade had a more formidable grasp, which exhausted my writing more.

The cutting edge itself is likewise secure. On the off chance that issues with another (immediately supplanted) make blade where the cutting edge came free, and haven't keep running over this with the True Control Knife.

The True Control Knife mold such that when it's topped, it doesn't move off the table—which you know is astounding on the off chance that you've at any point evaded a specialty blade that tumbles off your desk.

CRICUT MATERIALS

Numerous individuals guess a Cricut processing gadget is just for cutting paper or vinyl; anyway, it can accomplish such a great deal more noteworthy than that! More than 100 certain substances that a Cricut Explore PC can cut and the new Cricut Maker have a sharp revolving edge and a profound blade cutting edge that can decrease significantly! So, in case you're addressing what various materials a Cricut machine can cut, look at this amazingly great rundown underneath!

I likewise have a real data to the additional items and parts that every single Cricut tenderfoot wishes (and which ones are just "pleasant to-haves" that you can binge spend on the off chance you need).

Furthermore, in case you're in any case wavering or still have inquiries concerning the Maker, look at my post responding to all the essential questions regarding the Maker! A Cricut Explore processing gadget can decrease exceedingly an incredible arrangement for anything as long as it is 2.0mm thick or slender.

Cardstock and Paper

If you're doing any scrapbooking or making cards, you'll want to consider crafting your items with cardstock. You can choose some tremendous 65-pound cardstock for your crafting projects, and the nice part about this option is that it's pretty cheap. Cereal boxes, construction paper, embossed paper, even freezer paper can be used with your Cricut machine. Some users have had a lot of luck with the poster board, too, but you'll want to make sure you clean your blades if you plan on using this material since the poster board can be quite trying on them. Your blades could end up dulling over time, so make sure you clean them with aluminum foil. Craft paper is another option, as well, and if you're creating personalized boxes, this is an excellent material to consider – it can help bring a more personalized touch to your finished product.

Vinyl

This is one of the best materials for a Cricut blade, especially fine-point Cricut blades. You can adjust the settings and design the image onto the vinyl. Then, by ironing it on or using the Cricut press, you can create shirts and other appliques for outfits. You'll want to make sure that the iron-on setting is on your Cricut; however, before you think about using this.

You will realize that when you start to look for vinyl, the ideal type to choose is heat-transfer vinyl since you can simply iron or press it on. There are many different options, including fuzzy locked or glitter vinyl, that you can purchase.

Adhesive vinyl is another good one, and there are many different ways to use this. Containers, ornaments, and the like benefit immensely from this material. You can get permanent outdoor and removable indoor options. Again, Cricut machines are known for cutting vinyl, and this material is worth it if you're thinking about making decals, as well.

In case you're keen on endeavoring out vinyl with your machine, here's an essential instructional exercise on the most proficient method to lessen vinyl with a Cricut.

- Glue Vinyl

- Blackboard Vinyl

- Dry Delete Vinyl

- Sparkle Vinyl

- Reflexive Vinyl

- Holographic Vinyl

- Matte Vinyl

- Metallic Vinyl

- Outside Vinyl

- Printable Vinyl

- Stencil Vinyl

Iron-On

Iron-on vinyl, also perceived as warmth move vinyl, is one of my favored materials to cut with my Cricut! You can utilize iron-on vinyl to enhance shirts, tote packs, or any unique material thing.

- Ran Iron-On

- Foil Iron-On

- Sparkle Iron-On

- Shiny Iron-On

- Holographic Shimmer Iron-On

- Matte Iron-On

- Metallic Iron-On

- Neon Iron-On

- Printable Iron-On

Textures and Materials

The Cricut works admirably at lessening textures. However, you should sincerely like to include a stabilizer like Heat and Bond before you start cutting. These textures and materials cut with a Cricut Explore machine, yet there is much more than you can decrease with the rotating cutting edge on a Cricut Maker machine.

• Burlap

• Canvas

• Cotton Texture

• Denim

• Duck Material

• Artificial Cowhide

• Artificial Softened cowhide

• Felt

• Wool

• Cowhide

• Material

• Metallic Cowhide

• Oil Material

• Polyester

• Printable Texture

• Silk

• Fleece Felt

Different Materials

Other than texture, paper, and vinyl, many other solid point substances a Cricut can cut too. Here are a lot of energizing thoughts!

• Cement Foil

• Cement Wood

- Aluminum Sheets
- Aluminum Foil
- Balsa Wood
- Birch Wood
- Plug Board
- Ridged Paper
- Art Froth
- Channel Tape
- Embossable Foil
- Foil Acetic acid derivation
- Sparkle Froth
- Magnet Sheets
- Metallic Vellum
- Paint Chips
- Plastic Bundling
- Printable Magnet Sheets
- Printable Sticker Paper
- Psychologist Plastic
- Soft drink can
- Stencil Material
- Tissue Paper
- Impermanent Tattoo Paper
- Straightforwardness Film
- Vellum
- Washi Sheets
- Washi Tape
- Window Sticker

• Wood Facade

• Wrapping Paper

Cricut Maker

If you have the Maker, you can diminish considerably more noteworthy things! The Cricut Maker has 10x the cutting power of the Explore machines; in addition to it has a rotating edge and a sharp blade edge that empowers it to cut many more materials. The Cricut Maker can slice materials up to 2.4mm thick, in addition to over 125+ sorts of texture, including:

• Chiffon

• Cashmere

• Wool

• Jersey

• Jute

• Sews

• Moleskin

• Muslin

• Seersucker

• Terry Fabric

• Tulle

• Tweed

• Velvet

Contingent upon the Cricut model that you have, the materials that can diminish may likewise vary. So underneath, the full rundown of substances can cut with the guide of the Cricut Maker, and Cricut Explore has a record.

BOOK SEVEN: CRICUT JOY

Cricut Joy Key Features

The latest of the Cricut cutting machine series is the Cricut Joy and presently the smallest. It is designed to be super simple to operate and has no button on it. It is sorely operated from the Design Space app, which you can download and install on your PC, tablet, phone, or on all 3 of them.

There are several things your latest Cricut Joy can do for you apart from its portability including supers amazing labels, long cuts, cut vinyl without using the mat, cut repeated shapes for about 20 feet long, easier ways of making cards, and more.

The Cricut Joy is a compact machine that can create larger-than-life crafting projects. This little machine is designed to be used without a cutting mat, making it able to produce cuts repeated for up to 20 feet in length. It can also cut a single design up to 4 feet. This makes it an excellent little machine to cut longer projects.

It needs to use some of its accessories designed specifically for the machine due to its compact size. This means you will not be able to use the standard Cricut pens and some blades from the larger machines.

The little Cricut Joy is the best machine for children, beginners, scrapbookers, and greeting card makers. It can whip up small projects in no time, and as it is so small, it is portable too.

It can cut 50 different material types. To make your life easier with the Cricut Joy, Cricut has designed Smart Materials for use with this mighty little machine. These Smart Materials do not need a cutting mat and, as such, can be loaded directly into the cutting machine without the hassle of a cutting mat.

It should be noted, though, that the Cricut Joy is not a commercial-grade cutter, and it does require quite a few bits and bobs to get it going. Although the Cricut Joy can draw, emboss, do score lines, and cut, you can only do one function at a time. This means you will have to change tools a few times if you are cutting, drawing, and doing score lines in the same project.

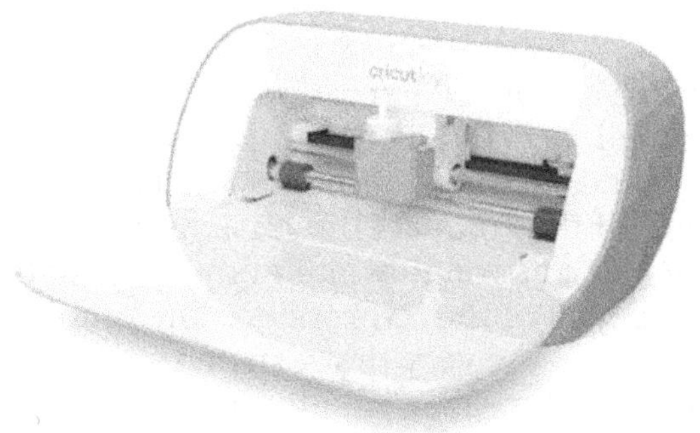

THE BEST CRICUT MACHINE TO PURCHASE

The Cricut Expression 2 Cutting Machine

The Cricut Expression 2 is a cutting machine that lets you cut stencils, transfer images, and design with precision templates. With this multi-purpose machine, you can easily create your own patterns and make professional-looking designs on any material.

And if that wasn't enough, there are even more ways to make your designs pop with Expression 2's extra tools designed exclusively for making designs on fabric.

When you have a Cricut machine, there are a few tools that you would need, which would make your crafting project easier and manageable. All these different tools help with cutting materials.

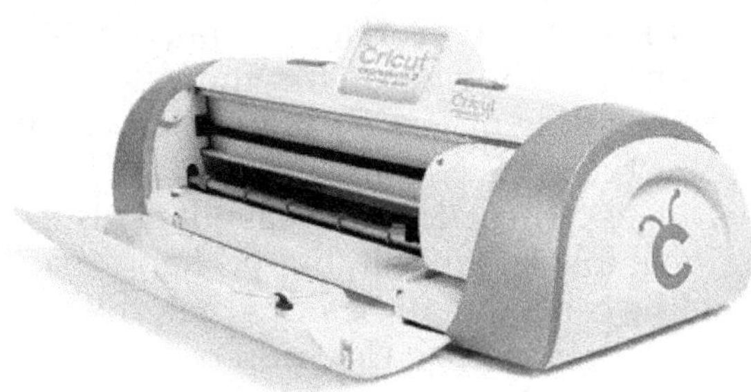

Cricut Expression versus the First Cricut

You Might Have heard about the Expression's Creator, the Cricut, also referred to as the 'small insect.' The Cricut Expression uses the same capsules and knife blades because of the first Cricut, allowing more flexibility. As a result of the compact dimensions, the first Cricut is only good at cutting edge designs roughly half of the sizes of these you're in a position to create using all of the Expression. The multiplier also has plenty of attributes not on the very first Cricut, the capacity to alter languages and elements of measurements, cut in portrait or landscape view, use hundreds of cuts for thicker fabrics, or even create mirror images using another attribute. The LCD screen is another new feature that permits you to see what you cut until you cut.

The Cricut Expression includes a few Disadvantages inside the very first Cricut. The Expression is more extensive and demands additional space on your desk or desk. If you would like to visit crops or friends' homes to concentrate on tasks, the plateau is much thicker and much more embarrassing to move. The expression could be costly.

On the reverse side, it empowers much more flexibility in your designs. The capability to reduce bigger things is useful for generating signage or banner and is quite valuable to folks who have to decorate bulletin boards or other significant distances.Generally, the Cricut Expression Cutting Machine is an exciting new alternative for crafters. It is especially useful for people with arthritis in their palms or whose palms are a little trembling. Most crafters may discover it won't take very long to represent the first cost of the Expression at the amount of cash and time they save in not buying or reducing their designs. The price has dropped considerably from the hefty first retail price tag of $499. If you shop carefully, you can now find the Expression for under $300. There is no pc or higher-tech understanding necessary to use this catchy machine. You will want to replace the knife cutting mat, and you may opt to purchase additional cartridges to broaden your layout skills. It's a good idea to buy the optional instrument kit, but perhaps, to create the paper a lot easier to lift from the central mat. Besides that, the Expression is almost carefree. The moment you've got a Cricut Expression Cutting Machine, then it will get such an essential part of your crafting, which means you could wonder how you ever got along without it.

Best strategies for Choosing the Ideal Cricut Personal Electronic Cutter

The Collection of Cricut Personal Digital Cutter machines create to automate several fiddly crafting tasks. In case you haven't ever heard of them before, then continue reading if you want to understand how to select your home crafts to a different degree.

In the event you know of them, you may be asking yourself how to determine which of these cutting machines will probably be acceptable for you. In the process, you're likely to observe the benefits and pitfalls of each device to aid you in producing an educated decision.

The Four variations we're going to be Studying would function as standard Cricut Personal Electronic Cutter, the Cricut Create," that the Cricut Expression, and the Cricut Cake.

The Easiest version to test at first is the Cricut Cake. It differs from other people, as it creates with one aim in mind. That is, to create expert looking decorations.

It might cut shapes from bread, fondant, gum paste, and additional raw materials. It is incredibly similar to that Cricut Expression method; however, the functional components alter to make them suitable for meals. It means that parts that need cleaning can easily remove. If you are looking to create edible ornaments, then this is the sole option from the range. This variant frees from roughly $270.

The Extra three Cricut Personal Digital Cutter models are appropriate for printing. They cut out of the same substances, such as vinyl, paper, card, and vellum. Which version you select will be contingent upon your budget and requirements.

#Budget

The Regular Cricut Personal Digital Cutter is the lowest price from the Scope, costing at least roughly $100.

Cricut Generate, Arriving at $160 and upwards.

The variety variant's surface is The Cricut Expression, which will place you back about $225.

Prerequisites

All Models are harmonious with the Entire choice of Cricut Cartridges. It typically means you've got a nearly endless source of cutting edge designs, as you can always purchase capsules. So there are two significant aspects on you should push your pick. These can be the measurements of machine and cuts, in addition to the variety of cutting edge options.

Sophisticated Cricut Suggestions for Your Craft Project

Capturing memories onto a virtual camera, even an HD camera, or a voice recorder makes life much more purposeful. When there's a unique moment you would like to catch and be in a position to return to at any certain time, you can certainly do this so easily with the assistance of these instruments. However, pictures continue to be the favorite medium by the majority of people. So, if you wish to put together those images and compile them onto distinctive memorabilia, then you flip into scrapbooking.

Scrapbooking is a technique of preservation of thoughts that's been in existence for quite some time and it's evolved up to now better. Previously, the invention of a single scrapbook was a monumentally crazy job. But now, with the creation of devices like the Cricut cutting edge machine, matters are made simpler. If you're looking to developing a scrapbook, this baby is the instrument for you. There are lots of good Cricut projects out there you can make the most of.

Scrapbooks are only some of many Cricut projects on the market. If you understand how to optimize it, this instrument makes it possible for you to create items that go past scrapbooking, for example, calendars. If you buy a Cricut cartridge, then there is a slew of layouts uploaded in each.

With calendars, you can design every month to represent the weather, the disposition, and exceptional events connected with that. The Cricut machine will take care of this. But in case one cartridge doesn't have the layout that you search, you can always go and purchase another. It's that simple

PRATICAL EXAMPLES
Vinyl Projects
The vinyl's versatility as a base for designing craft projects demands a section of projects solely dedicated to it. Following the instructions below

and feel free to further customize your designs with various colors and patterns.

Trick or Treat Bag

Step 1

Click on the "Images" icon and type in "Halloween" in the search bar and then click on "Insert Images" at the bottom of the screen. The image selected is shown in the picture below.

Step 2

You can edit either or both the image as needed by clicking on appropriate tools on the "Edit Bar."

Step 3

Select the entire design and click the "Group" icon. Then click "Save" to save the project.

Personalized Mugs (Iron-On Vinyl)

Step 1

Click on the "Images" icon on the "Design Panel" and type in "America" in the search bar. Click on the desired image and then click on the "Insert Images" button at the bottom of the screen.

Step 2

Click on the "Templates" icon on the "Designs Panel" on the left of the screen and type in "mug" in the templates search bar and select the mug icon.

Step 3

You can update the size of the template by clicking the "size" icon and selecting "custom" to change the "type" of the template to decorate non-standard size cups.

Step 4

You can further edit your design by clicking on the "Shapes" icon adding hearts, stars, or other desired shapes to your system.

Step 5

Click "Save" in the upper right corner of the screen, and then specify the desired name for the item, such as "Mug Decoration," and then click "Save."

Step 6

Design can be printed and cut.

Step 7

Using the "Cricut Easy Press Mini" and "Easy Press Mat," the iron-on layers can quickly transfer to your mug. Please wait for a few minutes before peeling off the design while it is still warm. (Since the system is delicate, use the spatula tool or your fingers to rub the letters down the mug before starting to peel the design)

Personalized Coaster Tiles

Step 1

Let's use our image for this project. Search the web to find a monogram image that you would like and store it on your computer.

Now, click on the "Upload" icon from the "Designer Panel" on the left of the screen.

Step 2

A screen with "Upload Image" and "Upload Pattern" will be displayed. Click on the "Upload Image" button.

Click "Browse" or simply drag and drop the image onto the screen.

Select the image type "Simple" and save the picture as a "Print Then Cut image."

Step 3

Choose the uploaded image by clicking on the "Insert Images" and edit the image as needed.

You can personalize the monogram by adding Text to the design by clicking on the "Text" icon and typing in "Your Name" or any other phrase.

Step 4

For the image below, the font "American Uncial Corn Regular" in Regular and color (green) select.

Select the Text and the image and click on "Group" then copy-paste your design for as many times as needed and save the project.

Step 5

You can resize the design as needed to match your coaster's size, although the recommended size is 4 x 4 inches for most common tile coasters. The system is ready to be printed and cut. Simply click on the "Make It" button and follow the screen prompts for using an inkjet printer to print the design on your printable iron-on vinyl and subsequently cut the design.

Step 6

Wait a few minutes before peeling off the system while it is still warm.

Vinyl Chalkboard

Step 1

Click on the "Projects" icon and type in "vinyl chalkboard" in the search bar.

Step 2

Use transfer tape to coat vinyl cutting strips on the blackboard. Lastly, use a chalk pen to write

messages.

Vinyl Herringbone Bracelet

Step 1

Click on the "Images" icon on the "Design Panel" and type in "#M33278" in the search bar.

Cloud Vinyl Wallpaper

Step 1

Click on the "Images" icon on the "Design Panel" and type in "#M4C5D3" in the search bar. Select the image and click the "Insert Image" button at the bottom of the screen.

Step 2

Using a weeder tool, remove the negative space pieces of the design. Use transfer tape to apply vinyl cutouts to the wall in a wallpaper-like pattern.

Printable Vinyl Easter Eggs

Step 1

Click on the "Projects" icon and type in "vinyl Easter eggs" in the search bar.

Step 2

I am using the dye to paint the hard-boiled eggs. Then, use transfer tape to cut the thinly sliced eggs into thin slices.

HOW TO MAKE MONEY WITH CRICUT MACHINE

Make and Sell Leather Bracelets

You can use either material. Despite what you choose, both are suitable materials to cut with the Cricut. Custom jewelry, like necklace pendants or earrings, are simple and stunning projects. These make beautiful and personal gifts or add the right touch to a particular outfit. Leather can also be used for making fashionable bracelets or cuffs.Having an intricate cut on a lovely piece of leather or faux leather, the bracelet can be attached to an adjustable band. Hair bows or bows to add to clothing or handbags are also possible. For a hair bow, hot glue a hair clip to the back when the bow is finished. Use hot glue or another adhesive to attach the bow to clothing or a purse. Other hair accessories can be made, like flowers and other shapes.These can be attached to hair clips, like the bows, or attached to hard or stretchy headbands. Leather can also be used as an embellishment to pillows or other fabrics, like chair backs, or made into manly coasters

Sell Iron-On Vinyl

Another way to make money is with the Cricut machine. You create an iron vinyl design.And sell to people. Iron vinyl can take the form of text or a pattern. You can also do it for any season or celebration, be it Valentine's Day, Halloween, Christmas, or Easter. Buyers can also order what they want.

Sell Stickers

This idea is for children. You can make money by designing educational and entertainment stickers for toddlers and other ages. You can create alphabetical stickers or city maps. Stickers are also used to decorate places like a wardrobe or cupboard

Make and Sell Party Decorations and Buntings

There is always a celebration in our day-to-day lives as human beings. It can be a milestone celebration or merely a fun-seeking escapade. Party decorations made with the Cricut machine can sell on these occasions.

Other Ideas to Explore
Create and sell parts and ornaments and banners

There is always a festival of people in our daily life. It can be a historic vacation or just a fun getaway. On this occasion, you can sell party decorations made with a Cricut machine

Window stickers

They all have a strange image, an object that practically obsesses us. A sticker on a vinyl window of your favorite photo contributes significantly to your decor. Making and selling window stickers is fairly simple and inexpensive.

Create and sell wall screens

Personalized wall art would make money quickly and easily. Get inspirational quotes or designs and turn them into wall art for sale.

Design and sell the body

Bodies or combinations are usually charming fabrics that can be enhanced with amazing works of art. Baby combinations can be made with many other texts in addition to "Papa time" or " Mom baby ". Other sweet words can be used to design a children's costume.

BOOK 8:CRICUT EXPLORE AIR 2

The Cricut Explore Air 2

This is the most youthful kin of the Cricut Explore line. It is the most awesome aspect the machines in this line. The Explore Air 2 is productive like different ones, however it manages its job stunningly better. It even has a superior plan, and it comes in various tones. The model highlights a Fast mode that speeds up the cutting cycle, basically on the off chance that you work with cutoff times. It likewise has the highlights in different frameworks like the German carbide premium cutting edge, inbuilt Bluetooth connector, double carriage, and auto-settings. The extraordinary thing about the Explore Air is that it is ideal for the two novices and progressed clients.

Characteristics of the Cricut Explore Air 2 Machine

The Explore Air 2 possesses some excellent features that make it easier for anyone to produce beautiful and professional-looking crafts. One thing you cannot find on the machine is a touch screen. Instead, every function is controlled by the dial and the software program on your phone or computer.

Cutting Width

Even though the Explore Air 2 is not suitable for heavy commercial use due to its small size, the compact size machine still offers an excellent cutting width to get the basic craft project done.

The machine measures 14 inches long and 12 inches wide. That is not the most significant width available to do a more massive cut, but it is the best you will get amongst the desktop home cutting machines. Also, note that the cutting width will further reduce in size depending on the type of material you want to cut.

Cricut Design Space Software

The Explore Air 2 can be used with the free Design Space software that is cloud-based. This action requires internet connectivity to log on to the software, and you can have access to an entire library of images and designs for your project. You can access the software seamlessly through your phone, tablet, or personal computer.

A major setback for the Explore Air 2 design space software is that you will need reliable internet access to design and to cut with your material. A new version only allows offline mode access but is only available for the iOS app.

Performance (2X Fast Mode)

The Explore Air 2 has a 2X fast mode, which enables you to cut common lightweight materials like vinyl, paper, and cardstock twice as fast as the regular speed setting. You can simply switching to fast mode to speed up your cutting when you want the project done quickly, although some thick materials may slow down the machine's speed.

Smart Set Dial

The machine comes with a Smart Set Dial to smoothly help you choose the type of material you are cutting, and the Cricut will automatically adjust the depth and speed appropriately. This saves you so much time or helps you to set up your work in real-time by removing any frustration you might encounter in guessing the amount of material needed for your project.

Pre-Installed Patterns

The Cricut Explore Air 2 comes with pre-installed ready-to-use designs that you can use to work on different applications for your project. With more than hundreds of pre-loaded printable patterns on the machine, you are given many choices to select a unique profile based on your preferences. You can also upload new printable images for your next cutting project, in addition to more than half a million printable images that come with the machine.

Useful Tips

Once you go through this process of getting your machine setup, the machine will be registered automatically.

In a situation where you couldn't go through with the setup when the Cricut was connected to your PC at first, you will need to get the machine reconnected and visit the design portal on the Cricut website, or visit the

Design Space Account menu, select New Machine Setup and follow the on-screen instructions that come up.

Basic Set of the Cricut Tools Kit

The tools should be packaged with the Cricut Explore Air 2 on purchase, and you can also get to buy them from Cricut directly or Amazon. It is sold for around $15 when purchased as a set. The craft tools set comprises of the following items;

Tweezers

This is designed in such a way that the handle can be squeezed open and also released to close. It is used in holding objects together while drying amongst other uses.

Scraper

The scraper is used in clearing the cutting mat and also works with vinyl.

Scissors

This is used as the name implies; to cut.

Spatula

The spatula helps in the careful lifting of materials off the cutting mat.

Weeder

The weeder is used in the removal of tiny little cuts or removing the vinyl from its liner.

Finding the Machine Serial Number

You will find the serial number of the Cricut machine on the underside tag of the machine. It is directly below the barcode for older machines. The serial number is composed of the following:

A 12 character alphanumeric code, It begins with the following letters:

Explore: E

Explore Air: A

Explore One: 1

Explore Air 2: S

Maker: Q

The Difference between the Explore Air 2 And the Explore Air

It is made up of the Rotary blade, which is mostly used for cutting fabrics. It is also used in cutting leather, silk, and other materials.

In the Maker, the scoring pen is replaced by the scoring wheel, which has more delicate scored lines and sharper.

The Maker is made up of the knife blade used for thick and heavy materials such as the balsa wood and heavy chipboard.

It is made up of the Digital sewing pattern library, which provides access to hundreds of fabrics plans for an instant cut.

It can cut hundreds of more materials ranging from the finest paper to heavy fabrics.

Unlike the Explore Air 2, the Maker comes without the dial. The Maker is also made up of a ridge that is used for placing your tablet devices as well as redesigned storage areas.

Cricut Explore Air 2

In terms of cost, the Cricut Explore Air 2 offers the best value for money. It has lots of great features despite costing up to half of the price of the Maker.

It can be used for a diversity of projects such as the patterned vinyl t-shirt, reverse canvas project, vinyl on glass water bottles, craft cutting, etc.

Cricut Access of the Cricut Explore Air 2 machine

The Cricut's premium access is called the Cricut Access, which gives you unlimited, though temporary, access to designs and fonts.

You can opt for purchasing your designs yourselves to have unhindered access anytime you need it.

The Use o the Bluetooth in the Cricut Explore Air 2 Machine

The Cricut Explore Air 2 machine is designed to connect to your computer, iPad, or iPhone wirelessly though they can also be paired together as well.

Important Notes

The design space can be used with any image you wish to use it along with.

You are advised to always make a test cut first on a small amount of material to save you from messing up the whole project, which can be a result of incorrect settings calibration or messy blade.

The Cricut Explore Air 2 Machine, if paired with an iPhone, iPad, or an Android device, can be used without an internet connection.

How to Open the Machine?

When you want to open the machine for use, you should click on where the red arrow is pointing at. You can raise the cover where the arrows are pointing below, to hide some of the accessories you will be using for making your designs.

UNBOXING THE CRICUT EXPLORE AIR 2 MACHINE

Unboxing the Cricut Explore Air 2

After purchasing the Cricut Explore Air 2 machine, it is essential to make sure it has all its accessories completely boxed in, and nothing is missing. If you find anything missing, you are advised to return it to where it was purchased or simply contact the Cricut support and inform them about the missing accessories. A complete packaged Cricut Explore Air 2 machine should have the following items in it:

- Cricut Explore Air 2

- Instruction manual

- Cricut cutting mat

- Cutting blade

- Silver pen and the accessory adapter

- Power and the USB cords

- The Cardstock and the Vinyl samples

It is to be noted that we have different kinds available, and depending on the kits you purchased, your Cricut Explore Air 2 machine might come with extra items included in it. The following are different kind of packages available for the Cricut Explore Air 2 machine:

- Ultimate Kit

- Tools Kit

- Vinyl starter Kit

- Complete Starter Kit

- The Premium Vinyl

Setting Up Your Cricut Explore Air 2

Once you can set up your Cricut Explore Air 2, it will lead to the machine's automatic registration to your account. To set up there Cricut Explore Air 2, you will need to take the following steps:

- Get the device plugged in and turn it on.

-Make use of the USB cord in connecting or the Bluetooth in pairing the Cricut Explore Air 2 to your computer.

- On the computer, visit design.cricut.com/setup.

- You will be prompted by On-screen instructions to create your Cricut ID and getting signed in.

- When started, download and install the Design Space plug-in.

- Once you are encouraged to begin your first project, the setup is complete.

Lighting

It is crucial that where you set up your Cricut Explore Air 2 is well lit. This lets you see what you are doing with the machine and lets you set it and change accessories with ease. Lighting could be natural (that is from sunlight) or artificial from bulbs and lamps. Lighting is very important as it prevents you from straining your eyes.

Power Source:

Since the Cricut Explore Air 2 is powered by electricity, a power outlet is important in setting it up. Set your Cricut Explore Air 2 as close to a power outlet as the power cable permits. This prevents the issue of entangling cables that make workspace untidy that occur when extension cables are used.

Work Space Configuration:

You will need to decide how you wish to configure your workspace before you set up your Cricut Explore Air 2. You need to decide where what needs to be kept. A good workspace configuration makes your craft making easy, convenient and enjoyable.

Ergonomics:

Such reverse-action tweezers have a good grip, precise points, and after extended use, they relieve cramping. The ergonomic grip helps you to maintain a firm hold on your materials during the whole process, giving you the extra pair of hands you'd always wish you had when you were made.

Linking the Cricut Explore Air 2 to your computer

The Cricut Explore Air 2 does not work by itself. To make the best out of it, you connect it to a computer. The Cricut Explore Air 2 works with PCs from Microsoft and Macs from Apple. Hooking up the Cricut Explore Air 2 to a computer is easy. Follow the steps below to get started

To get your Cricut Explore Air 2 working with a computer, you need to have Cricut Design Space installed and running on your computer.

Setting up the Cricut Explore Air 2 is easy! Use these steps and let's get started.

1. Open the box and unpack the Cricut Explore Air 2 and the accessories.

2. Place the Cricut Explore Air 2 on a flat work surface. Leave at least 10 inches of space behind the Cricut Explore Air 2. This is to allow the Cutting Mat roll forward and back conveniently behind the Cricut Explore Air 2 as the machine cuts the material.

3. Push the "Open" button

4. Carefully fix the accessory holder and the blades/blade housing in the tool holders.

5. Connect the USB cord to the Cricut Explore Air 2 and connect it to your computer.

6. Connect the power cord to the Cricut Explore Air 2 and plug it into a power outlet and switch on the power outlet.

7. Switch on the Cricut Explore Air 2 machine.

8. Your computer will detect the machine and install the drivers that are necessary.

9. If you wish you can connect the Cricut Explore Air 2 to your PC or Mac computer using Bluetooth.

10. Launch your browser and go to design.Cricut.com/setup

11. Login or Create your Cricut ID

12. Download the Design Space Plugin

13. Follow onscreen instructions and install the plugin.

14. As soon as the installation is finished, computer will alert you to make a project.

Linking the Cricut Explore Air 2 to your Mac via Bluetooth

1. Keep your Cricut Explore Air 2 within 10 feet of your Mac.

2. Go to Apple Menu and then select System Preferences.

3. Click the Bluetooth icon. Check to ensure the Bluetooth function is turned on.

4. Choose your Cricut Explore Air 2 from a list of available Bluetooth devices.

5. Click on Pair.

6. Use the code 0000 and select "pair".

Note that the Mac computer will only show connected when it is communicating with the Cricut Explore Air 2 during the cutting process.

Linking the Cricut Explore Air 2 to your Iphone via Bluetooth

1. Keep your Cricut Explore Air 2 within 10 feet of your iPhone.

2. Go to Settings on your phone then select the Bluetooth option.

3. Switch on the Bluetooth if it is off.

4. Select the Cricut Explore Air 2 from the list of available Bluetooth devices.

5. Click on Pair.

6. Use the code 0000 and select "pair".

7. Your machine can now cut from your iPhone.

Linking the Cricyt Explore Air 2 to your Android device via Bluetooth

1. Keep your Cricut Explore Air 2 within 10 feet of your android device.

2. Go to Settings on your mobile phone then select the Bluetooth option.

3. Switch on the Bluetooth if it is off.

4. Select the Cricut Explore Air 2 from the list of available Bluetooth devices.

5. When prompted for a code, use the code 0000 and select pair.

6. Your machine can now cut from your android device.

7.

Linking the Cricut Explore Air 2 to your Windows computer via Bluetooth

1. Keep your Cricut Explore Air 2 within 10 feet of your Windows computer.

2. Go to the Start Menu

3. Select settings

4. Select the devices option

5. Turn Bluetooth on and click on Add Bluetooth or Other Device

6. Select Bluetooth, the computer will sense the Cricut Explore Air 2 and show it in the list of available Bluetooth devices.

7. When asked for a pairing code, use 0000

8. Select Connect.

9. Your Cricut Explore Air 2 can now cut from your Windows Computer.

10.

Circuit Access

Cricut Access is something a lot of Cricut users don't understand. Hence a lot of misinformation flies around regarding it. The information I will provide here will help you decide whether you need it or not. Here is what you should about Cricut Access;

Cricut Access allows you to access thousands of images, fonts, and ready-made projects. All these come for a fee. Membership of Cricut Access comes in three major categories with different payment plans.

The perfect starter plans

This strategy is good for you if you just want to have a look before deciding whether you want to commit. It is a monthly plan and costs about $9.99

Annual Plan

This plan incorporates the benefits of the monthly plan. When you look at it closely, you'd realize you pay $7.99 per month – instead of $9.99. That means you pay upfront $95.88.

Premium Plan

The premium plan gives you all the profits of the other plans and also:

Up to 50% discounts on fonts, graphics, and ready-made projects.

Free economy shipping for purchases over $50.

Annually it costs $119.88. It would cost $9.99 monthly.

Whats Sets cricut Access And cricut design space apart?

Several people ask, what is the difference between Cricut Access with Cricut Design Space? The difference between both is very simple. Cricut Design Space is free software where you prepare your projects before sending them to your Cricut Explore Air to cut it. Think of it as a digital workshop you use to prepare your projects.

Cricut Access is a platform where you pay to get access to fonts, graphics, and readymade projects you can use in Cricut Design Space.

You can use Cricut Access images within Cricut Design Space. However, you will have to pay before sending them to be cut. You can pay as you go.

Cartridges

What are Cricut Cartridges? Cricut cartridges are a library of images that users can buy to use in creating their projects on their Cricut machine. Usually, these cartridges collect images focusing on a season (e. g Christmas or Easter), characters, or concept. A certain common trait links all the content of a cartridge together.

The Cartridges are physical devices that you plug into your Cricut Explore Air. You plug the cartridge into the cartridge port.

Within Cricut Access there are lots of "Cricut cartridges". These cartridges are not physical cartridges; they are digital libraries just like the physical cartridges. Once you purchase a cartridge, you can use it even without a subscription to Cricut Access. You can use Cartridges from your older machine on your Cricut Explore Air. Once linked to your account, you can have access to the content of the cartridge without even the physical unit. With Cricut Access there is little need to get physical cartridges.

Linking Cartridges with the Cricut Explore Air

While you cannot use your machine offline, your cartridges will work fine. Here is how to link your cartridge with the Cricut Explore Air

DESIGNING YOUR FIRST SAMPLE

Print and Cut

The Cricut Explore Air 2 comes with Print Then Cut features. With this, you can print out your images using your inkjet home printers and have your Cricut Explore cut them out with perfect precision. Say goodbye to inaccuracies caused by scissors!

Prepare Images for Printing

To make an image printable, you have to convert it to Linetype. This works on all images. You can also use the Flatten tool from Layers Panel to convert multiple layers for joint Printing.

Cricut library is filled with predesigned images that are ready to print. They appear on the design screen, where you can directly print and cut them. They are pre-aligned in the Layers panel as a single layer. They also possess a Print Linetype, which indicates that the image will be printed on your home computer and then cut using your Cricut Explore Air 2.

To locate Printables, click on the Filters icon and check the box marked Printables. Select your preferred image. A printer icon should be displayed on the image title. Include it to your canvas and click on "Make it to Print Then Cut."

Print The Cut Projects Things to Remember

After you have included printable images to your project, or switched the image Linetype to Print, click on "Make it" from Design Space. The preview image will be displayed, with a cut censor marking. Click on Continue to proceed to the cut interface.

The next screen comes up, where you will select your device from the drop-down menu. Click on Send to Printer to open the Print Then Cut interaction.

The images will be fitted with an image bleed, which will remove the white border from the cut image.

Utilize your Home Printer to print out the page. After, fix the paper on the Cricut cutting mat, and fix it in the Cricut machine. Your Explore Air 2 scans the sensor marking and accurately cut around the image.

Print Then Cut has a maximum image size of 9.25" × 6.75". The default material is 8.5" × 11". This is a permanent measure.

Consequential: Interference may be caused by colored materials, reflective materials, or materials with any pattern at all. The sensors might not be able to detect the cut sensor marks. You should use an Inkjet printer and 8.5" × 11" white materials for all your Print Then Cut processes with Cricut Explore. However, the Cricut Maker can Print Then Cut on light to medium-colored papers.

Print Then Cut Troubleshooting

Print Then Cut Calibration: These are a series of superficial cuts, questions, and answers, specially made to aid your Cricut in cutting precisely along the edge of your printed image.

Explore is not reading sensor marks: Visit the Cricut website to find out more about this and how to clear it.

Note: To use Print Then Cut with an iOS device, the printer must be equipped with AirPrint.

Significant: The Print Then Cut feature is NOT available on Android.

Using the Slice Tool

The Slice Tool can be used to make sentiments for your cards. You can find the Slice Tool from the functions at the bottom of the Layers Panel, right by the Weld and Contour. With the Slice Tool, you can cut the text or an image out of another shape. Just fix your image or word on top of the one you want to cut. Select the two shapes, then click Slice in the Layers Panel.

Slice Screenshot

This tool can be used to duplicate shapes. After use, click on the image you cut out. You'll get the shape itself and the shape you cut out of the background.

Use Stencils to Paint on Fabric

When designing for stencils, an important point to remember is to think about the negative space you are creating and how to keep the positive space intact. An excellent way to start is with a graphic of any kind, like an illustration, letters, or a whole design. You should also make a cutout for the Cricut that stays together. The last thing you want is a floating element or piece from your design.

Making a Letter Stencil Using Cricut

Letter stencils are arguably the hardest to make on Cricut. This is because it exhibits the floating design pieces more often than any other Stencils. However, there's a quick, easy fix to it. You can highlight the rectangle silver technique to slice your enclosed letters at their tiniest parts.

Top Stencil Fonts on Cricut

There are quite a number of Cricut fonts to choose from in the Design Space. These fonts do not possess floating elements. Some great options include:

- Doodle Type

- Dinosaur Tracks

- 3 Birds in paradise

- Girly Stencil

- Blippo Come Stencil

- Wednesday Stencil

- Cricut Alphabet-Circle

- Don Juan

- Glaser Stencil

Stencil Materials for Cutting Machines

Many diverse materials can be used to make Stencils, such as vinyl, paper, plastic, etc. Your decision may depend on the blank materials, the paint you intend on using, or your imagined design.

Top Materials for Reusable Stencils

If you're making use of a finite medium, you should make reusable Stencils. This is to ensure you do not waste materials. However, you should note that if your design contains floating materials, you might have to resort to using a silkscreen.

Some reusable stencil materials include:

- Mylar Sheets

- Stencil Roll Film

- Laminating Sheets

Top Materials for Cooking Related Stencils

Not all Stencils are food-grade materials. It is essential to know the ones you can use for your foods, not to endanger your health. Some top stencils include:

- Wax Paper

- Parchment Paper

- Grafix Clear Sheets

Top Disposable Stencil Materials

When stenciling with fabric, it is best to use a disposable material due to the paint's nature to avoid getting stains everywhere. These materials are sticky, making it much easier to operate with floating elements in your design. Some of them include:

- Transfer Paper

- Contact Paper

- Removable vinyl

Making Reusable Stencils with Cricut Explore Air 2

The recommendation for reusable stencils is to make use of Mylar Plastic sheets. They are straightforward to use and are very stable. Not to mention, very easy to wash.

Cricut Settings For Contact Paper

Contact paper sounds great, but is, in fact, considerably weak, which causes it to snag. It is advisable that you only set it on vinyl less for your Stencils. It might cut through, but it doesn't matter, as long as it is only used for stencils. You could also use a blue light pen for a more uncomplicated peel.

Making a Stencil for Painting with Cricut

There are several available surfaces to paint with a stencil. With the Cricut, you can make Stencils from the most popular materials. Among these materials are wood, canvas, fabric, ceramics, and chalkboard.

Adhesive stencils work best with painting. No matter how viscous your painting is, it will most likely run or bleed with a non-adhesive stencil. It is better to use adhesive stencil materials when painting, such as contact paper, sticky laminating sheets, removable vinyl, and transfer paper.

As for porous medium such as wood, you should use a mid podge to seal the cutout edges before painting. Just smear a layer of mod Lodge on the part that's been cut out of the wood.

You could also make use of a sponge or sponge brush when painting with stencils.

How Long Should Paint Be Left to Dry Before Removing the Stencil

Leave the paint until it is dry to the touch. It is best to peel it off after it has dried. This is to avoid smearing wet paint all over your work and yourself. If the base material is stretchy, you risk stretching the whole design in an ugly way when you peel off the paint wet. It's really not that complicated, so don't stress over it. Just peel when dry.

BOOK NINE: PROJECT 1

In this project, you are going to begin working with layers. You will be making a simple rose that needs two layers, one for each color. This transfer can be applied to a mirror or glass.

Materials

- Premium Vinyl — Permanent, in red
- Premium Vinyl — Permanent, in green
- Transfer Tape
- Mirror or glass surface
- Colorful builder's tape

Accessories

- Cricut Premium Fine-Point Blade
- StandardGrip Machine Mat (green)
- Cricut Weeder tool
- TrueControl Knife or a small pair of sharp scissors
- Cutting Ruler
- Self-Healing Mat (you can use any cutting surface)
- Cricut Scraper — This is optional

Finished Size

2.6" W x 2" H

Directions

1. Open Design Space on your preferred device.

2. Choose "New Project".

3. From the left-hand menu, choose "Images".

4. The images section is loaded with thousands of preloaded images from Cricut. You can also upload your own images. There are free images, images that come with the Cricut Access package, and other paid images.

5. For the sake of this exercise, the Cricut Access image of a rose has been chosen. This is a simple rose that should come with the Cricut Access package.

6. In the search bar of the "Images" screen, type in the following number: #M6DFDD42.

7. Choose the image of the rose and click on the "Insert Images" button on the bottom right-hand side of the "Images" screen.

8. Move the image to the top and left of the screen, if it is inserted near the bottom by default.

9. Move the rose to the following position on the screen: X = 2 and Y = 2

10. To do this, either drag and drop it, or type the coordinates into the "Position" option on the top menu.

11. Use the "Size" option on the top menu to change the size of the rose to W = 2.6 and H = 2.0

12. When you are working with layers, you will need to have a mark to align the layers with. This is called a registration mark.

13. The registration mark can be any shape from the "Shape" options on the left-hand side menu (except for the Score Line shape).

14. For this project, we are going to use the "Diamond" shape.

15. Choose "Diamond".

16. Click on the "Lock" icon on the bottom left-hand corner of the diamond.

17. On the top menu, go to the "Size" option.

18. Set the size of the diamond as follows: W = 0.32 and H = 0.56

19. Position the diamond above the rose. You can use the following coordinates if you used the previously suggested coordinates to position the rose: X = 3.347 and Y = 1.292

20. Select the diamond and the rose.

21. From the top menu, go to the "Align" option.

22. Choose "Center Horizontally".

23. This will center the diamond on top of the rose.

24. Once they are centered, make sure both images are still selected.

25. Right-click and choose "Group".

26. Once the images are grouped, right-click on them again to create a copy.

27. Move the copied image next to the original image.

28. Highlight the first rose.

29. On the right-hand side menu, you will see the two grouped roses.

30. Hide the image of one of the roses. You do this by clicking on the eye icon to the right of the image. You will see it has a line through it. On the screen, the rose will disappear, leaving only the petals.

31. On the second rose, hide the image of the petals, the same as you did for the image of the rose before. Only the rose should be left for this image, and there should be no petals.

32. You have to color sync the diamond above the image.

33. Select the first diamond on the screen.

34. If it is the diamond above the petals, you will need to color sync the diamond to green.

35. If it is the diamond above the rose, you will need to color sync it to red.

36. Once the diamond is selected, go to the right-hand side panel.

37. At the top of the panel beneath the top menu, you will see option tabs labeled "Layers" and "Color Sync".

38. Click on the "Color Sync" tab.

39. You will notice that it mechanically puts the colors of the objects in the panel below the "Color Sync" tab.

40. Match the diamond to the color of the image above it.

41. Repeat the "Color Sync" for the second image on the screen.

42. If "Color Sync" does not work, ungroup the rose and diamond object.

43. Select the diamond object. On the top menu beneath the option "Linetype", click on the square color box to the right of the drop-down menu.

44. Choose the corresponding color.

45. Select the diamond shape and the petals.

46. Right-click and attach the images.

47. Select the diamond shape and the rose.

48. Right-click and attach the images.

49. Click "Save" on the top right-hand menu.

50. Give the project an appropriate name, for example: "A Rose for the Mirror".

51. Click on the "Make it" button on the top right-hand side of the screen.

52. You will notice on the "Prepare" screen that there are two machine mats. There will be one for the petals and one for the rose.

53. Now it is time to get the materials and the Cricut machine ready for the project cut.

54. Use the Self-Healing Mat to cut a piece of the Premium Vinyl. As you can see, these images do not take up much material. You do not want to waste it, so only use what you need.

55. Match the color of the vinyl to the design image being cut. For instance, if the first image to be cut is the petals, load the green vinyl first.

56. Next, you will need to load the red vinyl.

57. Position the material on the StandardGrip Mat.

58. Use the Scraping tool to smooth the Premium Vinyl onto the machine mat.

59. Make sure the Premium Fine-Point blade is loaded in the right-hand blade compartment of the Cricut cutting machine.

60. Place the first part of the design at the mouth of the Cricut cutting machine.

61. Press the "Load/Unload" button. The Cricut cutting machine will load the machine mat.

62. Turn the Smart Set Dial to "Custom".

63. In Design Space, click the "Continue" button.

64. On the "Set material" screen on the right-hand side, click on "Browse All Materials".

65. On the "All Materials" screen, type "Premium Vinyl - Permanent" in the "Search" bar and click search.

66. Select the "Premium Vinyl - Permanent" option on the next screen and press "Done" at the bottom right-hand corner of the screen.

67. When the "Load tools and mat" screen appears, as long as you have the Premium Fine-Point blade and machine mat loaded, you can press the "C" button. The Cricut Explore Air 2 will start cutting out the project.

68. Once the Cricut has finished cutting, press the "Load/Unload" button to release the machine mat.

69. Gently pull the Premium Vinyl from the machine mat.

70. Repeat steps 55 to 60 for the second image.

71. Press the "C" button on the Cricut Explore Air 2 and the second image will be cut.

72. Use the Weeding tool to remove the pieces around the first image.

73. Once the second image has been cut, repeat step 68.

74. Use the Weeding tool to remove the pieces around the second image.

75. Pull the backing sheet off the second image.

76. Align the diamonds and press the second image onto the Premium Vinyl of the first image. When you align the diamonds, you will see how nicely the two images fit together.

77. Cut out a piece of Transfer Tape. Make the piece slightly bigger than the Premium Vinyl piece.

78. Remove the backing from the Transfer Tape.

79. Place the sticky part of the Transfer Tape onto the Premium Vinyl.

80. Be careful how you lay it over the design, and smooth out any bubbles or creases using the Scraper tool.

81. Place the Premium Vinyl with the Transfer Tape stuck on its face down on a firm surface.

82. Pull the backing sheet off of the Premium Vinyl, pulling from a corner of the vinyl at a 45° angle.

83. Use a bit of colorful builder's tape to mark out a boundary on the mirror or glass where you want to transfer the rose.

84. Place the design in the position you want.

85. Smooth the design out using the Scraper tool to make sure the design is properly stuck to the mirror or piece of glass.

86. Gently pull the Transfer Tape off the design.

87. Remove the builder's tape from the surface where the design is.

88. That's it! You have done your first vinyl layering project.

PROJECT 2

Heat Transfer Vinyl

Aheat transfer vinyl has a clear plastic back that allows it to adhere to fabrics when applied to it. Therefore, iron-on vinyl project is a great way to create your customized t-shirts, hats, bags, totes and more. You can use the Cricut Maker to cut the vinyl material and then do the heat transfer vinyl project yourself. This is an amazing way to be classy and creative. Here are tips on how to iron-on a vinyl project:

Prepare the project area and measure it correctly. There is no need for assumptions as this may prove costly later on. So, get a tape to measure the length and width of your vinyl material. Ensure that you use the same tape to measure all your project materials; this is very important.

Adhere strictly to the manufacturer's instructions and recommendations for your iron-on vinyl material.

Ensure that you mirror your image before cutting. Mirroring the image refers to flip it so that it can cut backwards. Though, a pop up may remind you to mirror the image if you have not done so. Mirroring the image will make sure that the heat transfer side of the image will appear correctly on the shirt or bag.

The right mat for this project is Cricut Standard Grip Cutting Mat.

Place any thin cotton material between your vinyl project and the pressing iron to avoid melting the vinyl material.

Use heat press to heat transfer vinyl to your project. This method will ensure that the right pressure and temperature is applied to the vinyl for bonding between the it and project then make sure that your pressing iron does not go higher than is required for the fabric you are using. Then, press the iron firmly on the cotton material covering the vinyl project.

Peel the liner off the vinyl. If some of the vinyl pieces are not firmly attached, put the cotton material back over it and again apply pressure on it with the iron. Do this at short intervals until you meet your aim.

Note that heat transfer should be applied only to fabrics or solids that can withstand the heat from the iron. These same steps are also applied when you create Christmas tea towels and other customized iron-on vinyl on fabrics. If there are steps you didn't get quite well, do well to go over and read them again. As you grab the content, allow your creative mind to roam and discover ways to beautify this design to come up with your customized design.

There are many designs that you already have, and you are eager to try your hands. Do not be afraid, just get busy and with the above steps to guide you, there is no problem.

How to Make A Simple T-Shirt

You can use your Cricut Explore Air 2 to make nice T-shirts designs and it's quite easy to do. Cricut cuts out an iron-on vinyl design in an easy and simple way.

In this tutorial, we will be using iron-on vinyl. Iron-on vinyl is a type of vinyl, like an adhesive that will stick to any fabric when applied using an iron.

1. Log into your Design Space.

2. Select "New Project" and then, click on "Templates" in the top left corner. Choosing a template makes it easier to visualize your design to know how good or bad it will be on your T-shirt.

3. Choose "Classic T-Shirt" and pick your preferred style, size, and color.

4. You will see tons of beautiful designs for iron-on T-shirts. Browse through the entire images before you make your choice.

5. Remember, if your preferred design isn't available, you can upload your pictures to the Cricut Design Space. We have created a tutorial on how to upload your own images to Cricut Design Space.

After you have selected the image, resize the image to fit the T-shirt. You can do this by clicking the resize handle in the bottom part of your design and dragging the mouse to enlarge or reduce.

When you are done, click the "Make it" button in the top right corner. You will be told to connect your Cricut machine.

Toggle the green "Mirror" button on. Toggling it on will make sure your design is not cut backward.

Face the shiny part of your vinyl design down on your cutting mat. Remember to move the smart set dial to the iron-on option.

Remove all the vinyl designs you don't want to be transferred to your project when it's ironed. Use your weeding tool to remove those little bits that will jeopardize your beautiful design. This process is called weeding.

Transfer your design to your T-shirt when you are done weeding. You can either use an iron or an EasyPress. Preheat your EasyPress before use.

Congrats! You just learned how to make a simple T-shirt on the Cricut Design Space.

WHAT IS NEW IN DESIGN SPACE?
Cricut Design Space
You can also create your projects from scratch, but if you're short on time or ideas, then from Design Space you can choose from over 60,000 plans and pictures.

You'll need a Cricut for these activities. The Explore Air 2 is also a good cutting machine. Once set up, it's just a case of buying the designs and following the directions to create them. You are free to combine it by adding the designs to separate colored T-shirts, or even jumpers and hoodies.

Before digging in, let's understand the meaning of the Cricut Design Space Canvas Area. This is where all the process occurs before cutting your projects.

Investing in a Cricut is fruitless if you don't know how to master the Design Space because to cut any project, you will always make use of this software. In my own opinion, Cricut Design Space is an excellent tool for beginners. If you don't have experience with any design programs such as Photoshop or Illustrator, you'll find it overwhelming in the beginning, but it's pretty simple. There's nothing to fear; you just need to get the hang of it.

On the other side, if you have expertise with any of Adobe's Creative Cloud applications or Inkscape, you'll see this program's a breeze. It's primarily to touch up your projects and produce minimal designs with shapes and fonts.

By logging into your Cricut Design Space account and starting or editing a new project, you'll do everything from a window called Canvas. Cricut Design Space's Canvas Area is where you do all your edits before actually starting to cut your projects.

Getting Started with Cricut Design Space

Do you know where to get the Cricut Design Space? Well, if you are on a desktop or personal computer, navigate to https://design.cricut.com. With an Iphone, find your way to your App Store and input "Cricut Design Space" on the search space.

If your smartphone runs on Android OS, enter the Play Store and use the same search term. Remember that downloading or installing this is completely free of charge. you will need a Cricut ID to sign in. This you can also get for free, even if you do not have a Cricut. Simply follow the prompts provided.

Once you have entered your email and gotten your ID, you will at once be taken into the main domain of the Cricut Design Space, the place where all of the magic happens. A quick tip: bookmark this page to your web toolbar so you can find it easily whenever you want to.

The Canvas you will be shown after, similar to a painter's whiteboard, is the big space where all your designs and progress will reflect; this space has a full grid by default to allow you to see everything about a single work without having to pinch-zoom and un-pinch. Nevertheless, you can choose the appearance and measurements of the grid.

Install on Windows/Mac

- Click on your browser and navigate to www.design.cricut.com.

- you need to create a Cricut ID otherwise sign in with your Cricut ID. Be sure that page is fully loaded before carrying out this activity to avoid the error.

- Select "New Project."

- Select "Download Plugin" from the prompt.

- Wait for the download finishing and then select the downloaded file to open/run it.

- Click "Next" when the Cricut installer opens.

- Read the Terms of Use and accept the agreement.

- Click "Install" to begin the installation.

- Click "Done" at the end of the installation.

Install Cricut Design Space App on iOS

- Tap on the App Store icon on your device.

- Search for Cricut Design Space.

- Tap the "Get" button to download. Please confirm the download with your iTunes password if prompted. The app will launch and display the necessary options that will be used to complete the process.

Install Cricut Design Space App on Android

- Tap Google Play Store App on your device to open it.

- Search for Cricut Design Space.

- Tap on the "Install" button.

- Tap on the Cricut Design Space icon to open it when the installation is complete.

- Sign in and start designing your project.

Uninstall the Cricut Design Space on iOS

- Press and hold the Design Space icon on your iOS device till it vibrates.

- Press the "X" button to delete it from your device. This is very easy, right?

Uninstall Cricut Design Space App on Android

- Go to Settings.

- Tap on "Apps" or "Applications."

- Swipe to the "Download" tab or "Application Manager."

- Search for the App you intend to uninstall.

- Tap the "Uninstall" button to finish, and the app will be gone for good.

Uninstall on Mac

- Move to "Finder" and open the "Applications" folder.

- Search for Cricut Design Space.

- Drag it to trash.

- Right-click on the Trashcan and select "Empty Trash" to remove the application.

Uninstall on Windows

- Click on the "Start" button.

- Select "Settings."

- Select "Application."

- Look for Cricut Design Space and choose "Uninstall."

Home Screen

It is not just enough to know that the CDS is an important tool; you must know how it works.

Navigating your way through the CDS can be a bit overwhelming, especially if you are new to the use of this space and the Cricut. This is because of the many functionalities that are found in it. If you are not trained to make use of these functionalities and to know what each of them stands for, you may not be able to make use of the platform and you will see that you will be at a loss for what to do every time you are about to create your designs or launch a project. We will take a deep dive into the CDS and help you better understand what it is all about how you can find your way around it.

When you log into your design space, you will be taken to the application's home screen. On the home screen, there are lot of thumbnail pictures. These are templates that you can customize to create your projects, and as a beginner, you may want to start by trying out this step. It may be a bit difficult to start creating your designs from scratch, so the best move sometimes may be to start out by customizing a template to suit your needs.

You can, however, start a new project if you feel that you have what it takes to do so immediately.

Canvas Screen

This is the Design Screen where you will create all of your projects.

The Canvas screen is split into the following sections:

Top Menu Bar — This is the top, dark gray Menu bar. When you are on the Canvas screen, this menu bar will have the following options on it:

- Canvas — This indicates the screen you are viewing.

- Untitled — This will remain "Untitled" until you have saved your current project. If you load a saved project, it will list the name of the opened project.

- My Projects — This will take you to the directory of your stored/saved projects.

- Save — This is the save button for your project. Once a project has been saved, there will be a second option listed "Save As". The "Save As" option is there so you can save a project as another name and keep the current one intact.

- Machine — This is the cutting machine selection menu. Once you have selected your default machine, it will load every time you log in.

"Make it" button — This button sends your current project to the "Prepare" screen to ready your design for cutting.

Top Drop-down Menu Bar (3 stripes in the top left-hand corner of the gray menu bar)

The Design Panel — This is the selection panel on the left-hand side of the screen. Sometimes, it is simply called the left-hand menu. The Design Panel is where you can select the object you are going to use for your design projects. These objects include Templates, Projects, Images, Text, Shapes, and an option to upload your own designs.

Edit Menu — This menu can be found below the top gray menu bar. It should be noted that this menu bar can change slightly depending on the object being designed. Some of the common features of this menu are:

Undo/Redo option — The first items on the left of the Edit menu are the Undo and Redo arrows. They are grayed out until there is an object on the screen or until an object has been changed. This is handy when you accidentally move, delete, or resize something on the screen.

Linetype — This is where the image or design linetype is determined. The default is always set to "Cut". The "Draw" option is for use with the Cricut Ink Pen accessories. The "Score Line" option is for marking a fold in the material.

The Linetype Color Swatch block — This is the small square next to the Linetype options. This option is used to determine what the color of the line will be.

Fill — The Fill option is used to change the color of the object on the screen. It is also where you will set the object to "Print". These are for features called "Print" and "Cut". This is when you send an image to the inkjet printer before cutting the material. It is for when you have various shapes, images, or objects that need to be drawn before they are cut.

The Fill Color Swatch block — This changes the fill color of the chosen object on the screen.

Select — This option will "Select All" images on the screen. Once the images have been selected, this option changes to "Deselect"

Edit — This is the standard editing menu that contains the "Cut", "Copy", and "Paste" options.

Align — This option aligns selected images either horizontally or vertically, or centers them. It also contains a "Distribute" option, which equally spaces out images either vertically or horizontally.

Arrange — This arranges the order of the objects.

Flip — This "Flips" the object either vertically or horizontally. It also rotates it by 90°.

Size — This option resizes the selected image(s).

Rotate — This option allows you to rotate objects to a certain angle. It allows for some interesting object positioning on the screen.

Position — This will place a selected object at the desired coordinates.

The Layers and Color Sync panel — This is the panel found on the right-hand-side of the Canvas screen. It is broken into two tabs.

Layers tab — The layers tab has a menu with the following options at the top:

- *Group* — Objects that need to be kept together on the screen to be moved, marked, colored, etc. are easier to work with when they are grouped.

- *Ungroup* — Ungroup is grayed out until objects have been grouped. Ungroup disconnects Grouped objects.

- *Duplicate* — This option is used to clone selected objects and make an exact replica of them.

- *Delete* — This option is used to delete selected objects.

Color Sync tab — This tab is useful when you have objects that you want to be drawn or printed in the exact same color. It will list the exact colors of all the objects on the screen for you to match other objects with.

Canvas Objects — The panel beneath the Layers panel menu lists all the objects currently on the design screen. As you get more familiar with working in Design Space, you will find this panel very useful.

Bottom Menu of the Layers/Color Sync panel — The bottom section of this panel has the following options:

Canvas — This hide or unhides any embedded objects on the Canvas, such as templates or background color.

Slice — This is for slicing up an object on the canvas.

Weld — Welds two objects together to form an outline.

Attach — Attaches objects on the screen that need to be printed together.

Flatten — Flattens an image with multiple parts into a single image.

The Design Canvas — This is the graphed space in the middle of the screen where you will do all of your designs. It is set in inches as a default, but the settings can be customized through the top right-hand Drop-down menu.

Zoom Control. This is grayed out until you hover the mouse cursor over it. By default, it is set to 100% scale. You can set it to zoom in or out of the screen by using the + and - selection icons on each side of the current zoom % marker.

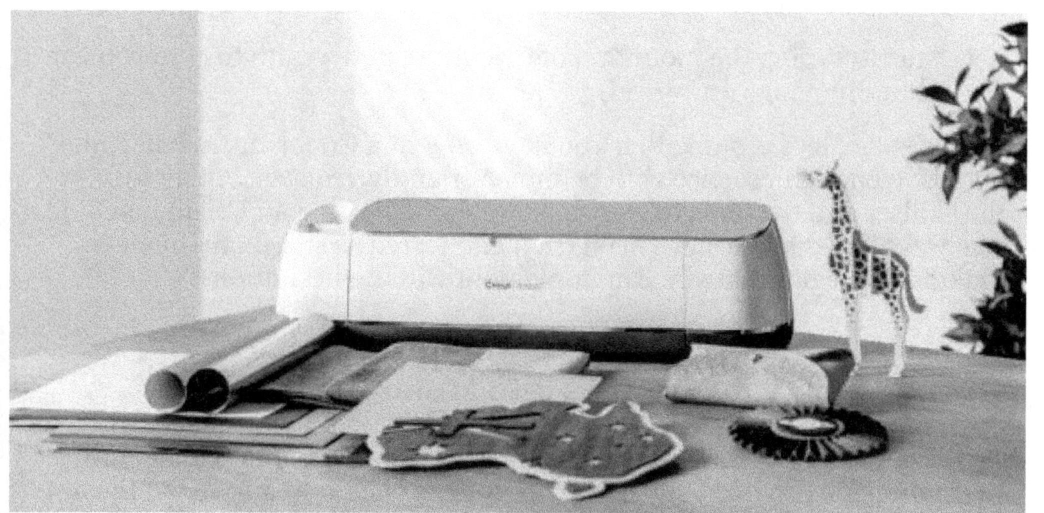

BOOK 10: HOW TO MAKE MONEY THROUGH CRICUT EXPLORE AIR 2?

Now, if you were to buy any of these machines during a holiday sale with a bundle deal that comes with a variety of tools, accessories, and materials for a practice project as well as free trial membership to Cricut Access, you would already be saving enough to justify the purchase for your personal usage. The cherry on top would be if you can use this investment to make more money. You can always get additional supplies in a bundle deal or from your local stores at a much lower price. All in all, those upfront costs can easily be justified with the expenses you budget for school projects that require you to cut letters and shapes, creating personalized gifts for your loved ones, or decorating your home with customized decals, and of course, your jewelry creations. These are only a handful of the reasons to buy a Cricut machine for your personal use.

Let's start scraping the mountain of Cricut-created wealth to help you get rich while enjoying your work!

At this stage, let's assume that you have bought a Cricut cutting machine and have enough practice with beginner-friendly projects. You now have the skillset and the tools to start making money with your Cricut machine. The ways listed below have been tried and tested as successful money-making strategies that you can implement with no hesitations.

How to Turn Your Designs into Money

So many people have asked the question, "How do I make money using my Cricut?" or "Should I buy a Cricut? Is the market too full? Can I still make money? How do I start?" Sometimes, it is hard to answer all these questions because some of the people using Cricut do not want to tell you how to make money from this craft. They do not want to share their secrets. But this book is here to give you all the inside information you need to know if you are in need of money.

When a lot of people are starting out and they are venturing into a craft—maybe they have a Cricut or another vinyl cutting machine, or perhaps they do not have one, and they want to get one—they have all these questions about how to get started, and it is overwhelming at first. It can be confusing and complicated, and then sometimes you will reach out to those that have one, and they do not want to share their secrets; they are afraid that you might become their competitor. But the truth is that everyone can succeed if you will build each other up there is room for us all to succeed. Let us start with the first question.

Let's now see how we can make money from all the knowledge we have gotten. Someone rightly said, "if you cannot make money from the knowledge you have gotten or if you have the knowledge and it is not useful to you in any way, then the knowledge is useless to you and the society." In order for this knowledge to be useful to you, I will show you how to make money from it. I'm not saying that the knowledge is useless if you use it to only make crafts for your family and friends; if you use it for that reason, then the knowledge is still useful.

Several of us are on Facebook, we go to marketplaces; you may have visited Etsy, and you've seen so many shops selling signs, selling shirts, selling one thing or the other, you probably wonder, "can I still make money with craft?" The simple answer to the question, "Yes, you can, and it is not that hard." With everyone specializing in a specific area where they know how to do better, the market can never be saturated. Take, for instance; someone might major only in the making of T-shirts, while another on making cups, another on woodwork design, and many more. The truth is that you will not find many people that are good in one particular area. So, the market can never get filled.

Now you are ready, you have gotten your Cricut, and you are wondering, "where do I start?" The easiest place to start is literally by making items for your friends and family. There are so many products you can make for your friends that they will appreciate and pay you for. Some of them are stickers, design their name on their T-shirts, and write motivational words on their T-shirts. You can brainstorm on some objects you think your friends would like and start designing for them. You can also make a design for your children and your spouse. When you are done with those designs, paste them on Facebook; you might get people who would want you to do the same design for them. This is the easiest way to start without investing so much money, and no one is buying it from you.

100+ Business Ideas You can make with your Cricut and Sell Wall Arte canvas

1. Calligraphy wall art

2. Customized lap desk

3. "Breakfast-in-bed" tray

4. Coffee bar sign

5. Cookie jar

6. Crafting stamps

7. Planner stickers

8. Custom calendar

9. Journal pages

10. Welcome mat

11. Wine gift bag

12. Silhouette art

13. Art storage

14. Labeled laundry baskets

15. Customized travel mugs

16. State silhouette signs

17. Forest themed nursery décor

18. Candleholders

19. Custom shot glasses

20. Wedding favors

21. Book tote bag

22. Patterned wood letters

23. Quilled art

24. Team T-shirts

25. Teacher appreciation mug gifts

26. Photo booth props

27. Personalized bottle cap catcher

28. Wine cork box

29. Paper succulents

30. Patterned scarf

31. Designed umbrella

32. Mandala hoodie

33. 3D stars

34. Doll clothing

35. Custom jigsaw puzzle

36. Glitter tumblers

37. Labeled pantry bins

38. Kitchen conversions chart

39. Family center

40. Paper straw party decorations

41. Headbands

42. Personalized tea towels

43. Stained glass wind chime

44. Ring dish

45. Monogrammed throw pillow

46. Giant bows

47. Kitchen mixer decals

48. Custom onesies

49. Car window decals

50. Hanging planter

51. Bumper stickers

52. Paper flower wreath

53. Nursery mobile

54. Food pun dish towels

55. Customized beach towel

56. Drink cooler

57. Pendant necklace

58. Leather tassel earrings

59. Finger puppets

60. 3D puzzles

61. Charity shirts

62. Glass cutting board

63. Wooden family name sign

64. Notebook covers

65. Flip flops

66. Decorative hand mirror

67. Makeup storage

68. Pop up paper animals

69. Felt flowers

70. Quilts

71. Vinyl banners

72. Custom potholders

73. Thank your cards

74. Leather purse

75. Dry erase weekly menu

76. Cookies for Santa plate and mug

77. Family tree wall art

78. Photo magnets

79. Window clings

80. Felt headband

81. Tupperware for food gifts

82. Sleep mask

83. Microwaveable rice pack

84. Leather cuff bracelet

85. Custom ballcaps

86. Decorated dog bandanas

87. Tooth fairy bags

88. Coloring books

89. Pop up cards

90. Polka dot vase

91. Winter shadowbox

92. Drink koozies

93. Custom drawer pulls

94. Photo board

95. Planner pages

96. Balsa wood jewelry

97. Etched pet tags

98. Water measurement bottle

99. Etched measuring glass

100.   Countdown sign

101.   Workout tank top

102.   Large wall decals

103.   Embossed cards

104.   Chipboard letters

105.   Striped coffee mug

106.   Teabag holder

107.   Decorative tea light holders

108.   Foam stamps

109.   Llama mask

Is the market too full?

You can target two avenues to sell your products: either by looking at how you can approach the market locally or online. It is advisable to concentrate efforts on one approach to start with as your target is to generate profits as soon as possible. Never forget that your goal is to grow benefit and reinvest it so that your business expands. The quicker you increase your sales, the more likely you will reinvest in new tools or new products, making, in turn, a stronger financial turnover. Understanding your marketing strategy is key to your success.

Where you should start from

Like any start-up business, initial questions need to be addressed to overcome possible difficulties. For example, addressing issues like defining my clientele, the products that might be of interest, where to find them, and how to make a profit margin of my sales are important to tackle from the start. In other words, you will need a good and well-defined business strategy to start with

Selling the craft, you have made with Cricut

The Cricut Explore Air 2 is the new top-selling craft plotter from Cricut and is arguably the best value for the quality they have to offer. This model cuts materials twice the two previous versions' speed, has Bluetooth compatibility, and the two adapter clamps on board.

The storage cup at the top of the unit features a more minor shallower cut to store your new blade housings while they aren't in use. If you want to change for a project with many different tips, they're all readily accessible during your project. Both cups have a smooth silicone rim, so you won't have to worry about getting rusty or scratched at the blades on your computer!

This is the right equipment for the job for anyone who finds themselves using their Cricut at some regularity. You will be likely to do your crafts twice as quickly, and each time, even at that pace, you will get a satisfactory result. There are a lot of things we have pointed out already that you can start doing and selling to your friends and neighbors. You don't have to convince your friends to buy many of those things because I know they will like it if you make personal designs for them. So, what you have to do is to find out what your friends like and make such a design for them. if you have a friend that likes football and has a team, you can design the logo of the team as a sticker for such a friend and write something good about the team for him or her too. You might also have a friend that sees clothes and likes what he or she does. You can make a lovely design with his business name for him or her. Also, you can make a sticker of his logo for him or her to put on every dress he makes.

Another way you can make money with your design is to look for people that would want you to iron-on their clothes for them. There are a lot of people looking for someone that would design their clothes for them.

Look for the people that sell in boutiques and sell your designs to them. This is how this is done. You can offer to do a free design for someone that sells plenty of plane T-shirts for him or her to see what you do. If he or she likes what you have done for him, you can then charge the person how much you would like to receive for designing each piece of clothing for such a person. So, look for local sellers around you that you think might need your design.

Another very easy way you can make money with this is through selling to groups. You can walk up to a group of people that wear a uniform and have a group name and ask to do a design for their group. This is easy to get because each person in the group would like to be identified as a member of the group and would like to pay you for your work. Examples of some of these groups are clubs, choirs, associations of friends, etc. offer to do a free design for the leader of the group first. if you can convince the leader of the group with your design, you can easily sell your work to every member of the group. Secondly, the group members will be seeing the design of the leader and would be asking where he did the design. Some will even suggest to him that why 'don't the group do the design for everyone. Then he will be forced to ask you to do the design for every member of the team. Get the leader interested, and you will penetrate the group easily.

Selling Pre-Cut Customized Vinyl

Vinyl is a super beginner-friendly material to work with and comes in a variety of colors and patterns to add to its great reputation. You can create customized labels for glass containers and canisters to help anyone looking to organize their pantry. Explore the online trends and adjust the labels. Once you have your labels designed, the easiest approach is to set up an Etsy shop. It's almost like opening an Amazon prime membership account. If your design is in demand, you will have people ordering even with no advertising. But if you would like to keep the tempo high, then advertise your Etsy listing on Pinterest and other social media platforms. This is a sure-shot way to generate more traffic to your Etsy shop and to turn potential customers into paying customers. An important note here is the pictures being used on your listing. You cannot use any of the Design Space images and must use your own pictures that match the product you are selling.

Create a package of 5–6 different labels like sugar, salt, rice, oats, beans, etc., that can be sold as a standard packager and offer a customized package that will allow the customer to request any word that they need to be included in their set. Since these labels weigh next to nothing, shipping can easily be managed with standard mail with usually only a single postage stamp, depending on the delivery address. Make sure you do not claim the next day or 2-day delivery for these. Build enough delivery time so you can create and ship the labels without any stress. Once you have an established business model, you can adjust the price and shipping of your product, but more on that later. Check out other Etsy listings to make sure your product pricing is competitive enough and you are attracting enough potential buyers.

Now, once you have traction in the market, you can offer additional vinyl-based projects like bumper stickers, iron-on, or heat transfer vinyl designs that people can transfer on their clothing using a standard heating iron. Really, once you have gained some clientele, you can modify and customize all your listings to develop into a one-stop shop for all things vinyl (a great name for your future Etsy shop, right!).

Selling Finished Pieces

You would be using your Cricut machine for a variety of personal projects like home décor, holiday décor, personalized clothing, and more. Next time you embark on another one of your inspiring journeys leading to unique creations, just make 2 of everything, and you can easily put the other product to sell on your Etsy shop. You will be able to keep safe your projects on the Design Space application for future use, so, if one of your projects goes viral, you can easily buy the supplies and turn them into money-making offerings. This way, not only your original idea for personal usage will be paid off, but you can make much more money than you invested in it, to begin with.

Again, spend some time researching what kind of designs and decorations are trending in the market and use them to spark up inspiration for your next project. Some of the current market trends include customized cake and cupcake toppers and watercolor designs that can be framed as fancy wall decorations. The cake toppers can be made with cardstock, which is another beginner-friendly material, light in weight, and can be economically shipped tucked inside an envelope.

Personalized Clothing and Accessories

T-shirts with cool designs and phrases are all the rage right now. Just follow a similar approach to the selling vinyl section and take it up a notch. You can create sample clothing with an iron-on design and market it with "can be customized further at no extra charge" or "transfer the design on your own clothing" to get traction in the market. You can buy sling bags and customize them with unique designs to be sold as finished products at a higher price than a plain boring sling bag.

Consider creating a line of products with a centralized theme like the DC Marvel characters or the Harry Potter movies and design custom T-shirts, hats, and even bodysuits for babies. You can create customized party favor boxes and gift bags at the request of the customer. Once your product has a dedicated customer base, you can get project ideas from them directly and quote them a price for your work. Isn't that great?!?!

Another big advantage of the heat transfer vinyl, as mentioned earlier, is that anyone can transfer the design on their desired item of clothing using a standard household iron. But you would need to include the transfer instructions with the order letting them know exactly how to prep for the heat transfer without damaging their chosen clothing item. And again, heat transfer vinyl can be easily shipped using a standard mailing envelope.

Marketing on Social Media

We all know how social media has become a marketing platform for established corporations and small businesses and budding entrepreneurs. Simply add hashtags like for sale, product, selling, free shipping, the sample included, and more to entice potential buyers. Join Facebook community pages and groups for handcraft sellers and buyers to market your products. Use catchy phrases like "customization available at no extra cost" or "free returns if not satisfied" when posting the products on these pages as well as your personal Facebook page. Use Twitter to share feedback from your satisfied customers to widen your customer base. You can do this by creating a satisfaction survey that you can email to your buyers or include a link to your Etsy listing asking for online reviews and ratings from your customers.

Another tip here is to post pictures of anything and everything you have created using Cricut machines, even those that you did not plan to sell. You never know who else might need something that you deemed unsellable. Since you will be creating these only after the order has been placed, you can easily gather the required supplies after the fact and get crafting.

Target Local Farmer's Market and Boutiques

If you like the thrill of a show-and-tell, then reserve a booth at a local farmer's market and show up with some ready-to-sell crafts. In this case, you are relying on the number of people attending and a subset of those who mayt be interested in purchasing from you. If you are in an urban neighborhood where people are keenly interested in unique art designs but do not have the time to create them on their own, you can easily make big bucks by setting a decent price point for your products.

Bring flyers to hand out to people so they can reach you through one of your social media accounts or email and check all your existing Etsy listings. Think of these events as a means of marketing for those who are not as active online but can be excited with customized products to meet their next big life event like a baby shower, birthday party, or wedding.

One downside to participating in local events is the generation of mass inventory and booth displays, topped with expenses to load and transport the inventory. You can or not be able to sell all of the inventory depending on the event's size, but as I said earlier, you can still make the most of this by marketing your products and building up a local clientele.

Becoming a Cricut affiliate
This includes being paid to make tutorials video by the Cricut company. These videos are uploaded to the internet for the netizen to make use of. To become a Cricut affiliate, you need to have a strong internet presence. You must also have a tangible number of followers on your social media accounts.

Making money through teaching
It doesn't mean to be an affiliate; rather, you create a blog for videos and upload tutorial videos, and get paid through the generated traffic

Other places you can sel your craft
You can make any of the crafts you find or create and post pictures of them online, announcing to those on your list that it is for sale. This works better because whoever is buying gets to see the picture of whatever they are getting before ordering it. Personalized crafts should also be included in your order of business.

Follow the holiday
Another way to make money is with the Cricut machine. You create an iron vinyl design and sell to people. Iron vinyl can take the form of text or a pattern. You can also do it for any season or celebration, be it Valentine's Day, Halloween, Christmas, or Easter. Buyers can also order what they want.

HOW TO SET THE PRICE?
It bothers me to see people selling their beautiful super elaborate creations at SO low prices. Those people are not even valuing their own

time. They are not taking into account your talent, materials, or other important things when setting prices.

Monetizing your Art

You have practiced, perfected, and established a style of that art that you like to do so much. You have decorated cards, personalized objects, created pictures with motivational phrases. With pride, you have shared your work on social networks.

Own studio or on-site?

What will be your minimum charge for small jobs?

Your Time + Energy

This is where the wellness factor comes in, where you need to think about how much your time is worth to you. It's worth a lot more than buying the cheapest combo at McDonald's, but there the questions come... Karissa, how much exactly? How do I find out? It is difficult to answer the frank, but there are certain guidelines that I can tell you that can help you.

The typical answer is that you put yourself a monthly salary with which you feel comfortable. I will speak in an imaginary way based on some local statistics of the Dominican Republic to speak with numbers and understand. Let's say (I made it up) that, on average, a monthly salary in my country is 15,000 Dominican pesos, and this is the number with which you value your time and energy.

This number will be divided by 4.3. This number is established as the average of weeks in the year since months have 30 days, another 31, and February with 28. Are you already starting to see the difference? Now try to use that math to calculate your hourly rate.

Start with the monthly salary you feel comfortable with:

____

Divide that number by 4.3 and put it here: ____________________________

Now divide this other number by 44 (remember that this number may vary). So, this result is your hourly rate that you will put here:

____

Cost of Materials

Are you using cheap store markers or artist quality paints? Do you use expensive papers and prepared inks? Are the special items you need? Do you have to order online specific to some part of the world or available near you?

The value increases with the quality of your tools and materials, as well as your knowledge of them. If you answer "What kind of paint do you have/do you use?" With an "I don't know ... I've had it for a long time and the label it has is no longer visible" or "a friend gave it to me, and I don't know where it got it. "Your work will not be as valuable as that of someone whose answer is" I use Winsor and Newton's lightweight, water-resistant watercolors. "

Artist-quality materials cost more, so you must know your materials' cost in case they run out.

Are you using cheap store markers or artist-quality paints? Do you use expensive papers and prepared inks? Are the special items you need? Do you have to order online specific to some part of the world or available near you?

The value increases with the quality of your tools and materials, as well as your knowledge of them. If you answer, "What kind of paint do you have/do you use?" With an "I don't know... I've had it for a long time and the label it has is no longer visible" or "a friend gave it to me, and I don't know where it got it." Your work will not be as valuable as that of someone whose answer is "I use Winsor and Newton's lightweight, water-resistant watercolors."

Artist-quality materials cost more, so you must know your materials' cost in case they run out.

Project Size

This is probably one of the first factors to value your project. How big is it? Creating something, for example, a lettering composition is an 8.5 by 11 inches sheet with 10 words that will take much less time and fewer materials than those same 10 words on an 8 by 10 feet board. You can have a price for measurements, let's say square inches, or better use your hourly rate that we work above.

Delivery-Shopping

You must indicate in your budget if the delivery is included or if is an extraordinary payment. That means you need to know where the piece is going. You may have to purchase parcel shipping quotes outside of your city based on the weight size and service you need. I recommend that you investigate the rates of the shipping companies and, thus, have a standard shipping cost.

Original or Continuous Use?
Will your client use your art once (like a wedding card), continuously (like a business card or blog), or multiple times (like a T-shirt to resell)? It's a good idea to ask this question in advance. The answer will help you determine how valuable your artwork is to the customer if it will be used continuously to promote or generate direct income for your client; the value increases.

Deliverables
What should you deliver to your customer as a finished product? An original art? Or is it digital? Both of them? What file formats? JPG, PNG, TIF, EPS, AI? Do you have experience digitizing, and do you have the best tools to do it?

Spending time digitizing and preparing multiple files takes time and experience, and therefore, should be priced accordingly. There are also those printed from digital art. Will you mail the file? In a memory? Digital start, and then you delivered it printed? All this must be taken into account, considering the time and effort it took to do it.

Note: A digital job is even more expensive since it can be reproduced. Using specialized programs requires previous experience and learning, which I suppose also costs you to acquire.

Location (In or Out of Your Studio)
Your hourly rate will also largely depend on where you will be doing the work.

When you have the luxury of your own space, you can perform several tasks simultaneously. That is, you can be working on two projects at the same time. This makes it easy to access all of your supplies and materials. The most convenient way for you to work in your place, at your own pace with everything you need at hand, you should not worry about traffic.

If the job requires you to be somewhere outside your study (let's say a restaurant, for example), the value of your time will increase significantly.

You will have to travel to and from the place (which needs to be included in your work time), carry all your materials with you, and only commit to that work during the assigned hours. That also means that you will be in an uncontrolled environment. This includes distractions, noise, and curious people. It can be a lot of fun working on site, and it can be a real headache.

Sometimes a combination of time in your studio and on-site works best. You can carry out all the designs and preparatory work in the studio so that you are ready to carry out your duties once you arrive on site.

This would be shown as two different hourly rates in the quote, breaking down your activities, so your client knows how they invest their money in you.

Project term

Only you know what time is most comfortable for you to work. If not, I recommend measuring the time you take doing your work to estimate and space if something unforeseen occurs. If a client comes out of nowhere with a crazy panic because they are the most important in the world, always add a fee for speed, clarifying the time it takes you in normal time for similar works, and that you will make an exception for them. Normally these prices vary between 50–100% of the labor price.

TROUBLESHOOTING

Problems with printing images

The Explore machine will work with a variety of printers but some printers will jam when using card stock. The best option is to use a printer that feeds the card stock from the rear. The less turns the card stock makes in the printer the less chance of it jamming.

Play it safe and don't use a laser printer for vinyl or sticky material.

Design Space has a printable area that is 6.75 by 9.25. This is a lot bigger than past versions. When you're working with an image, you're going to print select a square from the Shapes tool and place it behind your image. Make the size of the square 6.75 and 9.25. Then you can clearly see while you're working with you image whether or not it is within the printable area. Make the square a light color so you can see it separate from your image.

You can put more than one image in the box. Attach the images so you can move them all at one time. Delete the box before printing.

It's easy create custom designs for multiple uses just by changing their Line type instead of redesigning the whole project.

Pens

When you're inserting a pen into your machine, place a piece of scrap paper under the pen. This keeps the pen from marking up your material or your machine when you click it into the clamp.

There are different ways to breathe new life into dried markers sometimes just soaking the tip will work or refilling the pen with 90% alcohol.

Besides the homemade universal pen adapter I mentioned, the tube shaped pencil grips fit some markers making them compatible with the Explore.

Problems with cutting images

Before unloading the mat try to determine if the material has been cut to satisfaction. If not manually hit the cut button on the Explore and cut it again several times.

Use the Custom Material Settings in Design Space to increase or decrease the pressure, add multiple cuts, choose an intricate cut setting, or change materials. Within each category there are several listing for different kinds of paper or card stock for example. Just try selecting a different kind and see if that helps.

Tip: Create your own custom settings for any material by selecting Manage Custom Materials from the main menu. Then just click Add New Material and enter the information.

Some complex designs won't cut well in Fast Mode so just cut it regularly. Make sure the blade and mat are clean.

If your images are not cutting correctly be sure and wipe the mat and scrape off any access material left from previous projects. If the mat is severely scored or gouged replace it.

Try switching to another mat such as the stickier blue mat. If the mat isn't sticky enough the material can slip and won't cut properly. Or tape the paper to the mat.

Then carefully clean the blade. If there is still a problem it might be time to replace the blade. Using the new German Carbide blade is your best option for optimal cutting. Believe it or not there can be a slight difference in the cutting edge between one new blade and another.

Make sure the blade fits tightly in the housing. Regularly clean out the blade housing of fibers that accumulate and interfere with the cutting process. Blow into the housing or use a straightened paperclip and carefully loosen and stuck material. Since the angle of the deep cutting blade is different try using it on regular material when experiencing problems. If you get a message saying image is too large you simply need to resize the image to make it smaller. Some people think that since the mat is 12 x 12 they can use 12 x 12 images. But there is a slight space left for margins so the largest image size is 11.5 x 11.5. You can purchase a 12 x 24 mat to make larger cuts of 11.5 x 23.5.

If all else fails try a different material. Some users find that certain brands of paper or card stock work better than others.

Mats

If your mat is too sticky when it's new place a white T-shirt on it and press lightly or just pat it with your hands. This will reduce some of the stickiness. When using a brayer and thin paper don't apply a lot of pressure on the mat. This makes it hard to remove without ripping the paper.

Always clean your mat after each use. Use a scraper to remove small bits of lint or paper that have been left behind. These small scraps will cause problems with future projects.

You can wipe the mat with a damp cloth. Then replace the plastic cover between uses to prevent dust and dirt from sticking to the mat.

When the mat has lost its stickiness; tape the material to the mat around the edges rinse, let dry and it's good to go. Have you seen those food grade flexible cutting mats or boards? Some users are turning them into Cricut mats. Look for the thin plastic ones that are 12 x 12 or 12 x 24.

Use spray adhesive and cover the mat leaving a border so the glue doesn't get on the rollers or just spray the back of the card stock to adhere to the makeshift mat.

Load and unload

When you load the mat into the Explore always make sure that it's up against the roller wheels and under the guides. This assures the material will load straight when you press the load button. When the cut is complete never pull the mat out of the machine as this can damage the wheels. Always hit the unload button and then remove the mat. To extend the life of the mat turn it around and load it from the bottom edge. Position the images on different parts of the mat instead of always cutting in the upper left corner.

Curling

Here's how to avoid curling material into a useless mess. When working with new mats they tend to hold on for dear life.

When you're pulling a project off the mat, do not pull the paper (or whatever material) up and away from the mat. This will cause it to curl into a mess.

Instead turn the mat over and curl it downward. Instead of pulling the mat away from the paper, pull it away pulling the paper up and away from the mat.

It seems like a slight difference but it will save you from trying to uncurl and flatten a project. Just remember how curled the mat was when you first unboxed it had to wait till it flattened out.

Power Button Blinking Red

When you notice that the power button is blinking unexpectedly, observe at what time and what project you carried out that elicited such abnormality.

This issue sometimes happens when you are powering on your Cricut machine or updating firmware. It also happens when cutting a project or when loading a mat. The red light can serve as a warning or a notification that something had gone wrong with a project.

If you notice your power button is blinking red while powering on your machine and while updating firmware, contact Cricut support.

In the case of the power button blinking red when loading a mat, it is possible the roller bars have gathered specks of dust. In this case, power off the machine, move the carriage to and from and blow away the speck of dust.

When cutting a project, the red light could signify that the blade is stuck in a material or the machine is faulty. Contact Cricut support for further assistance.

Cricut Machine tearing Through Materials

This issue is similar to the problem no. 2. If the machine is tearing through materials, instead of cutting them, it could be for a variety of reasons that can be resolved. Follow these troubleshooting solutions to resolve this issue.

1. Ensure that the selected material and your Linetype have the recommended setting for that blade you chose. For example, if you are using the rotary blade, make sure your linetype is set to fabrics that the rotary blade can be used for, such as cotton. The blade installed is in concordance with the blade recommended by Design Space. The Cricut Explore Air 2 model might be slightly different in the selection of material. If the set dial is on customs, select material from the "Custom Materials" list.

2. Consider the size and texture quality of the image. If you are having difficulty cutting through small images, try cutting through larger ones.

3. If the blade is not suitable, open Clamp B and loosen the blade housing. Hold down the plunger, gently remove the blade and replace it. You can equally inspect the blade housing and blow away any dust.

4. Check the pressure settings for the material type. You may need to adjust accordingly to suit the material to be cut.

5. Attempt contacting Cricut support if problems persist.

Cricut Machine Not being Able to read Cut Sensor Marks

If you are getting an error that your Cricut Design Space cannot read the cur sensor marks, check if you selected the Print then Cut option. If the image is set to this, that means the machine cannot read the cut sensor marks.

You will need to change your image's linetype from "Print" to "Cut". This way, the Cricut machine will be able to see the sensor marks that will allow it to cut the images precisely.

Cricut Machine Having a Disturbing Noise

The type of noise your Cricut machine will make will determine the best approach to use to resolve the issue. Unusual noise is an indication that your Cricut machine needs help. If you hear a grinding noise, it could be the carriage is faulty or the configuration/setup is wrong. To troubleshoot the issue of grinding and unusual loud noise;

1. Check the carriage and report to support on what to do next.

2. Make sure you are using the power cord and the accessories that came with the machine. A different power cord and accessories may result in the machine producing an unusual grinding noise.

3. Check the pressure setting for the material type. If it is too high, try adjusting it to a lower level. Do this more than twice to see a change.

4. If you notice your Design Space is unusually loud, check if fast mode is activated. If it is not, contact support for technical support.

Cricut Machine Having Firmware Updates Issues

Firmware update issues are normal issues that users experience in their Cricut Design Space. If updates are failing to install or not completing, follow the steps below;

1. First of all, ensure your system meets the minimum requirements for Design Space.

2. If your system meets the minimum requirements, make sure also that the desktop or computer you are attempting to install the update is connected to your Cricut Explore Air 2. USB is faster and better than Bluetooth. If the update is failing with a USB cable, try another one.

3. Use Google Chrome browser as its more compatible to use.

4. If the firmware update is still failing, disconnect your Cricut Explore Air 2 from your system. Restart and attempt the process again.

5. Contact Cricut support if the issue still persists.

Cut Sensor Light Not Turning on During Print Then Cut

1. Ensure your Cricut machine is turned off.

2. Press down and hold both Clamp A and Clamp B at the same time. Release the clamps and power the machine on.

3. Attempt to Print then Cut the image.

4. If the sensor light doesn't come up, contact Member Care for further assistance.

Cricut "Print Then Cut" Calibration Not working

Sometimes, calibrating the Cricut machine to work with the Print then Cut option is difficult. This is because you get to a point in the calibration process and you are stuck.

You have to get the correct calibration sheet by downloading it online and loading it into your Cricut machine. This way you won't have to go through the calibration process. Ensure the sensor marks are showing to enable a good cut.

Cricut Machine not Powering On

You must never use an external power cord for your Cricut machine. Always use the same cord that came with your machine. The Cricut Explore Air 2 power cord is designed differently from the power cords used with other Cricut machines. This way, the chances of having power issues are reduced.

If you notice your Cricut machine has a power issue;

1. Ensure the plug, the power adapter is secure and connected properly to the power source.

2. Check the cutting mat. During movement, the cutting mat might unplug the power cord from the Cricut machine. So, check if the cord is inserted correctly.

3. If power is not coming on, try plugging to a different wall outlet.

4. try using another compatible power cord. It may be there is an issue with the current power cord.

Contact Cricut support with a video clip of the issue

Cartridge Issues

If you are experiencing issues linking your Cricut cartridge to Cricut Design Space:

1. Check if cartridge purchased has been used. It is possible the first user has already linked that cartridge to his Design Space account. Cartridges can only be linked one time according to copyright and licensing laws. If the cartridge has been used, return it and purchase another one.

2. If the cartridge is new, but still not recognized, clear the browsing history and cookies of your desktop computer or laptop.

3. Understand that you can only link a cartridge, through a desktop or laptop system. Also, check if there is any firmware update available for your Cricut machine.

4. If there aren't, contact Member Care for further assistance.

CRICUT EXPLORE AIR 2 MAINTENANCE

Blade Life

A blade can last between 500 and 1500 single cuts before it requires replacement. The life expectancy for a cutting blade mostly relies on the settings you use and the materials you cut. This is why you need to monitor the quality of your cuts, and when the quality decreases, that's when you will need to replace your cutting blade. In order to have the best possible results, make sure you only use Cricut Replacement Cutting Blades, available on the Cricut Shop, but also at other retailers.

Replacing the Cutting Blade

This is a process that you will definitely come across, especially if you are using the Cricut Machine on a frequent basis. Never replace the blade when the Cricut Machine is still on, in fact, you need to unplug it before replacing the cutting blade. After the machine is unplugged, you will need to take out the cutting blade assembly. Then, you will need to find the blade in the assembly and push it in, in order for the blade to emerge from the cutting blade assembly. Next, you will need to gently pull out the blade from the magnet that is holding it in place.

When you need to install a new blade, you will need to let go of the blade release and insert with caution the shaft of the blade in the hole at the bottom of the cutting blade assembly. Then, you will notice how the blade gets "sucked" inside the shaft and installed properly. Place back the cutting blade assembly into the Cricut Machine following the reversed procedure of removing the cutting blade assembly. Please be aware that the cutting blades are very sharp and should only be handled with extra care. Also, they can be considered choking hazards, so you need to keep them away from children.

Replacing the Cutting Mat

Nothing lasts forever and the Cricut Cutting Mat doesn't make any exception from this rule. It takes between 25 and 40 full cuts for a Cutting Mat to get damaged and at that point, it should be replaced. The life expectancy of this spare part depends a lot on the materials you cut and the settings you use. When the paper is no longer sticking to the Cutting Mat, it has to be replaced. It's always better to replace the mat with genuine Cricut Mats, and it's perfect if you can purchase the Cricut Self Healing Mat. Always remember to rotate the mats to prolong the overall life of each mat.

Cleaning and Greasing Your Cricut Machine

Every product can show signs of usage, and a Cricut Machine may collect some paper particles and dust, or you can even see grease from the machine building up in the carriage track. Luckily for you, cleaning up this machine is quite easy, but you need to consider the following tips first:

- Make sure you unplug the power from the machine first before cleaning it

- You can use a glass cleaner sprayed on a soft cloth to clean the machine

- If you notice static electricity build up leading to the accumulation of paper particles and dust, all you have to do is to wipe it off with a clean soft cloth

- If you see grease building up on the bar across which the carriage travels, gently remove it using a soft cloth, tissue, or cotton swab

Machine Dial Not Working

If you ever come across issues with dialing on your Cricut Machine, you can just follow the troubleshooting steps below

When Explore Smart Set Dial won't turn:

- In this case, you will need to look for your proof of purchase (any receipt or invoice your might have regarding the purchase of this product) and prepare a short video of the issue

- You will need to Contact Member Care, using one of the options for assistance

- Unfortunately, there is no way to troubleshoot this issue

- When the material is not changing in Design Space:

- Check the connection of the USB cable on both your Cricut machine and your computer.

- Unplug the Cricut machine from the computer and then power it off. Next step, reboot or restart your computer. When the computer is back on, turn on the Cricut machine and reconnect it to the computer, then try to see if it's cutting again. If it still doesn't work, make sure you try the following step.

- Consider reconnecting your Cricut machine through a different USB port on your computer. If it still doesn't help, move on to the next step.

- Check if the issue happens with a different Internet browser. If the issue is happening regardless of the browser you are using, please consider the next step.

- Try to see if a different USB cable works (if you have a standard printer you can try it with that cable and vice versa), just to see if the Cricut machine can cut with a different cable. If your machine is in warranty and you don't have another cable, you might want to consider contacting Member Care.

- Check for any possible updates (make sure the Firmware is updated) on your Cricut Machine.

- If there are no available updates, please get in touch withMember Care for further assistance.

Machine Tearing or Dragging Materials

There might be situations when the machine has some malfunctions and it tears through the material. However, all these variables can be fixed using some basic troubleshooting steps. Therefore, if your Cricut machine is dragging or tearing through the material, make sure you check the following:

1. Check if you selected the right material setting in Design Space, or make sure that Smart Set Dial is on the right setting:

   a. if you are making a Custom setting, you can make sure that you select the right material from the drop-down menu

2. Check the intricacy and size of the image. When you are cutting an image that is small or very intricate, try cutting it larger or simpler.

   a. If cutting a simple image fixes the issue, you can try cutting the more complicated one by using the Custom setting for Cardstock - Intricate Cuts.

   b. If you are using Cricut Maker or Cricut Explore Air 2 in Fast Mode, make sure you disable the Fast Mode and reattempt the cut again.

3. Take off the blade housing from the machine, then the blade and make sure there isn't any debris on the blade or inside the housing.

4. Decrease pressure settings for that specific material type in the Manage Custom Materials window by increments of 2-4. You can access the Manage Custom Materials screen from the account menu, or by going to the Edit Custom Materials option from the upper right corner of the Mat Preview screen (just after clicking on Change Material).

5. It may have to be done 2-3 times in order to change the cut result.

6. Try to cut a different material (I would suggest copy paper) using the right setting for that material. Try to see if the problem is only with the material that you are trying to cut, or the issue persists with other materials as well.

7. Consider using a new mat and blade. In this case, both of them can cause cut issues.

8. If you followed all the steps above, but the issues still persist, I encourage you to get in touch with Member Care for further assistance.

Machine Not Cutting Through Material

One of the most common issues of any Cricut machine is when it simply doesn't cut through the material, or it's just scoring the material, even though it normally should be cut without issues if it has the right settings applied.

In this case, you only need to follow the troubleshooting steps below:

1. Check if the material setting you chose in Design Space or on Smart Set Dial matches the material on your machine mat. If you are using Cricut Explore models, you can go ahead with the Custom option, and then select the right material from the Custom Materials list.

2. Go to the account menu and open the Manage Custom Materials page, and from this option, raise the pressure for your material setting by 2-4 increments. After this, try a test cut. You may have to increase the pressure settings by 2-4 increments 2-3 times, to check if there are any changes in the cut result.

3. Try cutting a different material (the best choice would be printer paper), but using the right setting for the material. Do you still have the same issue? If not, then perhaps the issue lies within the original material you are trying to cut.

4. On your browser, you can also clear the cache and cookies, and then try another test cut, and if the issue persists, may I suggest trying a different browser (I normally recommend Google Chrome or Mozilla Firefox).

5. If you have attempted all of the steps above, and you still have issues, please get in touch with Member Care for further assistance.

Cricut Explore Air 2 Cutting Machine Blades

The Cricut cutting blades do need to be changed from time to time. As they are cutting through materials, they will start to get blunt, just like a knife or any other blade would.

Types of Cutting Machine Blades Available for the Cricut Explore Air 2

The second clamp (right-hand side) of the accessory carriage in the Cricut Explore Air 2 holds the blade of the cutting machine. Most projects are done with the Premium Fine-Point blade that comes standard with the machine. However, the machine is capable of cutting a lot more material types, and as such needs the correct blade to do the cutting with. Blades compatible with the Cricut Explore Air 2:

Bonded-Fabric blade

- This blade does not come standard with the machine. It is an optional extra.
- It is used for fabrics including:
  - Stabilized fabrics
  - Bonded fabrics
- The FabricGrip (pink) machine mat is the mat recommended for use with this blade.
- Deep-Point blade
- This blade does not come standard with the machine. It is an optional extra.
- It is used for deeper cuts and thicker materials, including:
  - Leather
  - Chipboard
  - Cork
- The StrongGrip (purple) machine mat is the mat recommended for use with this blade.
- This blade comes standard with the Cricut Explore Air 2.
- It can be used on most medium weight or thin materials, including:
  - Cardstock
  - Paper
  - Vinyl

- o   Iron-On

  - o   Poster board

- It comes with its blade housing, which is either rose or silver in color.

- It can be used with the LightGrip (blue) and StandardGrip (green) machine mats.

Changing the Cutting Machine Blades for the Cricut Explore Air 2

All Cricut Explore Air 2 blades are changed the same way, as per the instructions listed below.

The Cricut blades have two parts to them:

- The blade housing, which is the cylindrical tube that fits into the Cricut accessory carriage and houses the blade.

- The blade looks like a sewing machine needle.

Always keep the small protective covers that come with the Cricut blades.

Remove the blade housing from the Cricut Explore Air 2 machine.

Place a small tub beneath the blade as you hold it, with the blade pointing down.

On top of the blade housing, you will find a small plunger.

Press down on the plunger to make the blade fall into the tub.

Be careful when handling the blade. It may be blunt, but it can still give you a nasty cut.

Remove the protective cover from the new blade and store it with your Cricut accessories.

Flip the blade housing upside down, so the plunger is facing down.

Make sure the blade is facing up, with its head facing down.

Drop the blade, with the head facing down, into the blade housing.

The inside of the blade housing contains a strong magnet that captures and holds the blade in position.

Load the blade housing into the right-hand compartment of the Cricut Explore Air 2.

Place the protective cap on the old blade and throw it away safely.

Caring for the Cutting Machine Blades for the Cricut Explore Air 2

To prolong the life of the cutting machine blades, you need to keep them out of dusty environments. When the Cricut Explore Air 2 is not being used, it is good practice to close it up and store it in a protective bag.

Cleaning the Cutting Machine Blades

The blade should be cleaned carefully with a cloth that does not produce cotton pieces or lint.

Storing the Cutting Machine Blades

Keep the protective lids on new or spare blades.

Keep any extra cutting machine blades in an airtight container in a dust free environment.

Caring for the Cricut Explore Air 2 Cutting Machine and Accessories

Taking care of your machine will ensure it lasts a long time. Here are a few maintenance tips for the Cricut Explore Air 2.

Cleaning the Cricut explore Air 2

You can try as hard as you like, but chances are at some stage your machine is going to get a bit dusty, or will be in need of a bit of grease if the carriage becomes sticky. Below is a brief overview of some cleaning maintenance tips.

Parts, Services, and Maintenance for the Cricut Explore Air 2

Cricut has extra parts for most of its machines, including the Cricut Explore Air 2. They have a friendly and helpful support line that you can call to find out who the local agent in your area is.

For services, repairs, or maintenance, it is best to trust your machine to a trained professional instead of trying to do it yourself.

Before cleaning the Cricut Explore Air 2, make sure to disconnect the power and USB cables.

Clean the outside of the machine with a cotton cloth. You can use a bit of glass cleaner as well.

Use a soft, anti-static cloth to wipe away dust particles.

To clean grease off the carriage rail that the blade and accessory housing run on, use a soft, anti-static cloth. You can also use a cotton bud, but be careful not to leave cotton bits behind.

DO NOT USE nail polish remover (acetone) or any other abrasive chemicals to clean the machine. This will damage it.

Greasing the Cricut Explore Air 2

Power off and unplug all cables, including the power and USB cables.

Slowly push the carriage to the left and run some tissue paper across and around the bar the carriage moves on.

Slowly push the carriage to the right and run some tissue paper across and around the bar the carriage moves on.

Slowly push the carriage to the center of the carriage bar.

Using a Cricut machine lubricant, open the packet and put a drop of the lubricant onto a cotton bud.

Drop a light application of the grease on the cotton bud to the left and right side of the carriage.

Be careful not to grease near the carriage itself. Try leaving at least a ¼" between the left and right of the carriage.

Once again, slide the carriage gently all the way to the left, and then gently all the way to the right before positioning it in the middle of the bar.

Wipe off any excess grease with clean tissue paper.

A grinding noise from the Cricut usually means that the carriage needs a little bit of grease.

Always make sure that the Cricut Explore Air 2 is closed when you are done working with it. Although it can be left plugged in, it is good practice to unplug the machine when you are not using it.

Cricut offers great storage bags designed specifically for their Cricut cutting machines. most of them include a handy accessory compartment. It is a good idea to store your machine in one of these storage bags and pack it safely away where there is no dust, or where it cannot fall or be damaged.

Transporting the Cricut Explore Air 2
If you are using your Cricut Explore Air 2 on the go or are taking it on a trip with you, you are going to need a machine-carrying case for it.

There are many excellent choices of machine carry bags, including ones with shoulder straps and wheels.

Make sure the machine is closed up properly before packing it away. Check that all the cables and accessories are packed safely and adequately.

TIPS ABOUT CRICUT AIR EXPLORE 2

These cutting machines are incredible. They are capable of a great variety of things, and the prospective venture consequences are genuinely limitless! Regardless, "Where do I begin!" was a common refrain in my house on the day I received my first Cricut machine, the Explore Air 2.

I made it through those first few days and now need to share with you 25 tips and tricks for getting started with your new Cricut machine. I mostly use the Cricut Maker these days, but many of these techniques apply to both versions!

1. Buy into Cricut Access

we recommend signing up for Cricut Access. You can pay a monthly fee of roughly $10 or a yearly fee that works out to be slightly less expensive each month.

Cricut Access offers you access to over 30,000 images, 1000s of activities, and over 370 different text styles. If you plan on using your Cricut a lot, this will save you a lot of money over buying each extension and picture separately.

2. De tack Your Cutting Mat

When it's brand new, the green cutting mat is clinging! After removing the plastic spread, place a clean, dry shirt over the tangle to prepare it for your first adventure. When the paper is at its most tenacious, it's pretty tough to get it off, regardless of whether you have all of the equipment!

It's not tough to damage the venture while attempting to get it off the ground.

3. Keep Your Cutting Mat Covers

The cutting mats accompany a plastic shield covering them. This can be pulled off and set back on effectively. We kept our spread and set it back on our tangle when we were done with it – it keeps the web spotless and clingy longer!

. Cleaning The Cricut Cutting Mat

Each now and again (if not each time you use it), give your cutting mat a wipe-over with some infant wipes. The non-liquor water wipes without scent are ideal.

5. Get The Right Tools

Ensure you have the Cricut Tool Set! It contains a weeding device, a scrubber, tweezers, a spatula, and scissors. It is advantageous to have the wedding device if you anticipate cutting either cement vinyl or warmth move vinyl.

6. Request The Cricut Scoring Stylus

The scoring stylus is required for a wide variety of card tasks. I didn't set one up with my machine right away, so I had to wait a long time for it to land before I could move on to other projects.

7. Start With The Sample Project

Start with the example venture when your machine arrives. Test cardstock is included with the Explore Air 2 to make your first card. You will be given a small number of materials to complete this special card.

8. Test Cuts

When working on your projects, it's a good idea to execute a test run befo re committing to the whole thing.

If the sharp edge is adjusted too low, your cutting mat will be destroyed.

If it's set too high, it can cut through your vinyl, cardboard, and other mat erials, ruining them.

9. Supplant Pen Lids After Use

It's all too easy to forget your pen is in the machine once you've finished a task. I usually get caught up in what I'm doing and forget that it's still there! However, it is vital to put the top on it as soon as possible once you've finished using it in order to avoid it drying out. They're far too expensive to throw out. The great thing about the Design Space projects is that they frequently inspire you to replace the cover!

10. Connect Your Cricut Cartridges To Your Design Space Account

You must transfer any old cartridges from a previous machine to your new record. This is a fundamental methodology. Every cartridge must be attached once; thus, if you're looking for some used, double-check that this hasn't happened yet.

11. Getting Materials Off The Cutting Mat

There is another trick to getting your cardstock or vinyl (e.g., Cricut Iron-On) off the cutting mat besides using the appropriate instruments. Rather than separating your task from the knot, which might result in twisting (or destruction), separate your commission from the tangle. Instead of going in a different direction, curve the net away from the card.

12. Request The Deep Cut Blade

Nothing is more frustrating than trust into a task only to discover you lack the necessary tools! The deep slice cutting edge allows you to cut through thicker materials, including card, calfskin, chipboard, and more. With the Explore Air 2, this cutting edge is ideal. It's critical to acquire the cutting edge, but the sharp edge must also be lodged. Request it now rather than waiting until you need it.

13. Set aside Cash By Using Free SVG documents

 You don't have to follow the blueprints in the Design Space store. You can either make your SVG documents or utilize one of the many free SVG files available online. A list of websites that provide free SVG records has been developed.

14. Different Pens Work In The Explore Air 2 Too

These pens incorporate, yet are not constrained to, Sharpie Pens and American Craft Pens. Cricut pens do appear to be of excellent quality. However, in every case, my enclosures keep going for quite a while.

15. Burden Mat Correctly

Ensure your tangle is appropriately stacked before you start cutting. It needs to sneak by the rollers. Your machine will probably simply begin cutting before the highest point of the lattice on the tangle or not in any manner if it hasn't been stacked right.

16. Utilizing Free Fonts For Your Projects

There are such a large number of accessible text style destinations for you to begin utilizing! See here for a rundown of thousands of free text styles. You essentially download the textual style, introduce it to your PC.

17. Introducing Fonts Into Design Space

After introducing a text style to your PC, you may need to sign out and over into Cricut Design Space before your new textual style will appear there. You may even need to restart your PC for it to appear (mine wouldn't occur without restarting my PC). For more data, read how to introduce textual styles in Cricut Design Space.

18. Supplanting Blades

Like everything, Cricut edges wear out. When the cuts are never so smooth and powerful again, it's the ideal opportunity for a change. Different signs that you need another sharp edge include: tearing card or vinyl lifting or pulling vinyl off the support sheet not carving right through (ensure your cut setting is right also)

19. When Your Mat Loses Its Stick

Cleaning your tangle is one way to help get more life out of your cutting mat. Yet, you have not requested another cutting mat if it's past that. You would prefer not to tape over a region waiting to be chopped, however down a few sides should carry out the responsibility.

20. Cricut's Custom Cut Settings

The Explore Air 2 accompanies seven preset choices on the dial:

Paper

Vinyl

Iron-on

Light cardstock

Cardstock

Fortified texture

Notice board

If the material you are cutting isn't on this rundown, there is a custom choice that you can choose on the dial. Go into Design Space, select your task and snap 'Make It.' You can choose your material from a drop-down menu.

21. Different Blades For Different Materials

A few people depend on utilizing separate sharp edges for cutting every material. For instance, you have one cutting edge that you use for cardstock and another for vinyl. This is because the different materials will wear differently on your sharp edges. Cutting vinyl is simpler on the short edge than slicing through a card.

Having a devoted cutting edge for vinyl implies it will consistently be prepared and sharp, instead of having one advantage for everything that rapidly goes obtuse and afterward lifts your valuable vinyl! We haven't attempted this stunt ourselves. However, we will do as such and report back our discoveries!

22. Remember To Mirror Your Image When Cutting HTV

You should reflect your plan if you are cutting warmth move vinyl with your Cricut! After you select 'Make It,' there is a choice to reflect your program (as observed beneath), and you should choose this choice for every individual tangle!

23. Spot Your HTV On The Cutting Mat The Right Way Up

To cut warmth move vinyl, you should put your gleaming vinyl side down on the cutting mat. Along these lines, the transporter sheet is underneath, and the dull vinyl side is on top. It's difficult to see which side the bearer sheet is on, so simply recollect sparkly side down, and you'll be fine!

24. Use Weeding Boxes For Small and Intricate Designs

If you are removing a little or unpredictable structure or removing a variety of plans on one sheet of vinyl, it can utilize weeding boxes.

Simply utilize the square apparatus in Cricut Design Space to put a case around your structure and gather the two components together. Then, open the shape in the base left corner to control it into a square shape.

25. Make sure To Set The Dial

How frequently have I neglected to change the material setting?! It's such a simple thing to overlook – particularly when you have at last completed your plan and genuinely need to get cutting! Interestingly, Cricut Design Space discloses to you what material the dial is set to when you are going to remove a structure. However, it is not entirely obvious that as well!

26. Keep up A Supply Of Materials

As we referenced before, it's a torment when you need to begin an undertaking, and you don't have the correct apparatuses. For instance, we've been in the situation of being without the scoring stylus, without the correct pen for an undertaking, and without a profound cut sharp edge

Processing of Cricut Explore Air 2

First of all, you want to create your projects easily, without having to know all the engineering of your Plotter how to adjust the pressure, speed, depth... which, in the end, becomes tiring and frustrating. Therefore, it was thought that the entire engineering technical team from Cricut designed it, focusing on ergonomics for its users.

First of all, the machine is totally made to guarantee maximum convenience and comfort during its use. Therefore, it meets all the requirements of precision and simplicity, so that you can focus only on the final result of the work.

Therefore, all facilities guaranteed by its developers are in some characteristic details of Cricut Explore Air 2 that you should want to know.

First, it has Smart Set Dial technology. In other words, one of the buttons at the top right allows you to choose between material options with pre-programmed functions, all before starting the cut.

In addition, other options that the Smart button provides is the configuration in your own way, just choose from the available buttons the option "customize". Later, just follow the instructions for each material when customizing and programming in the software.

Some physical and application characteristics that are interesting to mention are:

The Storage Slot: which makes it possible to store tools you use within the Cricut Explore Air 2 itself; it is ideal for when you use many accessories;

Cuts designed for materials up to 30 cm x 60 cm. The dimensions of the machine are approximately 60 cm wide by 24 cm high;

There are about 100 materials that you can cut with Cricut Explore Air 2, such as EVA, Paper and Fabrics;

Tools in Cricut Explore Air 2

The blades are responsible for making all the magic happen. Therefore, thanks to them you can create everything you imagine very perfectly.

However, what you should know about these tools is that each one has been adapted to cut different types of materials. As such, they apply different strength and pressure.

Therefore, I will give you an overview of all the equipment available for our Plotter machine.

Cricut Cutting Blades

Fine point blade: it is made of extremely resistant, durable and high-quality material. It was designed to cut medium weight materials. So, it is perfect for making fine and interwoven details

Deep-edged blade: it is ideal for you who need to cut thicker materials. So, it has a sharp angle of 60 ° degrees - higher in comparison to the 45 ° available on the thin point blade - this guarantee cuts in thick materials, up to 1.7mm thick.

Fabric blade: it was specially designed for use in fabric cutouts. However, use in other types of materials is not recommended. Therefore, to use it, the material must be glued to the cutting base, thus ensuring a more efficient result.

Premium blade: it has the same cut level as the fine-tipped blade; however, it lasts up to 3x longer. It is also designed to cut medium weight materials. So, it is ideal for making fine and interwoven details

In addition, other tools that Cricut has to use next to its blades guarantee an incredible differential to your final result are pens, markers and etc.

With them, you can write and score. So that with it you can create folds in the materials. It is perfect for making boxes and cards and makes your project much more beautiful and personalized.

There is also the option to print and cut. However, this option is not performed by a tool, but rather a feature of the Software Design Space, which allows you to print a drawing and then cut it out. This feature is wonderful, especially when creating custom stickers

What Does Cricut Explore Air 2 Cut?
If you work with crafts, DIY decoration, or even want to start, probably the material you want to use will be among one of the 100 that Explorer works with.

Thus, you will have access to a complete list of all of them. That way, you'll have information ranging from cutting pressure to the ideal blade type. It is important to check it out before setting up your project.

Another important tip is to always test before sending your project for cutting. Since, the settings vary according to the state of the blade and the cutting base.

Having chosen your material, what else do you need to know? Well, another important information that you need to be aware of is about the base / mat that comes with the cutting machine. Thus, like blades, each cutting base has an ideal application for different types of materials. And Cricut has 4 options available:

Cricut Cutting Bases
Light Grip Cutting Base of blue color was designed to cut thinner and lighter materials. Such as: plain paper; thin cardboard; some thinner types of vinyl, among others;

Standard Grip Cutting Base in green is the most common and affordable, designed to work with medium weight materials. It is usually what accompanies your Plotter. It cuts paper of thicker thicknesses being them: papers, cardboard, tape paper, thicker vinyl, etc.;

Strong Grip Cutting Base in purple color is used as the basis for thicker and heavier materials. For best results, an adhesive tape is needed to fix the material on the carpet. It is ideal for products such as: thick cardboard, leather, some types of finer wood (Linden), acetate sheet;

Fabric Grip Cutting Base in pink was specially created for use in fabric cutting, used especially in the Plotter Cricut Maker. It is the most recommended base to use when working with felt;

This information is essential so that you don't have a headache before you even start your project. What's more, it is important to be aware of the material that will be used and which base will be the best option that guarantees an excellent final result.

What Can I Do with My Cricut Explore Air 2?
If you are curious to know, "What can I create? What projects can I start with?" We agree that these are really issues that must be taken into account. In view of the efficiency that this machine has many ideas arise, but even then, you are not sure if it is really what you want, or do not know what to do.

Usually, even when programming with ideas, we suffer from creative blocks. On the one hand, if you are a designer or illustrator, and have been in the production market for a long time, it gets easier. Since, you already have your own creative characteristics and people come to you for recognizing your work. But, when it is starting, many doubts and insecurities arise.

Remember that it is important to be sure of what you want to do before you start. You need to prepare the material, choose which tools to use and the product you create will be your fingerprint.

Cricut Access
For that, you have a great option within the Design Space software the Cricut Access platform - which is a tool that you have access to sources, images and the most varied types of projects. It is wonderful for those who have no experience in creating, or do not find external inspirations.

In principle, when you sign up for Cricut Access, you immediately have access to the Cricut library of over 90,000 digital images, fonts and designs available. With Cricut Access, above all, you will have a very realistic idea of what your final project will look like. With it, it is possible to remove the most recurring doubts and concerns. For example, "Is the design / is it adequate? Does this or those colors match?" In addition to tracking your entire project, you can predict how it will look before it is ready. Is show!

Note: it is worth remembering that the subscription to Cricut Access is paid, but every week Design Space offers free cutting options for customers.

Ideas to Do at Cricut

Here, however, we have another option is to follow Cricut on YouTube. There, you can follow creative ideas and ways to fully explore your plotter, with the most varied types of materials.

Eventually, you will see several creative production manuals. Just search and you can get a sense of how wide the creation options your machine is capable of. Therefore, we have separated some very cool project applications that you can do with your Cricut. All with the help of the resources available in Cricut Access and Cricut's YouTube:

- Cards: this is an excellent low-cost idea to start producing;

- Decorative items for parties and events: imagine just a beautiful party with all the content produced in your homemade plotter;

- Home decoration: be it in the creation of accessories and prints;

- You can create fashion designs on t-shirts or any type of clothing;

- Personalized wall pictures and calendar: tell me who doesn't like beautiful decorated pictures, they harmonize the house;

- Children's items: baby bows, felt dolls, images of animals that little one's love, the list just grows;

- Personalized stickers: great options to stick on personal accessories, decorate the bedroom wall and several other places;

Design Space Software

The Cricut Design Space is an excellent tool and is easily accessible for those who are starting. So, if you have no experience with any other Design program like Photoshop, you will find that although it seems difficult, its use is quite simple.

The Software is available for Cricut Maker and Explore. In addition, it is compatible with smartphones and computers from IOS, Android, Windows and Mac operating systems.

Design Space allows you to upload images for free and convert them. However, only basic images are supported with file types in .jpg, .bmp, .png and .gif formats, where it is possible to edit the images during the upload process.

In contrast, the vector images (.svg and .dxf) available for upload, do not have this characteristic, they are loaded and saved as they were designed.

Another important point is that the beta version of Design Space offline for PC is now available for download

TURN YOUR CREATIVITY INTO A BUSINESS

The principal thing you have to take on is your business technique. You have to figure out what sort of item you're going to sell, the kind of clients you're attempting to reach, and how to discover them.

Who and Where are your Clients?

There are two spots where you can sell your vinyl items, locally and on the web. Except if you've chosen to stop your all-day employment, and you have the cash to contract staff, you'll need to pick only one to start. Your objective ought to be to do a profitable business at the earliest opportunity; that way, you can reinvest those benefits in your future development.

Numerous new entrepreneurs dismiss the intensity of benefit. We don't have the advantage of getting financing from a bank or funding firm when you start.

If you can begin getting profitable deals rapidly, while prior a touch of that additional cash before all else. The benefit can be piped into development openings like new machinery, product offerings, or advertising. Benefit is the best.

By separating the various gatherings you can offer to and understanding the spots to discover them for both nearby and web-based deals, you can measure where to put your valuable time and exertion best. A touch of procedure presently can spare you from sitting around idly, cash, vinyl, and stamina not far off.

Selling Locally

Neighbourhood deals can be separated into two fragments, business to business (B2B) and business to client (B2C). If you choose to be a nearby dealer, it's ideal for picking between one of these two sections.

These two gatherings don't have much cover in the things they buy, or where you can market to them. The astute entrepreneur won't burn through their time pursuing leads and tossing showcasing cash at customers; they aren't arrangement to help.

Business to Business –

Volume Sales - The objective here is to utilize the proficiency of creating in bigger numbers to drive the cost you pay per thing down. The bigger the creation run, the lower your expense for item and time per unit delivered. This is the most laborious work to get into for another Cricut or Silhouette based business. The open doors are less, and customer desires are stronger.

Models:

- A contract with the neighbourhood government or school to create shirts or signage.

- Annual occasion signage and promoting.

Pros–

- Often, legally binding work can be finished in a single session. This implies you can buy from sellers in mass, enabling you to arrange lower material expenses. You will likewise have less exchanging between vinyl hues or product offerings, which means you can accomplish more in less time. This leaves you with more opportunity for different activities or advertising endeavours.

Cons –

- It will be hard to get one of these agreements. It is sensible to expect that these open doors in your locale are as of now being served by another person. If they aren't, jump at the opportunity.

Custom Work – Custom work for business clients, can be an extraordinary gig with massive upside. Organizations are eager to pay as much as possible for quality, dependable work. You can work with organizations to help make a brand personality, make mindfulness, and make limited time advertisements.

Models:

- If a business is beginning, you can offer a business dispatch starter pack. At least, you ought to incorporate logo design, signage for a retail front, and establishment.

- You can likewise provide organization marked swag like shirts, cups, or mugs as an extra. Every one of these administrations can be independent for new or existing organizations.

Pros—

- You are making associations with developing organizations. After your first effective exchange, you become their place of contact for future business marking, decals, mindfulness materials, and even visual communication. This relationship can pay future profits.

- Business customers accompany numerous open doors for upselling. More often than not, it is a success win for both of you.

Cons –

- It can be hard to discover new, quality leads. For most existing organizations, they as of now have a sign organization they trust. They needed to get their unique signs someplace, isn't that so?

- Business proprietors will, in general, be clever, with exclusive requirements and a solid feeling of what is a proper cost for your administration. Try not to be shocked or insulted on the off chance that they get different offers and arrange cost before tolerating your offer.

Business to Customer

Volume Sales - These standards are equivalent to with business to business mass work, yet you're going to discover your clients in new puts and have various contributions.

You will sell things that retail clients need to purchase. This incorporates one of a kind shirts, tumblers, espresso cups, or whatever else you can concoct. The key is to have expansive intrigue, something you can create various with the desire that they will sell.

Models:

Renting space at a classical shopping centre or art fair. Make sure to survey how much space you need, the value per square foot, and the commission your proprietor is requesting.

Become a seller at nearby occasions. For instance, my better half was a merchant at the Mutt Strut in Nashville, Tennessee this year.

Find space in popup shops

Find occasional occasions in your town that offer shoddy or free retail space, similar to a rancher's market or occasion fair.

Pass out business cards to neighbourhood shops where you envision your items may sell well.

Pros –

Your inventiveness will be the driver of your deals. If you think of an astute thought with mass or specialty claim, and you are in the perfect spot to offer it, you will receive the benefits. Additionally, you get the chance to figure out what media and medium you work in. Shirts, mugs, or whatever else, the decision is yours.

Cons –

You'll require a retail space to offer your things. The spots with higher pedestrian activity will be progressively costly. However, pedestrian activity doesn't rise to deals.

To be fruitful, you'll be eager to try different things with various areas and item contributions.

Custom Work

- Unique shirts for a wedding party

- Wall decals with interesting statements and family names

- Monograms for wine glasses or vehicle decals

Pros –

- Custom work for nearby clients has the most minimal start-up cost of any of these methodologies. If you can locate a dependable merchant who offers materials in little clusters, you can concede putting resources into vinyl until you secure an undertaking.

- You can likewise do the majority of your work from home, maintaining a strategic distance from the need to put resources into a retail front or workspace.

- You will probably charge a premium for your work. Retail clients pay the most astounding costs, and your design customization will raise the cost as well.

- Cons –

- Again, leads will be hard to get. Toward the start, the verbal exchange might be the main instrument you have. You're going to need to concentrate on quality workmanship and reasonable evaluating to get your underlying deals. If you have a touch of cash, you can kick start the procedure by showcasing with a nearby Facebook promotion.

Selling Online

Concentrating on web-based selling requires a higher specialized information base. Be that as it may, as I can bear witness to, you don't need to be a software engineer to make it work. You can profit with vinyl online by giving quality custom work, turning into a data centre point, or giving mass contributions. Once more, it's not fitting to attempt to do every one of the 3.

Your time is best spent working in one of the three choices to start. Thus, on the off chance that you choose to give custom work, don't likewise attempt to turn into a data centre point simultaneously. After building up your underlying balance and getting productive deals, you can anticipate how to utilize that cash for developing into different classifications.

Custom Work – For the perfect individual, I genuinely accept this is an incredible method to the opening shot your Silhouette or Cricut vinyl business.

Progressively, individuals are going to a Google search to discover custom work. Through existing commercial centres or your site, you can turn into the one they go to.

Models:

- Existing sites that enable you to sell handcraft administrations. Etsy, Amazon Custom, and Amazon platform notable.

- Another alternative is to dispatch your site. An extraordinary case of this can be seen with A Great Impression. They propelled a persuasive divider decal site, alongside a handcraft administration. You can find and get any decal, in any size you need from them.

Tip: I would suggest their methodology. Discover a specialty little enough you can contend inside, and offer handicrafts from that point.

Pros-

- If you sell on a current stage, the start-up expenses are extremely low. The minute you dispatch, you're contending in the worldwide marketplace. You approach a huge number of potential clients.

- Additionally, one of a kind designs will enable you to charge an exceptional rate. Be that as it may, online custom costs will, in general, be lower than a similar work done locally. It's an opportunity to clean up and expand your design range of abilities too.

Cons -

- Access to the whole world additionally implies you are going up against anybody with a web association. The expanded challenge will prompt lower costs for your designs and trouble finding occupations if you aren't intensely valued or offering an interesting design point of view.

- Selling on the web implies you additionally need to learn coordination's. You're going to need to get entered in with a delivery organization, make sense of pressing material, and calculate that cost your valuing.

Volume Sales – The advantages of doing work in mass online are equivalent to nearby. By accomplishing more work on the double and lessening the occasions you make switches between hues, designs, and product offerings, you're driving the expense per unit delivered down. You'll discover your clients through existing sites or by creating your own.

Models:

- The most significant stages for mass design work are eBay and Amazon, even though Etsy has seen development in these sorts of offers in the course of the most recent three years. On these stages, you can sell window decals, persuasive idioms,

divider dabs, vehicle decals, shirts, and so forth.
Fundamentally, anything with an intense interest that you can
replicate various occasions after the underlying design.

- Another choice is to pick a specialty and offer a similar kind of
work individually site. Spotted Decals is an extraordinary case
of this strategy. They are a little organization that works in
divider spots just, nothing else. They are the specialist with
regards to spotted decals. Since it is specialty and repeatable,
the work should be possible in mass, and they face the
insignificant challenge.

Pros -

- You can begin to construct a genuine retail business selling
this sort of work. After some time, you will almost certainly
figure out what the interest for the designs you offer and plan
creation likewise. This will expand your proficiency and lower
the time you need to spend making items.

- You'll additionally be making more items. Without a doubt,
you will get less cash per deal, yet this will allow you to
purchase a vinyl in mass at a diminished cost.

Cons -

- You're going toward the world here. There's a huge amount of
rivalry so that the edges will be lower, and quite possibly
somebody can undermine your little margins with phony or
fake things anytime.

-

- It takes noteworthy stage information to sell on the majority
of the various commercial centers (eBay, Amazon, Etsy, and
so on.).

Data Hub – Have you at any point visited a blog for guidance on the most
proficient method to utilize your machine or task motivation? If you can
dispatch a site and become the expert in the field, there's a chance to
profit with your Silhouette Cameo or Cricut there as well.

Models - There are some extraordinary instances of sites offering the
specialized skill and venture motivation with a specialty cutter. Some
additionally couple their Cricut and Silhouette learning with a way of life
blog.

- Joy's Life

- Just a Girl and Her Blog

- Cutting for Business

- Ginger Snap Crafts

- Lia Griffith

- Salty Canary

- CutCutCraft

Pros -

- You're not making decals for clients any longer, and your undertakings pursue your course of events. This implies you get the chance to be particular about the posts you take on, and the time you put into a task. Additionally, you can express your inventiveness anyway you'd like and assemble the group of spectators you need.

Cons -

- Let's emphasize, and you're not making decals for clients any longer. This plan of action is not quite the same as the remainder of the alternatives I've spread out.

- You can adapt your site with advertisements, support posts, offering an information item like a book for your committed per users, or a physical object. As it is, regardless of which course you take, it's not as immediate, nor necessary, as selling a decal.

What Are You Waiting For?

Beginning by picking a business methodology may be unashamedly old school. However, I'm sure you can perceive any reason why it's the establishment for your future achievement.

Via cutting a couple of hours to consider where you can you are best situated, you'll immediately separate yourself from a large portion of your rivals. You'll know who your clients are, what sort of things you can sell them, and the traps to dodge.

The subsequent stage is to score that first deal.

CONCLUSION

Cricut machines are fantastic equipment to acquire because they can be used to make crafts for business as well as enhance creativity and productivity. Crafters may make nearly anything with Design Space, and they can even customize their creations to bear their imprints.

People use these machines all around the world to manufacture gift items, t-shirts, interior décor, and a variety of other crafts to decorate their homes, give with friends and family during the holidays, and even sell, among other things.

We have two types of Cricut machines: the Cricut Maker and the Cricut Explore. In terms of efficiency, there are no notable distinctions between them. Consider this: in the world of crafters, these two machines bring thousands of items to life every day, both for fun and for business.

The Cricut maker offers more advanced functions, which is the sole difference between the two.

One aspect of the Maker that distinguishes it from the Explore Air is its ability to cut thicker materials. The Maker opens up a world of possibilities for artisans, allowing them to create creations that were previously impossible with Cricut machines.

The 'Adaptive Tool System' is another feature that sets the Cricut Maker machine ahead of the Explore Air 2. Because it will be compatible with new blades and other accessories that Cricut will release in the near future, the Cricut Maker has been empowered in such a manner that it will remain relevant for many years to come.

We can find differences between the two machines, there are some instances where they are absolutely indistinguishable. Take, for example, project design in Cricut Design Space.

Before being cut, all designs are made within the Cricut design space software, which is a crucial factor in creating handcrafted material.

However, in this regard, when talking about Cricut maker and explore air 2 there is no real division because both use the same software to design.

As a scrapbooking enthusiast, you should be conscious of design space. You won't get very far if you don't.

Understanding design space is critical since it provides craftspeople with a variety of tools for working on projects.

Design space is unquestionably powerful program that should not be disregarded by everyone who wants to deliver their best. However, it is not only a necessary skill for those who wish to do business with the Cricut machine, but it is also a vital skill for those who do it as a hobby.

You can either develop your own designs from scratch or use pre-made templates with the software.

Cricut design space features a lot of cool tools that can help you get started crafting quickly and easily, especially since these tools aren't difficult to use.

Experienced users or crafters are familiar with all of the tools in the Cricut design area and their functions in creating products.

But what are these tools?

- cutting tool

- welding tool

- attachment tool

- contour tool

- flattening tool

and much more!

Cricut machines are sold with tools and extras at the time of purchase. They are critical to the machine's functionality. They are the essential equipment and accessories that crafters need to bring their innovative crafts to life.

But first, let's look at some design and production tips and tactics that you may use with the design space program.

When problems develop, solutions are readily presented, and there are various ways to address app-related difficulties in Cricut Design Space to improve user experience and functionality.

Because the Design Space program is web-based, some laptop PCs are ideal for the job. These laptops are ideal for a variety of reasons, including performance, storage, and design. In conclusion, the best five laptops are the Acer Aspire E 15, Asus Vivobook F510UA, Dell Inspiron 15 5575, Lenovo Ideapad 330S, Asus Vivobook S410UN, and Dell Inspiron 15 5575.

Everything on earth needs maintenance, including Cricut machines. These machines are constantly cutting out materials of different textures, shapes, and quantity, etc. Thus, they need routine maintenance in order to boost their productivity levels and increase their life span.

The routine maintenance of these machines does not require a lot, and as a matter of fact, the hardware needs cleaning after cutting out materials. Thus, non-alcoholic baby wipes are highly recommended for cleaning material residue on the machines. The cutting mat is another item that needs maintenance from time to time because excessive usage without proper care reduces its stickiness.

There are a plethora of products that may be designed and cut out using Cricut machines in terms of crafts.

These things can also be profitably sold on the craft market. Although some people use the machines for recreational purposes, the number of people who use them for commercial purposes is significantly higher.

Cricut machines are used by commercial users to design and cut out products to sell for profit, and the machines have proven to be a lot of fun.

People can sell objects generated using a Cricut machine for a variety of reasons, one of which being the ability to create creative and unique products that are not available anywhere else.

Cricut machines are fantastic tools that should be on everyone's radar, particularly crafters.

I hope you appreciate this book as much as I did!